How to Obtain Business Loans

An Insider's Guide

Addison Parker

PT Publications, Inc.
Suite C
2273 Palm Beach Lakes Blvd.
West Palm Beach, FL 33409

Library of Congress Cataloging in Publication Data

Parker, Addison, 1964-
    How to obtain business loans: an insider's guide/
    Addison Parker
        p. cm.
    ISBN 0-945456-16-6 : $17.95
    1. Commercial loans — United States. 2. Banks and banking —
    United States — State supervision. I. Title.
    HG1642.U5P37   1994
    658.15'224 — dc20   94-32763
                                                                         CIP

Copyright © 1995 by PT Publications, Inc.

Printed in the United States of America.

All rights reserved. This book or any parts thereof
may not be reproduced in any form without
the permission of the publisher.

658.15224
P238

How to Obtain Business Loans

AN IRREVERENT VIEW FROM THE VAULT

Section 1: What Happened

Preface:	**It's a Wonderful Life** How Jimmy Stewart's Building & Loan gave way to David Paul's Centrust Savings. The reaction of regulators, and the public's uphill battle to understand.	Page	1
Chapter 1:	**Why Banking Changed** Highly Visible Targets — A much maligned profession takes its lumps.	Page	5
	A. Industry Transformation — From a monopolized to highly competitive environment.	Page	6
	B. Bad Loans — Ludicrous credit extensions.	Page	7
	C. Abuses — Manipulating the system.	Page	10
	D. Loan Reserves — Capital adequacy and the opportunity cost of classifying risk versus making new loans.	Page	11
	People are Staring — Bankers react to on-the-spot public inquisitions.	Page	15

Section 2: The Most Important Differences

Chapter 2:	**The Evolution of Lending** What's Going On? — Fewer loans necessitate intensified cost control.	Page	17
	A. The Burden of Proof — From the 5 Cs of Credit to the Glass Half Empty method of analysis. How the decision making process of lending has changed.	Page	19
	B. The ABC File — A battle to verify repayment ability. How banks treat the evidence before them.	Page	22
	Who Turned Out the Lights? — Laboring in the dark.	Page	34

Chapter 3:	A New Agenda	Page	37

Chinese Water Torture — The effect of regulatory inundation.

A. What Banks Have Been Panhandling For — How the business of banking has changed from lending to fee-for-service. **Page 39**

B. How to Give Your Deposit(s) Clout — Ways to guarantee yourself preferential savings rates, and how to measure an institution's ability to provide the service they promise. **Page 46**

C. Customers Won't Settle for Less — America's failure to remember a lesson it once taught. The difference that makes the difference. **Page 52**

D. The Struggle for Business — Backing up lip service. **Page 54**

The Change Bank — A glimpse of the service-only future. **Page 58**

Section 3: Governmental Efforts

Chapter 4:	Big Brother Is Not Just Watching	Page	61

A Banker's Rebuttal — A CEO's response to fee-for-service.

A. Is Anybody Listening? — Lawmakers, and regulators need to take a first-hand look at what they impose. The results don't justify the means. **Page 62**

B. The Paper Chase — What it takes to fill a loan file. **Page 64**

C. When Not to Kill Trees — Using annual requests for financial data to your advantage. **Page 71**

D. Character Loans — Why the buzz phrase is only that. Regulator's claims hold little practical promise. **Page 77**

CD Loans Versus Residential Real Estate Extensions — Which is treated as less risky? You'll be surprised. **Page 82**

Chapter 5:	**The Legislative Impact**	Page	83

All in the Family — The assessment of risk on an uneven playing field.

- A. Uniform Application *Among* Institutions — How size makes a difference in how regulators treat banks. Page 86
- B. The Consequence of Uneven Regulation — Small banks take advantage of a void, then are eaten by bigger banks. Page 88
- C. Uniform Application *Within* Institutions — Bank and regulator risk as perceived by institutional department. Page 90
- D. May I Take Your Order? — How to sequence would-be simultaneous credit applications. Page 93

Banking's Peter Principle — A community banker's rise to incompetency and personal stress. Page 99

Chapter 6:	**Trickle-Down Banking**	Page	101

Reg Duh-Duh — Legislation, for remedial math students, which *simplified* yield disclosures on deposit accounts.

- A. Who Qualifies? — The Burden of Proof narrows the field of acceptable commercial applicants. Page 103
- B. Ellis Island — Entrepreneurs without sources of capital, jobs without entrepreneurs. How the "land of opportunity" applies to fewer and fewer. Page 108
- C. Community Reinvestment — The function banks are supposed to fill. The *divisional effect* caused by their failure, and how they still keep from serving certain markets. Page 111

APY Revisited — Protecting the little guy is the least the government can do after limiting his opportunities. Page 116

Section 4: Institutional Reaction

Chapter 7: **Turmoil On The Home Front** — Page 119
When Reg Meets Reg ... and policy contradicts policy, mass confusion persists.
    A. Harmony and Discord — An attempt to ensure uniformity in lending, and how often deviations are tolerated. Page 121
    B. What's Taking So Long? — Improperly conjugated verbs, flowery speech, and other transgressions which can delay and jeopardize a loan request. Page 125
    C. May I See Your Palm Please? — Your account officer's responsibility to foresee the future. Page 130
When Charity and Political Involvement Aren't Optional — Mandatory payroll deductions benefit the industry's image. Page 132

Chapter 8: **For What It's Worth** — Page 135
Just Fix the Form — It's much more important than substance.
    A. Who Needs Collateral Anyway? — How the Burden of Proof surrounding cash flow, and the accrual issue, overshadow any evaluation having to do with real risk of loss. Page 139
    B. Thank You Sir, May I Have Another? — When one appraisal isn't enough. Page 148
Made As Instructed — How all the legislation in the world affects the front lines. Page 156

Chapter 9: **Self-Inflicted Wounds** — Page 157
No Salvation — The public can misperceive an industry.
    A. In One's Best Interest — Loan pricing differential, default penalties, and compensating balances. Page 158

B. Dangerous Standards — How bank imposed covenants can be an institution's own worst enemy. Page 161
C. It's Due... Now What? — Calling it payable by department. How balloons differ. Page 171
Stopping the Masochism — It starts at ground level. Page 175

Section 5: Impaired Decisions

Chapter 10: Adjudicating Commercial Credit Page 177
Hunting for a Positive Outlook — Pessimism offers a poor backdrop to any event.
A. Sittin' On the Dock of the Bay — A marina loan is put off because... Page 178
B. From Docks to Doctors — "Marginally increasing risk" foils a physician's request. Page 188
Turn About is Fair Play — From banker to bankee. Page 192

Chapter 11: What's *Adjudicating*? Page 195
Don't Jump — Employees contemplate ending it.
A. Can You See Alright? — Obstacles are put in the way. Page 196
B. Going Through The Motions — When answers make no difference. Page 202
Stop the Fight — Throwing in the towel. Page 218

Chapter 12: THE Deal Page 219
THE sales meeting — Lenders try to figure out who they can extend credit to.
A. THE p.u.d. — If ever there was an ideal market to exist in. Page 221
B. THE Applicant and THE Request — An experienced, but perplexing, borrower. Page 223
C. THE Structure — Laying down the numbers. Page 226
D. A ~~Word~~ Litany from THE Sponsors — Secondary sources made available Page 232

| Chapter 13: | THE Deal Continues | Page | 239 |

Panic sets in — THE deal is restructured.
- E. THE Opportunity Cost — Weighing the return against a virtual absence of risk. Page 243
- F THE Expert(s) — A second wave of bankers are brought in. Page 244
- G. THE Newest Guarantor — The borrower counters. Page 251
- H. THE Last Gasp — A separate institution offers to come aboard. Page 252
- I. THE End — Polemics are discontinued. Page 255

THE moral — Don't put all your eggs in the same basket. Page 257

Section 6: Relations 101

| Chapter 14: | How The Bank Looks At You | Page | 259 |

Where deals come from — Choose a messenger wisely. Some are shot.
- A. All That Glitters Is Not Gold — Stacking up against your industry. Chiropractors aren't the only ones who do adjustments. Page 262
- B. Mind Your Own Business — The bank's treatment of contingent risk... a plague borrowers can't get vaccinated for. Page 269
- C. Are the Rumors About You True? — What your credit report is telling people behind your back. Page 270

Talk is Cheap — That's because there's so much of it around. Page 278

| Chapter 15: | How to Get Your Deal Approved | Page | 281 |

Know Your Opponent — What's a banker? Distinguishing characteristics will help in identifying them from the general public.
- A. Who Do You Think You're Dealing With? — What's in a title? A lot to the person wearing it. In banking, clothes don't make the man... titles do. Page 283

      B. Who Do You Think You'll Be Dealing With Tomorrow? — A discussion of why high turnover exists. **Page 285**
      C. Know Your Audience... and know how it receives your actions. Are you as important as you think? **Page 290**
      D. Make Every Sales Pitch Count — What's *the only thing*? And the absolutely essential item needed to obtain it. **Page 294**
Move 'em Out for New Ones — How banks throw out perfectly good credits. **Page 299**

Section 7: Closing the Vault

Chapter 16: The Close of (All) Business **Page 301**
Another Seminar — A sales culture without the sales.
      A. Healthy Banks, Anemic Economic Future — A profitable industry without industry. **Page 305**
      B. The Grapes of Wrath — Steinbeck gives a retrospective on the federal government's three-decade spending spree. **Page 310**
      C. Putting On Our Best Face — Dressing up the numbers makes you feel better. **Page 314**
      D. Paying For the Make-Over — When reality sets in, the obvious stares back in the mirror. **Page 316**
      E. Looking Ahead — Until the placebo is discarded, shining examples will be rare. How to handle the pressure and turn your loan application into a diamond. **Page 320**
As the Seminar Winds Down — What's essential is clear. **Page 321**

Glossary **Page 323**

Index **Page 337**

To my wonderful wife — The one person who has always supported and believed in me without limitation, and who went through so much to help bring about this book.

A thousand thanks S.
I love you.

Acknowledgments

Many thanks to the book's editor, Steven Marks, who had the unenviable task of deciphering the financial lingo I use as everyday English and keeping my sarcastic sense of humor within the boundaries of good taste.

Special thanks to Peter L. Grieco, Jr., Chairman of PT Publications, who enthusiastically found reason to publish a work so different from anything else in its field.

Also, thank-yous go to Kevin Grieco for his marketing expertise as well as his graphic designs, and to Mark Grieco for timely legal advice.

Off-the-record appreciation goes to a banker friend who helped make sure all my calculations added up.

And lastly, to all my past clients who waded through the trials and tribulations described herein: May all your future credit requests be pre-approved, or at least may the use of this book make it seem that way.

Preliminary Notes

This book has been written from the vantage point of a corner office within a regional bank. Thus, the information recounted should be considered typical form for most similarly sized institutions. The financial world for the largest of concerns (who have access to capital markets) varies drastically from that of the majority of American firms — who deal with the bank on the corner. Which is why this title should be deemed particularly useful to small to mid-sized businesses. *Breaking the Bank* gives you access to the vault.

This work is not intended to harm anyone. Special care has been taken to protect the anonymity of the parties involved. Names have been changed as have the figures reported, although in no way have they have been altered beyond sensible proportion to the example(s) with which they are intertwined.

My desire is to accurately depict what takes place within most banking institutions on a day-to-day basis... and leave a wake-up call for meaningful change to the existing system of intermediation.

Along the way, a few shots are taken at stereotypes and some sensibilities may be challenged. Hopefully, as eyebrows raise so will the corners of mouths, as the short story manner in which chapters are written is meant to be entertaining.

In closing, remember that in no case are any documents, or excerpts from same contained herein, direct examples of those used by a singular institution. The reader should understand that almost identical documentation is employed in widespread fashion throughout the banking trade.

And lastly, with regard to the specific verbiage of transaction documents, please be sure to seek the advice of an attorney. Certainly, in no way should the information detailed within this book stand alone and/or take the place of legal counsel.

Disclaimers aside, enjoy.

PREFACE

It's a Wonderful Life. At least it was for George Bailey of the Bedford Falls Building & Loan. If you remember, George was the recipient of his entire community's outpouring of affection in his hour of need. And why shouldn't he have been? After all, ol' George helped build most of the city by extending credit when needed.

Savings and loan administrators and bankers enjoy Jimmy Stewart's Christmas portrayal year round. Where else can they get the warm feelings created in that movie? Certainly not in their own home towns. In fact, over the past several years, most lenders have just been glad angry mobs haven't resorted to building gallows. (Out of pocket, of course.)

It would be a sizeable understatement to say bankers are not the favored sons and daughters of their communities anymore. They are being loathed to extremes previously reserved for attorneys alone. So what happened with the legacy George left his profession? How did we get to where we're at?

Let's start by answering a rhetorical question. How similar was Bedford Fall's S&L to David Paul's Centrust Savings? Not very. George ran an institution that provided loans for the construction of

How to Obtain Business Loans

homes, and for the operation of small business. David Paul ran an institution that joint ventured^g massive commercial developments (and provided him with a nice art collection).

We are all well acquainted with the debacle that was the savings and loan industry of the 1980s, and no one would suggest immediate government intervention wasn't necessary. The specter of the S&L bailout prompted Congress to enact legislation aimed at preventing a similar disaster in banking.

The question now is whether or not the regulations put in place go beyond ensuring safety and soundness. "Congress is like the fabled puritan who lived in fear that somewhere, someone was having a good time. They seem to worry that somewhere, some banker is taking a risk... so afraid are they of making the S&L crisis a twice-told tale. The General Accounting Office[g] seems similarly inclined to risk killing the industry in order to save it. 'There isn't a guy in the GAO who can't find World War III lurking behind every corner,' former Deputy Treasury Secretary John Robson noted not long ago."[1]

We all read how great efforts are being made to get money back on the street. Such is in the news almost daily. The Federal Reserve[g] has pushed the discount rate way down to induce lending activity, but they've done so in an increasingly restrictive regulatory environment that has seen the Office of the Comptroller of the Currency[g] tighten its examination of nationally chartered banks. As a result, "commercial lending" has become a vulgarity.

The public is not getting the real story of what's going on in its financing institutions. While politicians and governmental agencies continue to make noise about freeing up money for business, banks operate under the status quo. Which means a continuation of unduly limited credit.

Look at the motivating factors involved. Banks need to be at least as conservative as their regulators in order to receive good reviews. The regulators get their direction from Congress; and if Congress is to err, they want it to be on the conservative side. It is much easier for them to defuse discontent about a credit crunch, than address the public clamor that would arise from another insolvency crisis.

Those who expect banks to return to the operations of old are kidding themselves. I still hear people speak of "the pendulum swinging back," and lending parameters significantly loosening. These individuals assess the lack of credit solely as a function of the present stage of an economic cycle. They point to other periods in history when lending dried up, only to return in force as the economic outlook brightened. This group is ignoring a megatrend caused by the S&L fiasco, and exacerbated by the federal deficit.

Preface

COMMERCIAL BANKING WILL NEVER TOTALLY RETURN TO ITS METHOD OF PAST OPERATION. (Read this sentence several times and let it sink in.)

This leaves the marketplace to adjust to the new rules. And as I've heard many times from people in business, no one has informed the rank and file. That's what this book will do.

What follows is an education of how banks are currently set up, how they operate in the prevailing environment, how they look at you, and what you need to do to get the most out of your relationship with them. Rephrased, that's... who you need to be talking to at the bank, what loans they are willing to do and under what conditions, what's important on your application for financing, and **how to get your loan approved**. Along the way you'll be entertained and even shocked with tales from the inside.

This book is not some macro-economic report on the current status of the economy. You'll hear what's actually happening in institutions from a banker waste deep in regulation and bureaucracy. You'll come away with the knowledge of what really goes on in the boardroom, and how you must adjust to continue successfully obtaining credit. In short, you'll be getting the real story.

Mark McCormick, founder of International Management Group, wrote a very good book on the interpersonal dynamics of business. It's called, *What They Don't Teach You at Harvard Business School*, and sub-titled, "Notes from a Street-Smart Business Executive." This book could easily have been entitled, *What They Don't Teach You about Banking Anywhere*, sub-titled, "Notes from an Audit-Battered Commercial Banker." Let's get started...

---

[1] Dean, Virginia: "Onward and Downward," *Bankers News*, May 26, 1993, p. 6.

CHAPTER 1:

WHY BANKING CHANGED

I suppose it has always been part of a banker's job to remain highly visible within the community. Given that services have become all but completely homogenous, it's of paramount importance today.

So tonight I'm attending yet another dinner function. The scheduled speaker is to elaborate on the city's zoning changes. A less than scintillating topic that will have most of the audience napping in no time. However, I won't be. I'll need to stay alert for the question and answer session. At which time, no matter the presentation content, the gathering will probably move into a little banker bashing. Happens a lot.

It seems flat out amazing, so long as the discussion is remotely related to business, someone in the crowd will invariably bring up

How to Obtain Business Loans

the lack of money being lent by banks. This always livens up the group. Instantly you'll hear testimony on requests rejected, proposals altered to the point of being ridiculous, and the time that it takes to get any answer at all. "What the blank are these bankers doing anyway?" is usually the emphatically asked question.

Now being highly visible in the community means being a big red target. Boy, I can't wait to go tonight.

Industry Transformation

Let's have a review of basic economics. When a business holds a monopolistic[g] position it can be relatively assured of enjoying good profit margins. Accordingly, there is little reason for management to take excessive risks in operation.

In the event true competition arises and the business has to fight for its customer base, management will be forced to make more and more decisions that increase operating risk. They may lower the price of the product, pledge faster delivery, take on additional leverage to try and attain higher market share, etc. When this occurs, the firm's risk of bankruptcy rises. This is what happened in banking.

Regulatory protection once allowed the banking system to operate as somewhat of a monopoly. There wasn't an institution on every street corner, and alternative short term investment vehicles didn't exist. Your local bank's cost of funds was quite controllable. At the same time, if you needed a loan they were very often the only game in town. As a result, net interest margins[g] were high, most institutions returned their owners a nice profit, and insolvencies were almost nonexistent.

But as AT&T found out, monopolies don't exist perpetually in our country. (Except for baseball.) Commercial paper[g] entered the scene and abruptly took away banks' bread-and-butter earning asset... short term loans to quality large firms. To worsen matters, money market funds[g] followed soon after and swooped up a big percentage of shorter term deposits. What happened? Loan rates had to be dropped, and deposit rates had to be raised in order to retain customers. Margins contracted sharply.

What next? Interest rate deregulation. Deposit rates were further bid up to gain market share. At the same time, other forms of lenders were entering the arena: leasing companies, insurance firms, finance companies, and brokers of private money. Margins disappeared.

Chapter One

Every action demands an equal and opposite reaction. So, commercial loan volume had to be increased in order to meet budgets. As a result, banks made riskier and riskier credit extensions.

As the appetite for loans skyrocketed, loan-to-deposit ratios expanded drastically. Ratios in the 95% range became more the norm and less the exception. With liabilities increasing substantially, and no additional equity being infused, institutions made themselves ripe for bankruptcy **should** vicissitudes in the economy take place. (Back to basic economics. Capitalist society = cyclical economy.) **When** the downturn came, insolvencies began to occur.

Bad Loans

I've been employed by two quality regional size banks. Each had loans on the books that Michael Milken might have thought too risky an investment. (Too bad he wasn't on the board.)

One memorable credit was a loan to Trafalgar Development. (Throughout this book the accounts given are genuine, but names have been changed; as have numbers, although they remain in proportion to actual figures.) Trafalgar had been able to obtain a $1.5 million dollar loan to construct an office facility. They were a British concern with no holdings in the United States. Likewise, the company's principal, Colin Scott, was a British subject with no assets stateside. This meant the loan was basically without recourse to company or individual in the event of any default. The reliance was solely upon the real estate.

That in mind, you must be presuming the location of the building was outstanding, and that the majority of space was pre-leased prior to construction. Wrong and wrong. The site was located well south of the city. Although it fronted a main thoroughfare, it was in a sparsely developed area.

Leases. Ah yes, that would've helped. Too bad by the time construction was completed there weren't any; the few pre-leases that existed having fallen out. So there she stood, 20,000 square feet of concrete and glass. A shell whose only tenant, after 4 years, was the leasing agent.

The bank? Needless to say the estimated loan-to-value position had become something substantially different than that initially underwritten to. With the building generating no income, an up-

How to Obtain Business Loans

dated appraisal yielded a value much less than originally estimated. (To say the least.)

Value of facility as initially calculated:

20,000 SF @ $15.50 per	$ 310,000 in gross rents
Less 10% vacancy	31,000
Effective gross income	$ 279,000
Less 25% in expenses	69,750
Net operating income	$ 209,250
Capped^g at 10%	$ 2,092,500
	(say $2.1 million)
Original LTV (Loan-to-Value)	71%

Versus a valuation based upon an adjusted income stream, using more conservative rental rates and vacancy factors:

20,000 SF @ $12.00 per	$ 240,000
Less 15% vacancy	36,000
Effective gross income	$ 204,000
Less 25% in expenses	51,000
Net operating income	$ 153,000
Capped at 10%	$ 1,530,000
	(say $1.5 million)
Adjusted LTV	100%

Just like that, there's no equity in the collateral. This happened on a lot of real estate deals throughout the industry. Undertakings which really weren't feasible got done. The desire for volume was at such a premium, good sense didn't prevail during loan committee.

Another notable credit was a residential development known as Meadowood. This project was undertaken along a dead-end road outside of town. Again, the location was not what you'd call in the midst of anything. However, there were plans to construct a major hospital nearby. The developer was counting on the demand for

Chapter One

housing to increase as he assumed hospital employees would want to live close to work.

The bank approved the loan to complete the permitting, infrastructure^g, and entranceway. Lots were to be marketed in the $35,000-$40,000 range. End users were to find their own contractors to construct their homes. (Great idea.)

In fact, the developer convinced the bank that demand was going to be so strong, they'd miss out if they didn't finance another project of his across the street. Carillon Marsh was to offer the area "product diversity" according to the originating loan officer. Lots were to sell in a **completely** different price range, $45,000-$50,000. (**Really** great idea.)

It was so good... several other entrepreneurs had already thought of it and were developing adjacent parcels. No one but the lead officer was aware of this. Carillon Marsh was approved.

Soon this dead-end road in the middle of nowhere had no less than five residential subdivisions in process. A total of 215 lots (all priced between $25,000-$60,000) were to be made available virtually at once. Universal success hinged on it being a BBBBBIIIIIGGGGG hospital with lots of workers who hated to drive very far.

Things didn't go quite as everyone had planned. (Gasp.) The developer in question went belly up, and somehow the bank had not escrowed^g enough funds to complete either Meadowood or Carillon Marsh. The other projects didn't fare so well either, the hospital apparently having a staff full of driving enthusiasts.

The officer who underwrote the original credit was moved into the residential lending department. It was decided his "aggressiveness" would be better suited to the home mortgage environment than that of commercial lending. Guess who got the joy of cleaning up? Yours truly.

One fine spring day as we prepared for foreclosure, I decided to do a site visit to the most overbuilt dead-end road in the nation. No inspection had been done in some time, so I thought I might like to see the condition of our collateral. What I saw defines "failed project." As I drove to the end of the street where Meadowood was located, I was careful to skirt the broken bottles. Evidently, the teenage crowd found this an ideal place to congregate. What the heck, there certainly wasn't any traffic. Making out the project on my right through the three-foot weeds, I turned into the subdivision. The two-by-fours which fashioned the entrance had fallen and lay in disarray. A sign

How to Obtain Business Loans

announcing "reduced lot prices" was propped against a small tree. And there, in the middle of the road, were two buzzards eating a dead armadillo. (I think realtors call it "street appeal.")

It has been a few years, and to my knowledge the bank still holds both properties in its Real Estate Owned[g] category. No lots ever closed. The other projects? Well, one succeeded. Which is about all that ever could have. The desire for loan volume was at such a premium, good sense (again) didn't prevail.

These, and other credits I could cite, are examples of what happens when a bank becomes *too* dependent upon exceedingly high loan volume in order to turn a profit.

Abuses

Sure, sure, we've all heard about the wild happenings at the S&Ls, but those shenanigans were isolated to unregulated thrifts. Right?

I've seen many things that would do more than raise eyebrows at a committee meeting on ethics. There was the individual who was in the process of moving some investment property through eminent domain[g] proceedings. He offered lavish parties attended by prominent attorneys, city planners, town council members, local politicians, and bankers alike. Perhaps by coincidence, he was able to pyramid debt by means of changing borrowing structures, partners, etc. at a few institutions. (It's not what you know, but...)

I'm aware of bankers enjoying the boats, condos, and other toys of their borrowers; and I've noted them accepting significant gifts from same. In a probably unrelated matter, I've observed the borrowers obtaining additional financing on a nonrecourse basis for raw land speculation, with interest reserves funded by the bank. I even know of one such loan which was approved with a senior bank officer being one of the equity partners in the transaction!

Unfortunately, no amount of legislation and regulation is likely to completely eliminate these types of *indiscretions*. In truth, some of banking's problems mirror society as a whole. There are unscrupulous people, and they **do** engage in unprincipled affairs. The challenge is to police them, and other matters, without handcuffing an entire industry.

Chapter One

Loan Reserves

Capital adequacy[g] and loan loss provisions[g] are the focus of those inclined to ensure the safety of banking. A premium has been placed on banks classifying credits according to their perceived risk. Almost all institutions have a grading system in place that segregates loans by category, and assesses reserves accordingly. The following would not be considered atypical:

Class 'A' Loans which are considered essentially without danger of loss. For example, those collateralized by a certificate of deposit held by the advancing institution. (Banks will gladly lend you your money at 1-2% over the rate of interest paid on a CD. And usually with a minimal fee of around $50! Maximum LTV is typically 90% of the CD amount. The 10% cushion is in the event interest cannot be paid in full at maturity.)

Class 'B' Loans thought to have minimal to average risk associated with them. These are generally to major concerns. For instance, an equipment loan to IBM might be rated a Class 'B'. (Evidently banks have more stringent rating guidelines than do Moody or Standard & Poor.) Most banks wouldn't categorize a credit to a small or medium sized firm as a 'B' for fear of being chastised by regulators.

Class 'C' Loans with acceptable, but more than average, risk. It's humorous to consider banks classify the majority of their credits in this category. Meaning the **average** loan has **above average** peril associated with it! Think about that. The regulators have the industry so gun shy that bankers are saying the bulk of loans being made have above average risk, and that they recognize the related exposure. This is certainly easier than trying to sell an auditor on the fact you have a solid credit on the books with minimal to average risk. Better to be too conservative, so you won't easily be criticized.

Class 'D' Loans with significant risk. These credits have

How to Obtain Business Loans

specific weaknesses which could cause a default under certain circumstances. An example would be a loan to an individual who owns a strip shopping center. If it is discovered tenants have fallen out, the loan is likely to be classified a 'D'. This is because repayment was evaluated based upon lease income, and now the borrower must make restitution from other resources.

Class 'E' Substandard. Repayment to established term is considered highly unlikely. **It is important to note that credits are often graded substandard, even though they pay on a timely basis.** The loan described under the Class 'D' definition would be moved to Class 'E' if the bank could not verify other resources. Again... even if the individual was making his monthly payments. It is probable it would also be placed on nonaccrual[g]. This makes the credit a performing nonperforming asset[g]. (Isn't that an oxymoron? Kind of like jumbo shrimp.)

Class 'F' Loans which are, in all probability, uncollectible. Reasons persist why they are kept on the books, and not immediately charged off as a loss. (Although I can't think of any at the moment.) Banks are not quite as pessimistic in this area as others. It's one thing to downgrade a loan to sidestep reproach, it's a whole other ball game to actually write something off.

So, as I think you can see, the real benefit to the grading system is banks recognize losses on a t..i..m..e..l..y   b..a..s..i..s. Hmmm, something didn't work out right there.

Anyway, each classification carries with it a reserve component[g], which is figured as a percentage of the loan balance. For example:

Grades 'A' - 'C'	(not criticized)	1%
Grade 'D'	(risky)	5%
Grade 'E'	(substandard)	10%
Grade 'F'	(doubtful)	50%

Adherence to a tiered reserve system like this has put a huge

Chapter One

priority on file maintenance. To clarify, let's say a $500,000 loan is made to the owner of a small office building. She leases space to three unrelated tenants, and her own company occupies one-quarter of the facility. At inception, the risk rating is a 'C'. The bank carries 1% of the balance as a loss provision — $5,000.

Twelve months from closing the originating officer discovers two of the initial tenants have gone out of business, and the space they vacated is unfilled. The credit is moved to category 'D', and the provision becomes 5% — $25,000. Where does the money come from? **Basically, reserves are set aside out of income.** (Now there's an attention getter.)

For the next few months the officer attempts to collect updated financial statements from the borrower, who has become uncooperative. As a result, the loan must be moved to an 'E' classification because of the bank's inability to substantiate continued repayment without current information. Even if there is a perfect track record to date! Now reserves jump to 10% — $50,000. To compound matters, the loan will likely be placed on nonaccrual; the interest portion of payments received will not be taken into bank income.

Now let's look at the opportunity cost[g] associated with the lending officer's time. If an upgrade to a 'D' classification can be obtained, $25,000 will ultimately be removed from reserves and flow back to income. Conversely, using 1 point as a typical loan fee, the officer would need to originate $2.5 million in new business to generate $25,000 in near term income. Which is a more judicious use of time; working on upgrading one credit, or doing five medium sized loans? (Expect the lending officer to make a lot of calls on the individual not supplying financial statements.)

You can see why bankers have been so internally focused over the past few years. With auditors having downgraded so many loans, banks are better served to have their officers work for reclassifications. Think of it this way... if a "lender" gets one $500,000 credit moved from an 'E' to a 'C', he has earned his salary for the year.

I hear you. "That's all well and good, but can't the officer continue to make new loans?" Permit me to give you an idea of what would be needed to upgrade our example loan:

- An updated personal financial statement submitted on a bank supplied form.

How to Obtain Business Loans

- Verification of cash and other liquid assets.

- A copy of the most recent personal tax filing, including all schedules and K1s for each partnership and S Corp [g]. If the current return is extended, a copy of the extension should be provided.

- An updated company financial statement. Depending upon the size of the firm, audited reports [g] may even be required.

- A copy of the last company tax return, plus extension if applicable.

- Forecasts for the next twelve months.

- Quarterly operating statements on the building, along with similar material for any other rental properties the customer holds.

- Copies of current insurance coverage.

- The rental listing[g] should be obtained.

- The officer must do a site visit and complete a detailed narrative supplying commentary on the facility's interior and exterior condition, as well as the general repair of the surrounding grounds.

- All the preceding information would need to be analyzed (ad nauseam), and a formal package completed summarizing the findings.

- Then a committee would be convened to determine if the loan could be upgraded without possible outside criticism. (Read: "without regulators disagreeing.")

This process completed, the "lender" need only fill out a few forms and send them to the regional loan review officer for approval. Then, address any concerns he might have, obtain further supporting data as usually requested, await additional questions... and by that time their statements are almost outdated again.

Seriously, the procedures for changing loan classifications are

Chapter One

extremely time consuming. And remember, the officer must be acquiring and analyzing the same type of information on all borrowers so as to substantiate continued repayment ability. If not, other loans will be downgraded. What this amounts to is "lenders" have become clerks. The vast majority of their time spent chasing and pushing paper, **not extending it**.

Uh oh! The speaker's looking at me. Someone must have asked a question directed at bankers. **"I'm sorry?"** All eyes now focus on me as my collar tightens and the room temperature goes up 30 degrees.

An irritable looking man at the other end of the dining room repeats, "You guys are so tight... can you get any money out of the vault these days?"

I smile as if I've just kissed a baby on the campaign trail and say, **"Not much. In fact, we have a styrofoam cup set up in the employee lounge to collect for coffee purchases."** Everyone laughs, and for the moment I'm off the hook. Funny thing is, I wasn't joking.

Chapter Two

CHAPTER 2:

THE EVOLUTION OF LENDING

My wife and I are driving through beautiful Asheville, North Carolina on vacation. It's fall, so the leaves are turning, birds are singing, children are playing, and any number of other things are happening to occupy one's attention. However, at the moment, the entire town seems engrossed in something going on over at the bank. A large crowd has gathered, and all stand peering through the plate glass window fronting the street. Looks like there's a policeman on the scene. Must've been a robbery, or maybe somebody fainted in the lobby. **'Honey, roll your window down and let's see what the story is.'**

The policeman's voice resonates in the air, "Alright you people, break it up... move along now... get back to your business. I'm sure everybody has seen somebody qualify for a loan before."

Okay, okay, so that's just some cruel humor making the rounds

How to Obtain Business Loans

at the expense of bankers. Although things **are** incredibly squeezed right now, and not just in the lending area. The emphasis on cost control has never been greater than at the present. Merger mania is taking place as holding companies seek to expand market share without having to build it from the ground up. As this transpires, expenses are curtailed by consolidating as many back room operations as possible, and by tightening belts across the board. Particularly since fewer loans are being put on the books.

Gone are the days of taking a customer out for a round of golf under the heading of "business development." For two reasons; (1) no one is what you'd call aggressively in the market for commercial loans, and (2) with the yields on earning assets having been driven down, **cost control is king**. I really wasn't kidding about the coffee being sold to employees on a per cup basis. That's just the beginning. One institution I know inventories all items on hand within the bank. Not just computers and art work. I'm talking about staplers, hole punchers, scissors, etc. (The high ticket items.) Each carries a numerical sticker for identification, and you sign them out. The same bank issues initial business cards that look like this:

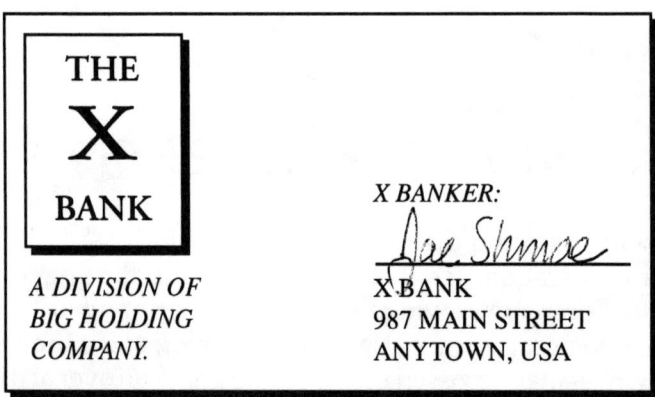

(Your cards have your name penciled in, everything in your office has been inventoried, and you're told you'll get a name plate if you get through the 90 day probationary period. Welcome aboard, feel secure?)

Departments have to adhere very closely to budgets. Codes are assigned by cost center^g for the copy machines, as paper usage is monitored. The tapes from desk calculators are reversed so both

Chapter Two

sides are utilized. And once when I was leaving a particular branch location, I was asked to white out the name on my business cards so that the incoming officer could use them.

A trip in the bank car requires a written request ahead of time. The journey must be logged to the 10th of a mile, and you should anticipate it being verified against your described itinerary. If you order the movie while staying overnight on business, don't expect to be reimbursed. The same goes for any meal fancier than what McDonald's offers.

In many instances, cost control is synonymous with cost abolishment. I know big business is turning to "temporary" or "project workers" as a means of saving on benefits, but where else would you hear of the same temp being used for a year and a half without interruption? Only in banking.

In fact, only in banking would you find management evaluating the revenue side of the business equation almost as an afterthought. In most industries, sales are immediately addressed when the bottom line begins to soften. But in banking, where so much income is derived from recurring interest payments, management tries to live off what's in the pantry. With the focus of underwriting having changed drastically due to regulation, there better be a lot in the cupboard.

The Burden of Proof

Anybody ever heard of the 5 Cs of Credit? They're what stone-age bankers judged loans upon. You know... character, credit, capacity, collateral, conditions... the 5 Cs. How did they work? Quite well. I'll bet you've even used them yourself and didn't know it.

Has a friend, or relative, ever come to you for money? Let's say cousin Bill did. He asked for an amount large enough to make you stop and think about it. What went through your mind? What did you base your decision upon?

Character You had known Bill for years, and always considered his integrity beyond reproach. No one ever had anything but positive things to say about him.

How to Obtain Business Loans

Credit Things had been tight for Bill a few times, but he'd always kept up his obligations. (You knew this because his wife talked about the family finances a little more than she should have.)

Capacity Bill had worked at the lumber mill for almost 15 years. He'd certainly never be rich, but it was a decent living and he was a fixture there. Becoming foreman five years ago made him almost indispensable to the company.

Collateral Never one to take straight charity, Bill offered you the title to his old Chevy until the loan was repaid. It wasn't brand new by a long shot, but it was worth more than what he wanted to borrow.

Conditions The local economy was actually holding up better than that on the national horizon. Demand for lumber was pretty solid, so the mill's outlook for the future was good.

After considering these things, you went ahead and made Bill the loan, which you agreed to have paid back in equal installments over 24 months.

A year goes by and Bill never misses a beat on his payments. He even mentions when he gets his Christmas bonus he's going to retire the debt early. Question: At this juncture do you sit down and re-evaluate whether or not Bill can repay the loan you gave him? Seems a little silly doesn't it? Welcome to the 6th C of Credit. **Continuous**... as in monitoring.

In banking there is no such thing as an assumption of extending capacity. A 10-year term note could have paid perfectly for 9 years, you would still be obligated to "prove" cash flows for the ensuing 10th year; or potentially downgrade the loan. I call this the regulator's **Glass Half Empty Stance**. No matter what the track record of a credit is, in the absence of current financial information, there is a negative supposition about the loan's future.

Let's suppose Bill's debt was a bank financed commercial obligation. At the end of the first year, the account officer would need to

Chapter Two

obtain an updated personal balance sheet so as to recognize differences in financial position. (Note: Even if the officer were aware of the small changes which had transpired for Bill in the last year, he wouldn't be able to just write out another statement for him and have it signed. If he did, the bank could not legally rely upon it... even if Bill attested to the information. Judges have ruled that since the entire document is not in the handwriting of the borrower, the bank cannot "prove" it was thoroughly reviewed by them.)

The bank would also need to acquire a copy of Bill's last complete tax filing, signed by he and his wife verifying its authenticity. (No kidding.) The return would be analyzed to come up with a recurring income figure. This would be adjusted gross income less capital gains, lump sum distributions from partnerships, non-repeating interest income, etc. Bill's continued ability to service the bank's loan would be "proven" by showing that his annual income stream covered the current portion of all debts disclosed on his financial statement with some room to spare. The expenses listed would have been verified against an updated credit bureau report. The bank will also validate that Bill's other obligations are being paid on a timely basis. If one isn't, the bank might reclassify its loan even though the credit is being kept current, and Bill shows the capacity to keep it that way. (Better to be safe.)

I know what you're thinking. "We're confirming future repayment ability based upon past cash flow information." Well you're right, but you're ignoring the 11th commandment... **Thou shalt not trust a borrower's projections**. They are always considered too optimistic, and *if* supplied are often tossed out. (Thanks anyway.) You see, suppose they were kept in file and then the following year cash flow doesn't turn out to be what was expected. Internal review often would treat this as a "red flag," a warning of danger ahead. Accordingly, there is a good chance the credit rating would be dropped. (Better to be safe.)

So what are we doing? We look at last year's numbers to see if Bill paid the loan... hmm, let's have some fun. What if the statements indicate he did not generate sufficient income to make the payments that he did? (This happens more than you might think.) **The loan is downgraded.** Okay, then what happens if the statements show he had enough cash flow to make timely restitution, but he actually ran a little slow? **The loan is downgraded.** (That darn glass is half empty no matter how you look at it.)

How to Obtain Business Loans

In either case, an additional loss provision would be set aside. The scenarios we discussed would probably mean at least a 'D' classification, and possibly an 'E' rating with a 10% reserve. Further, the note might be a candidate for nonaccrual. In the past, this category was utilized for loans 90 days or more delinquent. It now includes many paying credits where THE BURDEN OF PROOF has not been met.

The ABC File

One such loan was to ABC, a general partnership. If the cousin Bill example was an over-simplified illustration of how the criteria for assessing credit has "evolved," then discussion of The ABC File will be an expanded clarification of the extent to which the new methodology is implemented.

Bernard Gettz was the proprietor of Guns-R-Us. He operated his retail firearms business out of space leased from a James Duncan. Desiring expansion, but without the capital to accomplish it, Mr. Gettz offered Mr. Duncan an opportunity to invest in a building to be constructed. A larger facility would allow Guns-R-Us to set up a shooting range to complement merchandise sales. Mr. Duncan liked the idea and brought in his associate, Bob Harvey, as a third partner in the venture.

Messrs. Duncan and Harvey were long-time customers in good standing. The bank having previously extended monies to them for two major condominium projects in the aggregate amount of $6.5 million. Both loans were paid according to term.

ABC approached the bank with a request to finance a portion of the proposed undertaking. Based upon the previous successes with two of the individuals, a loan of $400,000 was approved. Duncan and Harvey put the balance of funds necessary in on the front end, $120,000. The facility was constructed without incident, and Guns-R-Us made the transition to operating from a new venue. Over time, the partners contributed another $130,000 to customize the building. Upgrades included exterior wall fortification, sound barriers, firing divisions, etc.

Three years went by with monthly payments being made as agreed, and the loan was ballooning at about the point I went to work for the institution in question. As a signing bonus, I inherited the ABC relationship.

Chapter Two

The loan had been downgraded some time ago due to... (guess what)... a failure to "prove" continued timely repayment. The bank's president made it the highest priority of my new job to get the credit placed elsewhere. (Read that: Paid off by another financing institution.) Or restructured in such a manner as to ensure a more favorable loan classification. (Meaning one without almost $40,000 in reserve requirements... which, coincidentally, was my salary.)

I thought before I just arbitrarily began pushing the relationship out of the bank, I'd at least take a cursory look at the file. Here's what I found... ABC's tenant, Guns-R-Us, had posted a terrible statement for their fiscal year ended November 30, 1991. A simplified funds flow looked like this:

Net Income	($46,299)
Adding Back:	
Depreciation	6,194
Rents Paid	44,732
Available	$ 4,627
Annual Service	(44,504)
Shortfall	($39,877)

What's more, the company's trend was quite negative. Apparently, (legal) weapon sales were on the decline.

	1988	1989	1990	1991
Sales	$677,929	$910,321	$878,486	$690,620
Gross Profit	$142,176	$336,818	$210,836	$145,030
Gross Margin	21%	37%	24%	21%
Quick Ratio	1.25:1	2.35:1	.75:1	.20:1

Taken by themselves, these numbers substantiated an 'E' classi-

How to Obtain Business Loans

fication, and nonaccrual status. However, one must remember credit was extended not on the basis of Guns-R-Us' cash flow, but on the strength of the investors' joint and several guarantees.

As of 4/30/91 Mr. Duncan reported the following financial position:

Assets:		
Cash & Marketable Securities		$ 249,300
Note Receivable—Mashburn Corp.		11,250
Subordinated Debenture—Mashburn Corp.		31,500
Investments:		
Watkins Glen Insurance	(33% interest)	753,750
Mashburn Corp.	(25% interest)	101,250
The Caldwell Agency	(33% interest)	225,000
Pikesville Properties	(100% owned)	225,000
Minority Real Estate Holdings:		
Parson Properties	(25% interest)	123,750
LBJ Partnership	(20% interest)	191,250
Gunnison Corp. Center	(6% interest)	50,625
Duncan Enterprises	(25% interest)	1,017,000
Charleston Properties	(50% interest)	218,250
Watkins Glen Partners	(33% interest)	134,064
Ben Davis Limited	(13% interest)	337,500
Pikesville Partners	(26% interest)	1,120,500
Georgetown Properties	(20% interest)	274,500
BMT, Limited	(17% interest)	349,875
Other Assets:		
Automobiles		56,250
Residence		1,068,750
Boat Slip		67,500
Personal Property		325,125
Total Assets		$ 6,931,989
Liabilities:		
Tax Provision (on the difference between estimated current asset values and their corresponding liabilities, less their cost basis, at the marginal tax rate)		1,725,000
Net Worth		$ 5,206,989*

Chapter Two

*Contingently liable for the following:

Watkins Glen Insurance	$1,687,500	
Mashburn Corp.	196,875	
The Caldwell Agency	168,750	
ABC Partnership	400,000	
Total		2,453,125
Net of Total Contingencies		**$ 2,753,864**

Adjusted gross income on Mr. Duncan's last two tax filings was in excess of $250,000. His personal debt ratio^g appeared to be in the 10-15% range, as most of his expenses were netted from business and partnership cash flow rather than being passed through to him individually. However, the bank was not in possession of detailed financial information on the 14 different enterprises he was involved in. Therefore, it had been concluded Mr. Duncan could not be relied upon to support the $39,877 paper shortfall left by Guns-R-Us. **(Wow!)**

Mr. Harvey's financial data was also on file for review, and was even more impressive than Mr. Duncan's notable disclosure. (Assuming that you, as I, thought Mr. Duncan's statement was impressive.) On a summary dated April 1, 1991 Mr. Harvey reported:

Assets:

Cash		$ 56,250
Autos		56,250
Cash Value of Life Insurance		22,500
Residence		652,500
Nolin Property Management		4,000,000
Nolin Realty		28,125
1st Settler's National Bank		2,250,000
Cajin' Rage Clothiers		28,125
River City Farms		56,250
Winter Centers		585,000
Adams West		3,037,500
Minority Real Estate Holdings:		
House, Jackson St.	(25% interest)	39,375
House, College Ave.	(25% interest)	196,875
Gunville Lakes Land	(5% interest)	28,125

(summary continued on next page)

How to Obtain Business Loans

Oliver's Place	(6% interest)	28,125
Johnson Mobile Homes	(25% interest)	281,250
Main St. Apts.	(25% interest)	393,750
Griffith Ln. Offices	(20% interest)	54,000
Cobalt Manors	(45% interest)	225,000
G & J Bldg.	(53% interest)	337,500
Polly Square	(2% interest)	5,400
Streams Plaza	(15% interest)	225,000
Old Smokie Views	(9% interest)	16,875
Seascape Retirement Home	(14% interest)	143,640
Indian Towers	(5% interest)	281,250
MTV Partners	(50% interest)	112,500
St. Matthew Partners	(50% interest)	168,750
Total Assets		**$13,309,915**

Liabilities:

Home Mortgage	315,000
Mortgage on Nolin R.E. Bldg.	900,000
Unsecured Note 1st City Bank	337,500
Winters' Mortgage Edgewater Bank	84,375
1st Settlers' Mtge.	843,750
Tahoe Company Purchase Money Mtges.	365,625
Costigan Mtge. MidTown Bank & Trust	1,800,000
Total Liabilities	**$ 4,646,250**
Net Worth	**$ 8,663,665***
***Unspecified contingent liabilities total**	3,495,800
Net of Total Contingencies	**$ 5,167,865**

Mr. Harvey's recent tax filings caused the bank great consternation. Memorandums in file attempted to explain the returns, but coming to a definitive cash flow figure was not easy; as each filing was about as thick as a New York City phone book. To say the least, they were quite complex. Due to losses carried forward, a negative adjusted gross income was posted annually; then offset by non-cash expenses such as depreciation, and further bolstered by tax free income.

The problem was not coming to an **exact** number for cash flow, just one in the ball park. Estimates for 1990 ranged from $100,000 to in excess of $1 million. This *minor* discrepancy was never resolved, as

Chapter Two

the bank gave up trying since they were not in possession of all K-1s information. In the absence of which, they reasoned any attempt to quantify past cash flow would be nothing more than guesswork.

Mr. Harvey had balked at supplying all his K-1s, as forwarding copies of the *New York City directory* to various lending institutions was already beginning to become a real expense. Adding the cost to duplicate and send K-1s about the country was a bit much in his estimation. Instead, he supplied a summary statement of all contributions and withdrawals^g. Unfortunately, the bank felt uneasy about relying upon the information. (What... trust a borrower?)

Still trying to help, Mr. Harvey furnished an accountant prepared estimate of his cash flow for the next twelve month period. It indicated he would receive in excess of $1 million, without the benefit of any capital gains (which, by the way, amounted to $4 million dollars during the prior year).

The bank's conclusion on Mr. Harvey? Sure he had a lot of assets, but the majority of them were minority interests. What kind of real control did he have over those affairs? How could one depend on any cash flow projections without the benefit of analyzing the 23 different enterprises he was involved in? Without articles of incorporation on the solely held companies, and partnership agreements on the other endeavors, no credence could be given to an assumption of ongoing stability. There were just too many unknowns.

Additionally, without the separate balance sheets and tax filings for the corporations, the K-1s for the partnerships, the operating statements for the income producing properties, the assessment of possible environmental problems on his vast real estate holdings, the status of his marriage, the knowledge of his childhood behavioral patterns, the scouting report on his ability to dribble to his left, abcd, efgh, ijkl... well, how could **anyone** count on Mr. Harvey's ability to support $39,877 in annual debt service? There were just too many unknowns. (If any of this makes sense, stop reading this book now. Drive directly to your local bank and apply for a senior management position in the audit division. You're a cinch to be hired.)

Notations in the file indicated the bank was quite pleased with Mr. Gettz's financial disclosure. I assume because it was fairly straightforward, having only one business concern. His personal statement showed a net worth of about $200,000; which, when adjusted for his guarantee of ABC's debt, left him in the red. Cash totalled only $2,000; and his last tax filing showed personal income

How to Obtain Business Loans

of less than $50,000. In my eyes, Mr. Gettz offered little support to the credit.

However, the bank had set forth the opinion that any hope for an upgrade lay in the operation of Guns-R-Us and Mr. Gettz's personal cash flow after the fact. They felt if it could be shown he had monies left over after living expenses, maybe a reclassification could be justified. The prevailing suspicion was that the other gentlemen could not be counted upon due to their "far flung affairs." (You are entering the fifth dimension. A dimension known only as The Twilight Zone.)

To recap the bank's conclusions to this point:

1) $305,550 in cash and marketable securities between Messrs. Duncan and Harvey were disregarded due to the uncertainty surrounding potential contingent liability claims.
2) $20,241,904 in total assets were discounted because a large portion were held in partnerships with others.
3) $13,870,654 in net worth was ignored because of its... its... Well, I'm not sure why.
4) Mr. Duncan's $250,000 annual cash flow, plus Mr. Harvey's $100,000 to $1 million, was adjudged "undependable," and not "thoroughly verified."
5) The bank, rather, chose to rest its hopes for an upgrade on Mr. Gettz's $50,000 a year, to be derived from Guns-R-Us' deteriorating financial statements.

(Quickly I began to search the hallways for someone with normal brain wave activity.) I debated from the position of common sense. (Wrong stance.) I was told: "Of course ultimate repayment is dependent upon Mr. Duncan and Mr. Harvey... and they certainly appear to have the wherewithal... but we're talking about classifying risk here." (Huh?)

"Isn't the assessment of whether or not you're going to be repaid the same as the evaluation of a loan's risk classification?" I asked.

"Well, ummm, ah... you don't understand."

You're right. Especially given that the individuals have stated they've never had to support Guns-R-Us' monthly payments to the bank. I offered, **"Perhaps Guns-R-Us might be enjoying some unreported cash flow? I mean, they make payments even though their statements show they can't."**

Chapter Two

"That's not even appropriate for discussion."

In other words, don't cloud the issue with any facts, let's get back to analyzing those statements. Having ascertained there was little or no chance of garnering the leap of faith required to assume Messrs. Duncan and Harvey could support $3,231.42 per month between them, I decided to try and push the loan out of the bank. (This is a touchy task. Even if the bank president has instructed you to do this, let a borrower call to complain about mistreatment after years of being a good customer and you could promptly be martyred into the unemployment line. Notwithstanding, if you don't get it moved out, you are "not handling the relationship properly.")

James Duncan was in my office to discuss the matter just days before maturity. As I illustrated how the bank was unable to verify continued timely repayment, and explained how the inability to do so resulted in a **real cost** to us, Mr. Duncan's face turned an unfriendly shade of red. He burst into a 10 minute tirade on how "the *blank blank* banks in this country wouldn't know a good loan if it bit them in their *blanking blankes*." And this was "nothing but a bunch of *blanking blank blank*." He then eloquently stated that neither I nor anyone at my institution "knew our *blankes* from a hole in the ground." More *blankity-blank* followed until we were both shouting at the top of our lungs from behind an office door which as yet did not carry my name plate. I decided to calm the situation down in a hurry.

Time to interrupt the flow of things. **"Cough, cough."** I faked a suddenly dry throat. **"Cough, cough."** He stopped yelling, and I asked, **"Do you want something to drink? I seem to have something in my wind pipe, I'm going to get a Pepsi. You want one?"**

"Well, ummm, ah... sure." His face began to return to its more normal pigmentation, and the vein in his neck receded from the enlargement which had made it the size of a garden hose.

I left my desk and opened my office door. **"Louise..."** I called to my secretary (who was busy canceling the order for my business cards). **"Would you get us a couple of Pepsis, please? Thanks."**

She returned shortly with two sodas, which I would have to reimburse her for later. By that time, *James* and I were wrapping up our banter on the virtues of a tropical climate. "Look, I'm sorry I lost my temper," he said, "but you guys have got to work with us. There is no way, in the current environment, we can get this loan placed elsewhere in less than six months."

How to Obtain Business Loans

I knew he wasn't exaggerating. He was speaking both of the credit crunch, and the unwritten "bigger fool theory." Which, simply defined, means if another institution no longer wants to house a loan, then there certainly must be something wrong with the credit. Taking away the other bank's position would make you a "bigger fool" than they. This doctrine could also be called "The Ostrich Axiom," or the "I'm-Going-to-Stick-My-Head-in-the-Sand-and-Not-Listen-to-Your-Request-Since-I-Know-Where-It's-Coming-from Postulate." (But that's not as catchy.) Ol' Jimbo was right, it would be tough for them to place this elsewhere. Wait a minute, hold the Pepsis, who's manipulating who here? Oh well, I **was** sympathetic with ABC's position in the first place. I always felt the bank's stance on the credit came from somewhere outside of Pluto.

"Jim, maybe we can work out a renewal under some very stringent parameters."

"How stringent?"

"Well, I have to be able to prove continued cash flow." His color started changing again. **"Jim, as ridiculous as it sounds, I cannot substantiate future cash flow to our auditors with the type of holdings you and Bob have. They are just too diverse for us to conclusively analyze. The successful way in which you've amassed your substantial net worth through partnerships is a little too complex for us to readily understand. At least, without asking for every piece of financial information you yourself are privy to. And I feel that would be too time consuming and cumbersome for you to deal with."** He was enjoying a prideful little smile, and was again headed out of a red hue.

"I have an idea. Suppose you and Bob post an irrevocable letter of credit from your northern bank, in an amount equal to one year's principal and interest payments?" (His thermometer was on the rise once more.) He bellowed for a few minutes in anger, frustration, and disbelief. I broke to ask Louise for another round of Pepsis (throwing a mostly full one in the trash).

"Jim, I know this will cost you money; but it's going to cost you a lot less than the alternatives. Let's say you were able to move the credit tomorrow. You'd pay the next bank a fee, and you'd have title insurance and recording costs, not to mention legal expenses. Or let's say, only hypothetically, we begin foreclosure. In that case, you're just going to feed some lawyer for over a year while trying

Chapter Two

to protect the equity you have in the building. Which, between you and Bob, is over a quarter of a million dollars." (This sounded infinitely more than two-hundred-and-fifty-thousand.)

"Alright, suppose we get you the letter of credit. What else would you need to feel all warm and cozy with us?"

"We'd need an updated appraisal. And, although we would have to order it, you'd be responsible for the cost." (Major tantrum. Major, major tantrum. The Pepsi trick wouldn't work this time. Better hold onto my seat and ride this one out.)

"You did the original *blanking* loan at 77% LTV, and you know we've put in another $130,000 in improvements. Which leaves you in a better position than you originally took. Why and the *blank* do you need another appraisal?"

"Jim, on a cost basis you're exactly right. We're at about 60%. However, as you know, value doesn't necessarily equate to replacement cost. Many of the improvements you've added are only useful to Guns-R-Us. The bank must look at the value of the facility based upon the income which would be derived from its rental to another party. One who just wanted the building for warehouse space.

"A new appraisal law, FIRREA[g], requires the bank order another appraisal in this instance... where we are contemplating the renewal of a credit and believe our collateralized real estate may have declined in value. You see, our area has experienced fairly high vacancy within the warehouse market segment. Rental rates have been driven down, and as a result, we've experienced declining property values. Your building's appraised value will not reflect the cost of specialized improvements, and will be effected by the high level of vacancy."

"Well, Addison **(that's me)**, even if it appraises lower, what the *blank* are you going to do about it?"

"If it's significantly lower, I'll have to require the outstanding balance be reduced to bring it back within 75% LTV." I really began to worry about a possible heart attack. I mean he was working himself into a froth. As time went by, I found myself not listening very closely. Instead, I thought about the irony involved. A short time ago, I vehemently argued the capacity of the guarantors to carry this obligation. Then, as a matter of self-preservation, I switched hats and futilely tried to push the credit out of the bank. Finally, I lay down the requirements for a massive restructure of the loan... some points being necessary, but most amounting to overkill. Perhaps literally.

Over the next forty-five minutes, we worked out the other points necessary to renew the loan. As we ended our meeting, Mr. James Duncan gave me a totally disgusted look and said, "I don't know where the *blank* your industry's going. You guys make no sense to me." It was a telling comment that saddened me as I thought of the direction of banking, and I was actually more than a little ashamed to be one of "the guys."

Trying to be upbeat, I focused on the hope the credit could now be renewed and classified a 'C'. There were a few more battles to be won, though. The appraisal did come back with a lower valuation than the original report, $476,000 versus $520,000. Accordingly, the individuals would be required to drop the outstanding balance by $40,000 to bring the bank's exposure within 75% of the new value. After a few more rounds with Mr. Duncan, the reduction was made.

Then the Regional Credit Administrator, Louis Elmerton, insisted I cut the amortization[g] from the 22 years remaining on the original schedule, to 15 years. Needless to say, this made a significant difference in the monthly payment amount. Which seemed rather contradictory to me. The bank spent an eternity trying to decide if the borrower could support the annual debt service actually paid the previous year. It was concluded the borrower could not. So shorten the amortization and raise the monthly payment by several hundred dollars?

When I questioned this, Lightning Lou as I liked to call him, replied, "Doing so will get our principal reduced much more quickly... putting us in a more favorable position come the next balloon.[g]"

Follow me here. Continuing along the original amortization would have meant a three year balloon amount of $340,303 or 71.5% LTV. Dropping the amortization to 15 years meant a balloon figure of $320,106 or 67.2%. A whopping 4.3% difference. Would you consider this a huge change in your collateral position? (Me neither.)

The bank appeared to argue out both sides of its mouth, each in a way detrimental to the borrower. I could not convince anyone that common sense seemed to dictate guarantors with a combined net worth of $15 million had enough resources at their disposal to cover any shortfalls created by Guns-R-Us. Nevertheless, the bank wanted to raise the annual remittance. Question: If you truly thought your

Chapter Two

borrower was having difficultly making timely payments at 'X' amount per month, would you raise the payment? Lightning Lou would. And did.

The final loan classification? Well, internal review struggled with this for more than a month after the credit was renewed. They reasoned the bank still had not proven the capacity for continued timely repayment, and the rating should remain an 'E'. I argued they could not show me another loan in our institution where debt service was more absolute for the next twelve months. All I had to do was draw upon the letter of credit. Are you sitting down? There response was that I had no idea as to whether or not the issuing institution could fund the letter of credit if called upon to do so. Now I had to analyze another bank!

I contacted Filmore R. Denkins, President of Second Bank & Fidelity of Tall Pines, Michigan. Believe it or not, when I explained I was trying to verify his bank's ability to fund a $45,000 letter of credit, he did not go into hysterics. He noted that it was a sad commentary on the state of banking, but agreed to forward me his institution's financial statements.

Upon receipt of the information, I did a written report indicating the institution was indeed strong enough to fund a $45,000 loan in the event of an emergency. Upgrade right? (Ha.)

"You are misdirecting the emphasis of your credit analysis. We're not just trying to prove payments over the next twelve months, but continuing indefinitely."

(Speaking of playing both sides of the street.) I felt there was an obvious answer to this comment. **"You want this to run two different ways. You won't let me assume continued repayment on one loan when the statements on file are outside of a year old, right?"**

"Correct, the financial information is stale after that and cannot be relied upon. You can only forecast the next twelve months based upon the statements from the past year."

I moved in for the kill. **"Okay, so by having the irrevocable letter of credit in place, I've proven the next twelve months of repayment perpetually."**

"You don't understand."

(Right, again.) After being counseled on the need to get in touch with the "spirit of loan grading," and not the "literal interpretation," it was suggested I contact the guarantors for more detailed financial information on their various holdings.

How to Obtain Business Loans

"You know, they might not be too amicable about providing another bushel of statements for us," I offered.

"Why not? *We're their bank.*"

"Let's just say they're not pleased with all the requirements, and the overall difficulty in procuring the recently completed renewal."

"Well, that's the way things are. Try and get more information anyway."

After a few months of unreturned letters and phone calls, I finally touched base with Mr. Harvey. Surprisingly, he took my latest salvo of requests with relative good humor, commenting only that banking was "in a sad state of affairs." He declined supplying the entirety of what I asked for, but agreed to forward statements for Nolin Property Management, his largest holding. Upon receipt, I found that the company generated earnings of over $500,000 in each of the last two years, and had a current cash position in excess of $400,000.

At long last, internal review relented that there was enough sustenance to the guarantors to assume continued timely repayment was *likely*... but not assured. As a "compromise," they moved the credit to a 'D' classification, and that's where it sits today. Of course, I have requested additional financial information...

Monday mornings it pays to get into the office before anyone else. It always seems you can get twice the work done without being constantly interrupted.

I'll leave the common area lights off until later, I'll just be in my office. Click. Hummph. Click. Now what in the world is wrong with my lights? Click. Click. Click. Boy those things are hardly putting out any light at all. Maybe I will turn on the common overheads. Click. Alright, what's going on. These aren't putting out any more light than mine. Looks like I'll be working in a dim glow until maintenance gets in around nine.

(9 A.M.) "Al, good morning, this is Addison on the second floor. You need to stop by as soon as possible, there's something wrong with all the lights."

"No sir, the lighting all got changed last weekend. Senior management decided to go with lower wattage tubes."

"What in the world for? It's dark in here Al."

Chapter Two

"Myron (Executive Vice President of branch administration) said everyone would get used to it. He said the yellow tone would be relaxing. Less stressful... what with no glare coming off what you were reading."

"Well there certainly won't be any glare, to have a glare there has to be light... and as I mentioned Al, it's dark in here. If you don't mind, I'll pass on the dungeon atmosphere. How about replacing my old lights?"

"Sorry, Addison. I can't. The change is mandatory. Myron said the bank will save money using the new lighting tubes. They're supposed to give off less heat, so the savings will be in the electric bill... we won't have to run the air conditioners as much. Besides, Myron had me bust all the old tubes."

Things are tight. And the future doesn't seem too illuminating, either.

Chapter Three

CHAPTER 3:

A NEW AGENDA

So your banker hasn't been out to see you in awhile. As a matter of fact, you haven't heard from him in ages. Used to be he'd get in touch regular, just to see if you needed anything. Constantly wanted to remind you who to call if help was needed. "Yessir, you can always count on us," he would say. What in the world happened to that fella? What's he been up to?

His neck in paperwork. Just how heavy is the regulatory burden? William F. Denton, President, First National Bank of McGehee (Arkansas), told *Bankers News* that in one three month period, he received 1,158 pages of regulations.

"Noting 60 percent of each week's officers meeting is devoted to dealing with new and revised regulations, Denton adds that a 'considerable amount of time is spent interpreting the information, condensing many to revisions in our written bank policies, writing

How to Obtain Business Loans

operating procedures, writing audit procedures, and finally employee training.'" [1]

Bankers News notes in an editorial that "none of the time and talent spent on compliance produces a single new loan or investment in Denton's community." [2]

Ouch! 1,158 pages of red tape per quarter. Which is almost 18 pages per business day. Under the "banker's hours" now kept at most institutions (7:30 a.m. - 6:00 p.m), that equates to a page every 35 minutes. (Yes, your banker's average work day extends on either side of lobby hours.)

So, how'd you like to get a fax from the government every half hour telling you how to run your business? How efficient would you be? How responsive to your market?

I liken the nonstop interference to Chinese water torture. In and of itself, a drop of water on your forehead wouldn't bother you; but, a few thousand in a row will drive you out of your mind. Same thing with all the new restrictions. Those imposing them will say, "It doesn't take much to comply with what's being asked." And if you take snapshots of singular requirements, that's true to a large extent. However, if you look at what's taking place on an aggregate basis... drip, drip, drip, drip, drip, drip, drip, drip, drip, drip, drip, drip, drip, drip, drip, drip, drip... you'll understand the urge to run screaming into the night. (However, vocal outbursts in a bank *are* against government regulations.)

A lot of the directives imposed are excessive. Witness The ABC File. Consider the lack of productivity, and the lunacy, associated with "proving" repayment to the Nth degree. Think of the hours wasted on meeting government requirements for loans already made.

Are you ready for this? The same level of "diligence" is dictated for loans yet to be made. (Huh?) That's right. Letters of credit[g] which are committed, but unfunded, carry the same *evidentiary rules*. Failure to meet THE BURDEN OF PROOF, which in this case would be the borrower's ability to have repaid the loan **had** it been disbursed last year, means setting aside reserves. Could he have paid back what he didn't need to borrow? It's the chicken-and-the-egg riddle. Which comes first, the loan or repayment? This is the Yin & Yang of banking.

Now I'm not suggesting there isn't the need to qualify the borrower prior to committing a line of credit. But, if the unfunded

Chapter Three

line has remained on the books for over a year, is it an efficient use of time to convene a committee to discuss the "debtor's" cash flow? Should specific reserves be necessary for a non-loan loan? (Is the buggy before the horse?)

At this juncture, you're beginning to understand banking doesn't know which end is up. You've been introduced to the level of analysis needed to maintain an institution's existing loan portfolio, and you can see the opportunity cost associated with this priority. But, based on the cost reductions previously described, you also know additional revenues are essential. So what kind of business does the bank want? What is the business of banking today?

What Banks Have Been Panhandling For

Two words... FEE INCOME.

Traditionally, the business of banking has always been lending. And the revenues of the industry have historically been interest payments. However, as the servicing demands of existing portfolios increased due to regulatory requirements, fewer and fewer new loans could be made.

It's really a case of simple mathematics. For instance, one institution I worked for had a commercial real estate portfolio comprised of 411 loans, totaling $227 million. Maintenance was split between three officers. That meant, on average, each of us had 137 loans to monitor.

Assess the time involved to analyze and meet THE BURDEN OF PROOF on 137 loans each year. Working Monday through Friday for 50 weeks of the year sets a pace of almost 3 "reviews" per week! Consider the volume of work necessary to secure internal concurrence on the capacity of this many borrowers. There's not much of an opportunity for "loan officers" to prospect for new business. Furthermore, from the officer's perspective, it would seem almost masochistic to seek more business when you can't properly service what you have.

So the obvious question is why not add to staff? FTEs (banking lingo for full-time employees) are hard to come by. If additional staff wasn't in the prior year's budget, you might as well be asking for an employee swimming pool to be constructed off the west wing.

This is flabbergasting when you contemplate the swings in bank income a loan officer can effect. As previously discussed, upgrade one substandard loan of $500,000 to a 'C' classification and a $45,000

39

How to Obtain Business Loans

salary is "earned." Do $3,000,000 worth of new loans with 1.5% fees and the same wages are secured. For the average loan amount at the aforementioned institution, that's only about five credits.

Nevertheless, prying money loose for an FTE is like taking away a dog's favorite bone. Your only chance as a department head is to get one in the upcoming year's budget. Sadly, banks perennially believe the talk of reduced regulation, and with that in mind forsake adding to their work force. Ironically, senior management is then aghast when high turnover transpires as overworked and frustrated personnel flee to different professions.

But I digress. Suffice it to say fewer loans are being made simply because of the time constraints associated with servicing existing portfolios. Further, credit standards are tougher, which means fewer qualify.

How tough is tough? Witness the sign posted at Security First Bank of Plymouth, Ohio — "Get the Credit You Deserve, Apply for a Secured Visa Today!" Allow me to clarify this terminology for those of you unfamiliar with it. A secured credit card is one backed by a liquid deposit held by the card issuing institution. In other words, bring in a $2,000 CD and you can get a Visa with an $1,800 limit. As long as the CD is assigned for collateral.

As you might imagine, the consumer demand for this type of facility is not overwhelming. So fee income is the name of the game. The industry's motto is, "If you can get away with it, charge for it." For example:

Regular Checking Account
    Average balance less than $ 1,500 $ 8.00
    Minimum balance less than $ 750 $ 8.00
    Minimum balance less than $ 650 $ 8.50
    Minimum balance less than $ 550 $ 9.00

Interest on Checking
    (for those of you wanting the bank to pay for the use of your money)
    Average balance less than $ 2,500 $ 8.00
    Minimum balance less than $ 1,500 $ 8.00
    Minimum balance less than $ 1,000 $ 8.50
    Minimum balance less than $ 750 $ 9.00

Chapter Three

Business Checking Account
    Monthly fee $ 14.00
    Cost per item paid $ .20
    Cost per item deposited $ .15
    Cost per item credited $ .35

Miscellaneous Services
    Incoming Wire Transfer $ 10.00
    Collection Item $ 11.00
    Returned Deposit $ 6.00
    Insufficient Funds $ 25.00
    Stop Payment $ 25.00
    ATM Withdrawal $ 1.00
    Cashier's Check $ 4.00
    Money Order $ 2.00
    Traveler's Checks $ 2.00
    Draft $ 6.00
    Notary Acknowledgment $ 5.00
    Signature Guarantee $ 10.00
    Photocopy $ .25
    Balancing of Statement (per hour) $ 25.00
    Research (per hour) $ 25.00
    Closing Account within First 90 Days $ 6.00
    Outgoing Wire Transfer $ 12.00
    Dormant Account Monthly Fee $ 15.00

Let's look at how fast these charges add up. Suppose you're a native New Yorker who's just sold his business and are in the process of retiring to sunny Florida. There's an immediate need to set up a local banking relationship so the darn grocery stores will accept your checks! You decide to open an interest-on-checking account at The Vault & Savings Bank on Main Street.

You carried cash on the trip down and the account is opened with the remainder of your traveling money — $250, along with a $175 rebate check for some radials you just purchased at Tire Palace. The customer service representative (CSR) assures you no service fee will be incurred, because your average balance will be much higher once the remainder of your funds can be moved south. She indicates the best way to handle the transfer is by having your northern bank wire monies directly into your new account. She says she'll take care of all the details, but there is a $10.00 fee, adding, "It's the safest and fastest way!" You agree to have her handle the matter, although you could

How to Obtain Business Loans

just have written a check off your northern account and let it clear (which would have taken about a week).

While waiting for her to finish typing up some documents, you off-handedly mention to your spouse the need to arrange for proceeds of a recent stock sale to be sent. "I can do that for you! I'll just forward a collection item to your brokerage house, and they'll remit a check to the bank. Of course, there is a small fee for handling the transaction... $11.00... but it's the safest and fastest way!" your CSR offers.

"Faster than a wire?" you ask with a smirk.

"Well, no, but brokerage firms usually don't wire funds."

You decide it might be more convenient for her to take care of it, so you agree to stomach another fee. As she finishes up, you realize you'll need a couple of cashier's checks to get the water and power turned on. "I can get those for you, but there is a charge... only to defray our costs... it's $4.00 per check..." Well, you don't have much choice in this one, so after some grumbling you relent.

As you're leaving the bank, you ponder the $29 in fees you just shelled out for 15 minutes of that young lady's day. Heck, her time was worth almost as much as many high priced attorneys.

Several days go by and closing documents for the sale of your northern residence arrive. They call for your signature to be witnessed, notarized, etc., so you decide to have that done while visiting the bank to check on your incoming deposits. You meet with your CSR and are informed none of the funds have been received as yet. She's not sure what the delay is. "It never takes this long." Concerned, you request she investigate to make sure everything is alright. She promises to, "right after my sales meeting... which I'm a little late for."

"Well, before you go, I'd like to get these documents witnessed, and there is a place for a couple of notary acknowledgments... then I guess the deed requires my signature be guaranteed. Oh, and when we're done I wonder if you might make me copies of everything?"

"Sure, however... just so you know... I have to charge $5.00 for the notary acknowledgments, $10.00 for the signature guarantee, and $.25 for each copy."

You explode. **"What! That's ridiculous. I'm not paying an arm and a leg just to get a little service!"**

"Well, I know it may seem like a lot, but you have to understand

Chapter Three

the bank is incurring a risk by notarizing and guaranteeing documents. Not to mention the time involved. And the charge for copies is just to keep senior citizens from coming in with reams of papers to be duplicated. Which, when it happens, takes up so much of our time we can't attend to good customers like yourself."

Second trip to the bank. Two notarized signatures — $5.00, one guaranteed signature — $10.00, and twenty five copies — $6.25. Total cost $21.25 for 10 minutes work. On average, that "service" bank is billing you at a rate in excess of $120 per hour.

Quite early the next morning, you receive a phone call from the bank's branch manager. She not so politely informs you of your account being overdrawn, and requests an immediate deposit. You make an effort to sort the matter out over the phone, but she's in a bit of a hurry.

Off to the bank. When you arrive, your CSR tells you the manager is "in a meeting, and will be tied up all morning."

"Well, perhaps you can explain. She called to tell me I'm overdrawn. How can that be?"

"I see. Well, maybe we can discover the problem by bringing the account up on my computer. However, if in fact we get into reconciling your checkbook... I'm afraid I'll have to finish for you after lobby hours. We're happy to help people with those things, but we must do so after the branch closes... that way we're not tied up during the day, and unable to service good customers like yourself. And, just so you know, we do charge $25 an hour for research and balancing."

Somehow the $95 reduction in her billing rate did not appease you. **"I'm not leaving my checkbook with you! Just bring up my account and let's see if we can tell where the mistake is."**

"Okay... let's see... alright... here it is. Yes, you're overdrawn by $5.32... well, that's before the NSF[g] and returned deposit fees... actually you need to make a minimum deposit of $36.32."

"How in the world can that be? Haven't my stock proceeds been received? Didn't my wire come in?"

"No sir, and I need to check on the wire today. Unfortunately, I didn't get a chance to yesterday. Anyway, that's not the problem... you had an item returned. The $175 check deposited did not pay. Personal checks and withdrawals totaled $255.32, and only $250 in collected funds were available."

"So I'm overdrawn $5.32."

Her eyes roll. "No sir, as I said, you're overdrawn $36.32."

How to Obtain Business Loans

"How's that?"

With a bit of condescension, "We charge $6.00 for deposits which have to be returned, and there's a $25.00 fee for having insufficient funds to pay a presented item."

"Wait just a minute. You told us it was alright to begin writing checks... that our funds from up north would be transferred very quickly..."

"And usually that's the case. As I told you, I have no idea what is taking so long. However, it's the returned deposit that's your problem."

"Well, that's at least partially true. Listen, just yesterday I wrote Tire Palace a check for installing a new muffler. I'd like to put a stop payment on it."

Your CSR pulls some paperwork from her desk. "Fill this out please, and include the $25 stop payment fee along with the $36.25 to bring your account back to a zero balance."

The last straw. You launch into a totally unproductive tirade about the quality of service you've gotten, and the distaste you have for the glut of fees you've been hit with. You end with, "Miss, I'm closing our account!"

"Hummph... well, if you feel that's absolutely necessary. It'll just be a moment as I prepare the documentation. Please include the $6.00 early closure fee along with the $36.25 you are overdrawn..."

Such is the fee oriented world of customer service. $87.25 in a matter of days! And nothing but headaches to show for it. A word of warning here with regard to your personal banking affairs. Seek out the branch manager. CSRs are typically lower paid individuals ($15,000 - $18,000), and as a result, their position experiences very high turnover. Result: Few really know what they're doing. Think about it. How competent is a freshly trained individual commanding an hourly wage of $5.75? Should this person handle the wiring of your life savings? Save yourself some aspirin, take special needs to the branch manager.

At any rate, you see how banks will attempt to nickel and dime you to death. On a volume basis, small change can add up to a large sum of money. Which reminds me of a story. A few years ago, I heard of a bank controller who was arrested for embezzlement. (Okay, so actually I heard of several.) But one was in a class by himself. He wasn't your run-of-the mill grifter. He didn't divert incoming wires, or shave money off of construction disbursements. He didn't shift

Chapter Three

funds from dormant accounts, or misappropriate bank investments. His ploy was much more ingenuous, but just as illegal.

You see, he apparently was something of a computer hacker. And he used that knowledge to alter his institution's software so as to affect interest payments to customers. For instance, say your savings account was earning (a whopping) 2.5% annually. The calculation of your monthly credit would look like this:

July

Account balance	$12,986.38
(12,986.38 x 2.5%) x 31/360	$ 27.96 Interest

However, that's not entirely accurate. The actual interest earned was $27.95679028. The figure on your statement has just been rounded up. What if it wasn't? Evidently the controller asked himself this question. Or more specifically, what if each time interest was compounded the rounding portion was split off and placed into a slush account? How much money could be set aside over time? Particularly given many accounts now offer daily compounding!

The arithmetic went something like this:

Total deposits compounding daily	$2.8 billion (BIG bank)
Average account size	$5,500
Total accounts	509,091
Average rounding amount	$0.005
Amount diverted daily	$2,545.46
Amount diverted over 12 months	$929,091.08

By the time a comprehensive year-end audit caught him, he had almost become a millionaire. And it had been accomplished half a penny at a time. A similar ambition compels banks to charge small fees for all miscellaneous services. (Well, at least that's legal.)

The deposit/service side of banking has long been regarded as some sort of quasi-public utility. An inalienable right on a par with

How to Obtain Business Loans

water, power, trash collection, and network TV. People really resent the emphasis on fee per service. The sentiment most declare is, "If I'm a depositor, I should receive services free. After all, the bank's making money on my deposits."

The displeasure the populace has over THE NEW AGENDA is unmistakable. Composition of deposit market share is in a constant state of flux. For a while, Bank 'A' will retain the largest segment of a community until, dissatisfied with service, an exodus occurs to Bank 'B' which is offering incentives for new customers. Who will remain patrons until, fed up with poor treatment, they leave for Bank 'C'... and so on and so forth until the cycle begins anew with Bank 'A' offering the toasters. Further, while some institution's market share may vacillate within a reasonably small range over a period of time (say 10-20%), the makeup of depositors will have turned over to a large extent. Customers who have been with the same institution for years on end are few and far between. They are often called "Directors."

Management at the holding company level recognizes this *megatrend*. Hence the move to purchase market share through merger and acquisition rather than building it from scratch. Starting from ground zero demands a philosophy centered around top quality service with an absence of incremental fees. It also necessitates a credit culture ripe for lending. Recently, you'll note some of the greatest success stories of the industry come from small banking concerns. Those who have been able to realign their revenue structure with the operating norms of yesteryear.

However, by and large, most institutions follow the pathways fashioned by regulatory reform. They suffer the ebb and flow of market share as consumers perpetually try the bank on the next corner (as there always is one). To worsen matters, deposit rates are the lowest they've been in ages. Many people are withdrawing their money and placing it with brokerage firms. Mutual funds being a popular alternative to paltry CD rates.

How to Give Your Deposit(s) Clout

What does deposit base volatility mean for you? Opportunity. Folks have been changing banks almost as often as they take out the garbage. Which has led to a new means of setting deposit rates. Typically an institution will publish its rates in the local newspaper.

Chapter Three

The breakdown looks something like this:

Account Type	Stated Rate	APY*
Checking Plus Interest	1.50%	1.51%
Regular Savings	2.00%	2.02%
Super Savings	2.30%	2.32%

Account Type	Stated Rate	APY*
Money Market	2.25%	2.27%
Super Money Market	2.66%	2.68%
7 - 89 day CD	2.00%	2.02%
3 mo - 179 day CD	2.25%	2.27%
6 mo - 364 day CD	2.80%	2.83%
1 year CD	3.20%	3.24%
2 year CD	4.00%	4.07%
3 year CD	4.00%	4.07%
4 year CD	4.50%	4.59%
5 year CD	4.50%	4.59%

(* Stands for Annual Percentage Yield. A new term mandated for disclosure by Congress under The Truth in Savings Act. Equates to the percentage yield considering interest paid on an account, based upon the stated rate and the frequency with which compounding takes place over a 365 day period. More on this later.)

Most people don't look at advertised rates as they would sticker prices on a car. Those are negotiable. Bank rates are etched in granite. While haggling over the purchase of vehicles, houses, art work, furniture, major appliances... even clothes in some instances... is commonplace, dickering with the bank over what will be paid for the use of one's own money is considered taboo for the everyday individual. (How crazy is that?)

I hear you. "But Addison, aren't rates set by senior management in some board room way up the line?" True enough. What no one realizes, however, is most banks also have secondary terms. Rates given to "preferred customers," or new ones offering "significant deposits."

As a general rule, branch managers and CSRs have the leeway to offer between a quarter (1/4) and a half (1/2) of a percent better than

How to Obtain Business Loans

what's advertised. So how do you qualify as a "preferred customer"? If you have even a moderate amount of money in an institution, ask for a better than published rate. You might hear **"no"** to start with, but if you calmly explain that ol' Mortimer Starch down the street at Cornerstone National has promised you a better rate on your next CD... you've probably just qualified yourself as a "preferred customer." Which defined is — any depositor who has not yet left for greener interest, but who is threatening to do so. (Note: If you're going to bargain with your existing bank, it is invaluable to throw out the name of a banker at a competing institution. Through industry meetings, civic organizations, social events, and due to the fact many have flip-flopped between companies, most bankers in an area will know of each other. However, they won't call a rival to test your claim, and having the name presented adds weight to your declaration.)

Consider this. What else can a banker do to keep your business other than offer you an equal or better rate? *All banks have the same products.* One can't sell you a niftier CD than the other. They don't come in unique shapes or special colors. As yet, no one has come up with the quintessential deposit instrument which cannot be copied by the cache across the street. All an institution can claim, is better service. **Period**. And we'll soon cover the realities of such an assertion.

Perhaps you're already disgusted with the efforts of your current institution, and aren't willing to stay regardless of what's offered. How do you get the movie-star treatment from an alternative bank? Simple. You need to grasp one solitary concept. The income of a branch manager is tied very closely to his office's performance. Particularly to the volume of deposits attracted.

Guarantee the most leverage possible for your intended deposit (whatever its size) by finding a branch location within the most impoverished area of town. Holding companies with a major market presence in a community will often have branches in the least affluent areas. Doing so benefits them greatly under the Community Reinvestment Act[g]. Your patronage at those locations will be well received. Any deposit will look good in comparison to the deposits of their "average customer." The amount of your opening deposit will be magnified by the contrast.

You won't have to conduct all your affairs at said location once the accounts are started. So long as you're within the same county,

Chapter Three

you'll generally be able to use whichever affiliated branch is most convenient. (The Trust & Savings Depository of Elm Street is the same one on Sycamore.)

On the initial visit, see only the branch manager. Imply confidentiality and poor service were problems at Bank 'A'. Indicate the desire to move your deposits, but express concern about the rates of interest offered. A branch manager pushing to make budget should now jump like a hungry salmon after a fly. Set the hook by dropping the name of a third banker, and land preferential rates.

A couple of points here: 1) If asked your home address, you may feel the need to explain the wish to bank outside of your immediate neighborhood. If so, just explain business takes you through the area regularly. 2) You'll have the best luck with this approach in late fall-early winter. That's when the branch managers are really swimming upstream. Inevitably, the year's almost over and they are always outside of their budget's incentive range.

So now you're saying, "Sure these ideas sound good, but didn't you just tell me about a new customer being brushed off with service fees?" Very observant. Here lies another major contradiction in banking. A branch can be deposit-starved according to its internal plan, and there may be a tidal wave of exiting customers. However, in the true fashion of bank management, the branch is often severely understaffed. This means that while great efforts are made to lure new depositors, little is done to cultivate the continuing business of existing ones. Strangely, new deposit volume and not an aggregate total of deposits is often used as a barometer for bonuses. Which, of course, further exacerbates turnover.

A typical CSR may have anywhere from 350-1,500 accounts apportioned to him or her. What level of service can one reasonably expect to be offered? Use the following as a guideline for qualifying banks according to service capacity: (The model assumes only 1/10th of an institution's customers need servicing on a weekly basis.)

$$\frac{\text{Total Deposits (in annual report)}}{\text{Avg. Account Size (ask Manager)}} = \text{Total \# of Accounts}$$

(guideline continued on next page)

How to Obtain Business Loans

$$\frac{\text{Total \# of Accounts}}{\text{\# of CSRs (ask Manager)}} = \text{Accounts per CSR}$$

$$\frac{\text{Accounts per CSR}}{10} = \text{1/10th of CSR's Customers (Weekly Servicing Base)}$$

$$\frac{\text{Weekly Servicing Base}}{\text{Five Day Work Week}} = \text{Avg. \# of Accounts Handled on a Daily Basis}$$

9 AM to 4 PM, Minus Lunch Hour = Six Hours/Day on Floor

$$\frac{\text{Avg. \# of Daily Accounts}}{\text{6 Hours}} = \text{\# of Accounts per Hour}$$

$$\frac{\text{\# of Accounts per Hour}}{\text{60 Minutes}} = \text{Avg. Time CSR has for Each Customer}$$

Plugging in some numbers for comparison:

Bank 'A'

$$\frac{\$500,000,000}{\$5,000} = \text{100,000 Accounts}$$

$$\frac{100,000}{\text{65 CSRs}} = \text{1,500 Accounts per CSR}$$

$$\frac{1,500}{10} = \text{150 Weekly Customer Account Base}$$

Chapter Three

$$\frac{150/5}{6} = \text{5 Accounts per Hour}$$

$$\frac{60}{5} = \text{One Account per 12 Minutes}$$

Bank 'B'

$$\frac{\$250,000,000}{\$5,000} = \text{50,000 Accounts}$$

$$\frac{50,000}{50 \text{ CSRs}} = \text{1,000 Accounts per CSR}$$

$$\frac{1,000}{10} = \text{100 Weekly Customer Account Base}$$

$$\frac{100/5}{6} = \text{3.3 Accounts per Hour}$$

$$\frac{60}{3.3} = \text{One Acount per 18 Minutes}$$

Bank 'C'

$$\frac{\$100,000,000}{\$5,000} = \text{20,000 Accounts}$$

$$\frac{20,000}{40 \text{ CSRs}} = \text{500 Accounts per CSR}$$

$$\frac{500}{10} = \text{50 Weekly Customer Account Base}$$

$$\frac{50/5}{6} = \text{1.6 Accounts per Hour}$$

$$\frac{60}{1.6} = \text{One Account per 38 Minutes}$$

How to Obtain Business Loans

If customer service is important to you, and all other considerations are equal, which institution do you want to bank with? I'll take Bank 'C', where CSRs have two or three times longer to help customers than their competitors do.

Using this formula will help prove who can really deliver on customer service claims. I think you'll find smaller institutions your best bet. That's where you'll discover the smallest *account load per CSR*, the key ratio to consider when searching for the service your deposits deserve.

Customers Won't Settle for Less

The fees previously listed are included in most bank literature. They are disclosed in order to establish the right to charge for described services. However, most institutions also include special programs allowing the "preferred customer" to circumvent everyday tariffs. Unique marketing approaches which group accounts enable individuals to receive virtually all indexed services "free"... so long as they meet certain qualifying requirements. For example:

Silver Partners Only 55 and older qualify. Must maintain both checking and some type of savings instrument. Must keep a minimum of $5,000 between the two accounts, or are charged an automatic fee of $13 per month. "Free" benefits include personal checks, copies, travelers checks, cashiers checks, notary service, money orders, wiring services, and $150,000 worth of common carrier life insurance (payable upon proper claim any 5th Thursday of the month when Venus and Mercury are simultaneously aligned with the sun).

Portfolio Patrons Targeting the up-and-comers. Must maintain $20,000 in deposits, and qualify for/receive a $5,000 credit card. Annual fee is $50, and benefits include custom checks with a check book cover of your choice. Plus "free" travelers checks and money orders. Simplified account summaries and statement balancing are available upon request. An additional $20 monthly charge applies whenever deposits fall below the $20,000 minimum.

Chapter Three

Note that if the minimums aren't met, a hefty service charge is immediately applied (and automatically deducted from your balances). Funny, the special relationships provide only what banking used to for free. A little service for your patronage. Seems a tenet of business these days. Repackage your product, advertise to develop interest, then mark up the price. Offer the same thing, maybe even at lesser quality.

People are fed up. Witness the success of various magazines designed around providing unbiased information on retail products. Consider the number of activist groups conceived to fight for consumer rights. Companies whose motto include some form of *caveat emptor* better beware themselves. Not only will there not be any **repeat** customers, the information in the marketplace is sufficient to ward off first time buyers.

Americans want the facts. No more small print under the advertisement. No more rapid fire disclaimers after the sales pitch. If your product is no good — you're done. If you can't offer the service you profess — you're done. For the time being, such will mean a transient deposit base for most banks. People will continue to search for the quality of service they feel their money deserves. The public's perception of a product or service will define a company's level of prosperity.

In a society which offers alternatives for almost anything one desires, an industry whose product line is completely undifferentiated will... in particular... see the breadth of its customer base parallel perceived quality. People will not abide poor value when the same commodity you offer is available on the next corner.

Take, for example, the story of Chrysler's Plymouth Laser. The car is exactly the same as the Mitsubishi Eclipse. Identical style, corresponding 1.8 liter 92-horsepower base engine, matching drive train, interchangeable disc braking system, same wheel base, and coinciding options available under directly comparable pricing variations between $12,000-$20,000. The vehicle is actually manufactured for Chrysler by Mitsubishi. There is no difference.

Sales comparisons would have you think otherwise. A study was done after the sports cars' simultaneous introduction in the states. It demonstrated Chrysler was selling an average of 14 Lasers per dealership... to Mitsubishi's 100 Eclipses per dealership! What could possibly be the explanation? **Perceived quality**.

A follow-up survey was conducted. It concluded that although

How to Obtain Business Loans

Americans truly profess a desire to buy a vehicle sold by a U.S. car company, the feeling is outweighed by the notion that the quality of what's offered isn't up to Japanese standards. How did this come to be an accepted belief? Well, while American labels were engrossed in cutting costs, and doing little to innovate their product line, the Japanese were doing just the opposite. American manufacturers focused on short term profitability, as is the nature of a management style necessary to maximize dividend yields and near term stock prices. (It is not just the American youth who have short attention spans.)

How are the Japanese continually beating us in the marketplace? Many books have been written which would have you believe the Japanese culture is solely responsible. Not so. After World War II, General McArthur remained in war ravaged Japan in an effort to help rebuild the country. Encountering obstacles at every turn, he teamed with leaders of Japan's scientific and industrial communities to bring Dr. Edwards Deming over from America. Dr. Deming went about teaching the necessity of focusing on product quality, and on quality of service. He taught, that in the end, devotion to these principles of business would always be the most cost effective. In his estimation, the problems endured by failing American firms were often due to management's two pronged approach — increasing revenues and cutting costs.

Dr. Deming was able to convince the Japanese that the focus on quality would lead to customer loyalty. And continually improving quality would be the only way to become a power in the emerging global markets. Nowadays, within Japan, Dr. Deming is widely regarded as the father of the Japanese economic miracle. I would offer he could be called the father of Japanese management as well.

The Struggle for Business

At least a few American banking institutions see the handwriting on the wall. Some spend thousands of dollars annually (which you know is no small feat) in an effort to instill a sales doctrine among its front-line people. They recognize the tellers, the CSRs, the branch personnel are what often make or *break a bank*. The result is training in how to "sell yourself."

The theory being, given that products are all similar, what can be sold other than the trite promise of better service? The server. Experts

Chapter Three

feel if a customer likes a representative, they are more likely to become... or remain... a client. The push is to be friendlier. More likable. More agreeable. More slavish.

I had occasion not long ago to have a joint meeting with a residential builder, Tom Griffith, and the branch manager (BM) who serviced his deposit accounts. Fannie, the BM, set up the meeting as an introduction, as Tom was looking for a line of credit for personal investments.

He turned out to be a gruff, but quite likable man in his late 50s. On the day of the meeting, he was outspoken to say the least, expanding on the lack of customer service he received while previously banking elsewhere. He added, **"The restrictive covenants sought on my line there were totally unsatisfactory."**

He'd been carrying on for some time giving other testimony about his prior banking relationship. Then turned his attention to the present.

"Addison, I refuse to incur transaction charges for the deposit accounts I've opened with your bank. I've put in too much money to be charged penny ante fees for every little thing!"

At this point, Fannie decided to use some of the sales tactics she'd been educated with. She leaned forward. "You don't want to pay fees for every little thing... of course not... no, we certainly understand what you're saying."

For the moment unaffected, Tom continued, **"And I'll tell you what else, I don't think it's fair to charge me Prime + 1 1/2% on the line... considering the deposits I've brought to the table."**

Fannie, even more eagerly, gushed, "Of course not, you don't want to pay more than you think is fair. Especially since you've deposited so much money."

Now a little taken aback, but still pushing forward. **"Uh huh... and I'll tell you, Addison, you don't have any risk in this loan given it's backed by AAA bonds[8]. So I don't expect to be inundated with requests for financial information."**

Fannie seemed to have shifted into some trance, her eyes a little glazed over, but focused on her sales principles. "You're right, there isn't any risk in lending you money... not with the bonds as collateral... and certainly not with your character... we definitely understand you don't want a lot of unnecessary questions about your financial statements... we know you're busy."

Tom shot me a glance. He must have been feeling like Alan Funt

How to Obtain Business Loans

was going to step out at any moment and tell him the camera was behind a picture frame. **"Uh, well, um... maybe we should talk about this later."**

Now completely in a world of her own. "Sure, sure, you have other things to do. Maybe we should get together on this later."

At this point, Tom and I were awkwardly smiling at each other. I think we both felt we had been transported into a scene from *The Stepford Wives*.

Although a little annoying, and somewhat silly, Fannie had followed her sales rules to a T. She was agreeable, unargumentative, agreeable, without a doubt slavish, agreeable, and friendly to a fault. It was tough for Tom to be gruff with someone repeating exactly what he said. It would have been like arguing with himself.

Tom remained a customer. Although he did contact the bank president and request another individual be placed in charge of his deposit relationship. To which our president reportedly replied, "You're exactly right... you don't want someone handing your accounts who's too agreeable."

What other ways have banks stepped up their efforts in the area of customer service? One institution has begun a campaign which pays customers fees for poor performance. Recently, 3rd Street Bank of Augusta, Georgia advertised the following schedule of self-induced penalties:

Service Problem	Fee Paid to Patron
Customer forced to wait in line more than 5 minutes	$ 1.00
Customer finds ATM out of order	$ 2.00
Customer suffers impolite or discourteous service	$ 5.00
CSR does not get back to customer on an inquiry within the same day	$ 5.00
Customer locates a bank error in monthly statement	$10.00

Chapter Three

In form, the program is quite an attempt to solicit deposits based upon service assurances. But, in substance does it fall short of a true commitment to excellence? Note the most important area to customers, time spent waiting for service, carries the most watered-down pledge.

Sure, potential depositors respond to an advertisement such as this, as it appears to ensure quality service. But, do the numbers bear out the implied claim?

$$\frac{\$150{,}000{,}000 \text{ in Total Deposits}}{\$12{,}500 \text{ Avg. Account Size}} = 12{,}000 \text{ Total Accounts}$$

$$\frac{12{,}000 \text{ Total Accounts}}{14 \text{ CSRs}} = 857 \text{ Accounts per CSR}$$

$$\frac{857}{10} = 86 \text{ Customers in Weekly Servicing Base}$$

$$\frac{86}{5 \text{ Day Work Week}} = 17 \text{ Average Accounts Handled Daily}$$

$$\frac{17}{6 \text{ Hours on Floor Daily}} = 2.83 \text{ Accounts per Hour, or One Every 21 Minutes}$$

Not too bad, undoubtedly better than average. And what's the cost of their campaign? Say a full 25% of the customers serviced weekly receive a fee. Suppose the amount paid out averages $4.00.

$$\frac{12{,}000 \text{ Total Accounts}}{10} = 1{,}200 \text{ (Weekly Servicing Base)}$$

$$\frac{1{,}200}{4} = 300 \text{ Customers Receive Fee}$$

(chart continued on next page)

How to Obtain Business Loans

300 X $4.00	=	$1,200 Paid out per Week (Or $240 per Work Day)
$240 X 22 (Avg. Work Days/Month)	=	$5,280 in Monthly Promotional Cost

---

The cost of alternative methods to attract customers? Paying 1/4 of a percent more on deposits would result in the following: (say 2/3 of total deposits are interest bearing)

$100,000,000 (1/4%)/12	=	$20,833 per month

Which is why you see special incentive programs, and not increased interest rates offered.

In this bank's case, in order to drop servicing times to the lowest end of the industry, another 34 CSRs would have to be added.

Cost @ $15,000 each annually	=	$42,500 per month

Is management really devoted to quality, or are they strictly focusing on cost control and the repackaging of services to attract depositors?

The clamor to acquire deposit and transaction business reminds me of an old *Saturday Night Live* skit. It opens with a view in front of *The Change Bank's* pillars... then takes us in to the teller line. Where we find a paunchy, visor-clad male banker, and we listen for the pitch:

"Afternoon. Step right up. What can I help you with? I think you'll find us up to the task... We here at *The Change Bank* pride ourselves in finding creative solutions to customer problems. Skeptical huh? Got a minute?

"Let me tell you. Last week a fella came in with a twenty. Needed to know his options. Took me only a second. 'Will that be two tens, a ten and two fives, four fives, or maybe twenty ones?' Blew him

Chapter Three

away. He had so many choices on his hands he didn't know what to do... had me write them down so he could think them over.

"Then yesterday, this gorgeous lady comes in with a ten spot. Says she needs advice. 'I've got your answers,' I tell her. 'How about two fives, or a five and five ones, or ten ones?' Then just to show off a bit I say,' Or how about 40 quarters?' Earned myself a dinner date on that one.

"So as you can see, we know our business here at *The Change Bank*... it's making change... that's all we do."

---

[1] Smith, Ed: "The Regulatory Burden," *Bankers News*, June 8, 1993, p. 7.

[2] Smith, Ed: "The Regulatory Burden," *Bankers News*, June 8, 1993, p. 7.

Chapter Four

CHAPTER 4:

BIG BROTHER IS NOT JUST WATCHING

Stephen L. Price, President and CEO at The First Bank of Immokalee in Immokalee, Florida might offer contrast to my opinions on methods of fee imposition, but we would agree the marketplace should decide what can be charged... not our government.

Mr. Price recently sent a letter and a copy of an editorial about government interference in banking from the *Fort Myers News Press*. In its response, *Bankers News* noted that the newspaper editorial "took to task the Consumer Federation of America, the Public Research Group, and members of Congress who are sponsoring

How to Obtain Business Loans

legislation to require government check-cashing and the offering of low-cost bank accounts." [1]

> "Said the editorial: 'After the government gets through telling banks how much they can charge for checking accounts, automated teller and check-cashing services; maybe it can run price controls on cinnamon rolls, underwear, toothpaste and calculators.' [2]

The newspaper editorial concluded that it was best to leave banking alone and let the market determine bank fees. If Bank 'A' sets them too high, Bank 'B' will price its rates a bit lower to entice more customers to bank there.

Mr. Price was particularly upset, however, with "consumer groups' complaints that banks are using fees to make money." [3] He defends the practice by saying that it is the bank's responsibility as well to earn a profit so that investors will continue to put their capital into banks. He points out that this investor capital "'provide[s] depositors with the primary source of insurance against the loss of their deposits.'" [4]

(Psst... Hey Steve... make a loan would ya... procure some interest income in lieu of a check cashing fee.)

Bankers News concluded their response by noting that a bank's need to make a profit is something that the "legislative do-gooders would do well to address before they rush to micromanage (read: mismanage) American business into zero productivity." [5]

It might be too late. As this chapter will illustrate, there has already been a governmental stampede to impose controls at every level of bank operation.

Is Anybody Listening?

Not too long ago, the American Bankers Association (ABA)[g] brought aboard a banking regulatory official. Let's call her Jane Noe. She was added to the ABA's government relations staff. More than a few bankers in the Midwest had made Ms. Noe's acquaintance while she was across the desk as a safety and soundness examiner for the federal reserve district out of Chicago. They may like her much better now, as it appears her new job has acquainted her with the other end of regulation. Early on, she admitted as much, proclaiming

Chapter Four

something to the effect of "My goodness, there's a lot of paperwork to be done on this side of things. I had no idea."

A similar story has been attributed to any number of individuals. The theme is the same. Someone, formally of a regulatory background, takes a position which gives them firsthand insight into the paper flotilla that is the banking bureaucracy, and they exclaim in wonderment, "I can't believe the amount of work necessary to comply with government directives."

The question is, aside from every auditor taking an obligatory turn in bank management as a prerequisite to enforcement in the field, how will the message get across? In truth, it probably won't. At least not in a relatively short period of time. And certainly not without other compelling influence.

Meaning this. The government, and its regulating agencies, are not overly concerned with the burdens placed on bankers. Change will come about only when forces outside of the ABA become strong enough to warrant reform. What type of "forces"? Quite possibly, only those created by a national economic crisis.

Banking controls have paralleled what might be called the government's societal policy. In so many ways, we protect the rights and opportunities of the few, at the expense of the masses' quality of life.

We also do something else which is uniquely American. We take a good thing to excess (more often than not). Witness the effect of the American Disabilities Act (ADA) on banking. This piece of legislation was designed to offer greater equality for handicapped individuals. It required public facilities (banks, places of lodging, restaurants, schools, law offices, etc.) to remove architectural barriers in existing facilities, as well as provide special accommodations in new construction. The cost to be incurred by the property owner so long as no *undue hardship* would be imposed.

You're a United States Senator. Now let me ask you a question. Do you want to go on record as voting against legislation that would improve the lives of handicapped citizens? Of course you wouldn't, and neither would I. The problem is, no one properly understands the unabridged results of many well-intentioned bills. The wheels get put in motion, and the momentum just crushes any common sense.

As a result, **we now have drive-thru automatic teller machines equipped with braille.** Many times I've seen my blind neighbor

How to Obtain Business Loans

leave his home, accompanied by his seeing-eye dog, on the way to the bank. How frustrating it must have been to drive all the way to the branch, only to be unable to make a withdrawal because braille wasn't provided. Now if we can only get Congress to do something about those darn drive-thru menus at the fast food restaurants.

I know, I know, it is not "politically correct" to speak in such blunt language. And I don't wish to sound insensitive. However, the fact remains that lines must be drawn as to what's feasible... and what's reasonable.

Look at it this way. Speed limits were lowered to save lives (with a byproduct of saving gas). When we went from 75-80 mph as a maximum, to 55 mph, road deaths plummeted. So why didn't we make the speed limit 45 mph, or even 35 mph? Think of the lives that would have been saved. Instead, we ended up raising the limit back to 65 mph. Why? Because we viewed the slower speeds as impractical. We looked at the marginal gain, and decided the overall cost to the public was too much.

In these times of constant media scrutiny, filled with the ever present danger of being "politically incorrect," our elected officials do a poor job of drawing reasonable lines. This is what has happened in banking as we legislate against a minority of problems, at the expense of the overall system... and the national economy.

The Paper Chase

In the last couple of years, as an explanation for being less than active in commercial lending, I have heard bankers proclaim their institutions were "loaned up." This justification for the credit crunch would only be accepted by those woefully uninformed.

True, many had already employed their earning assets, but not in the form of loans. Loan-to-deposit ratios frequently were as low as 75%, and institutions still had a need to borrow fed funds to cover the purchase of various securities. Fannie Mae^g and Freddie Mac^g certificates, as well as government backed instruments, became the choice of comptroller allocation as a substitute for commercial loans.

And why? Two reasons. (1) In a falling rate environment they were able to lock in higher returns, providing for increasing spreads as the cost of funds dropped. (2) The administrative expense of commercial credit had spiraled. THE BURDEN OF PROOF placed a strangle-hold on the corporate lending department at most institu-

Chapter Four

tions, monopolizing the staff's time with file maintenance, and limiting the types of acceptable advances. What's more, even loans which were ultimately approved took an eternity to consummate due to the increase in required documentation.

As it continues to be an area of great aggravation for the small to mid-sized business owner, I will attempt to delineate the information characteristically needed to procure certain types of credit.

FINANCIAL INFORMATION

Borrowing Entities:

INDIVIDUAL or SOLE PROPRIETOR	PARTNERSHIP or SYNDICATE	CORPORATION (SUB S OR C), & PAs
Personal financial statement certified to the bank. On bank's own form if possible.	Two years balance sheet information.	Two years balance sheet information.*
A minimum of two years complete tax filings. K-1s are always required to determine actual cash flow.	Two years income statements, corresponding tax filings if possible.	Two years tax returns.
Verification of liquidity. Copies of recent bank and/or brokerage statements.		Probable liquidity verification needed. Often a list of trade references are required.

* Note: Banks will set their own guidelines as to the quality of statements required. As the company size and borrowing exposure increase, requirements will go from in-house prepared to accountant-compiled, from compiled to reviewed, and from reviewed to audited. As a rule of thumb, once your company size reaches $5 million in sales, you'll need to move to reviewed statements as a minimum. It should be obvious, the more comfortable the bank is with the information you supply, the more likely they are to approve your deal.

How to Obtain Business Loans

Remember this, any entity which has a "significant" interest in another entity or venture, will be required to shoulder the burden of disclosure relative to that affair. Some examples would include: an individual with partnership concerns, or a controlling interest in a company; a partnership formed to take a position in another partnership or syndication; and a company which either holds, or is a subsidiary of another firm. Generally speaking, two years balance sheet and income statements will be required on peripheral activities.

When in doubt what to supply in the way of financial statements, consider this question: **"Have I furnished the bank the information which will allow them to reconstruct an accurate cash flow for the past two years?"** If your answer is **"no,"** then get the Xerox machine humming.

And don't kid yourself with the statement, **"I've supplied them all I'm going to, and it darn well better be enough for them to make a decision."** I've heard this proclaimed by many folks who had overestimated their importance to the bank. They got their answer alright... "Good day."

Why not make things easier on yourself by providing full disclosure upfront? Without debating the merits and justifications for the laundry list of information now needed (because I'm not sure I can provide an airtight argument), suffice it to say you'll save time and effort if you swallow your ego and surrender everything from the outset. If you don't, you're only supplying the bank with a ready-made excuse for dragging its feet. "We can't offer any commitment without being privy to such and such." Banks can find enough reasons to frustrate your requests, don't give them any candy-hop bounces. Make them work to get you out (of there)!

And remember, a battle over THE BURDEN OF PROOF is being internally waged. When you withhold information, you only deny your advocate (the loan officer) details he could use to get your deal accepted. Arm him with everything you have. You stand a better chance of not just being approved, but getting a deal with terms and conditions you can live with.

With that in mind, you might consider it in your best interests to have an accountant prepare a cash flow on behalf of the bank. No doubt you'll pay nicely for this, but in the long run it may be less expensive than relying upon the bank to come up with its own favorable analysis. Particularly if you have a complex financial

Chapter Four

picture and you've submitted a request to a smallish institution. They simply may not have the expertise to unravel your statements. In which case, they will in all probability manufacture some reason for passing on the deal. Ask yourself, "What's the opportunity cost of not being approved in a timely manner?"

The second area of information needed to procure credit coalesces around legal documentation.

LEGAL DOCUMENTATION

Borrowing Entities:

INDIVIDUAL or SOLE PROPRIETOR	PARTNERSHIP or SYNDICATE	CORPORATION (SUB S OR C) & PAs
Picture ID such as a driver's license.*	Copy of partnership or syndication agreement.	Articles of Incorporation
		Certificate of Good Standing.
Proof of social security number.	Minutes of meeting authorizing borrowing.	Corporate resolution.
	Resolution with tax ID number.	Copy of minutes from meeting setting forth borrowing.
	Affidavit signed by all partners setting forth managing party, along with rights and responsibilities, and stating entity is still active.	Tax ID number.

* Note: Believe it or not, people routinely come to closings without proof of identity.

For the record, Trust structures need to provide a recordable copy of the Trust Agreement. They must also furnish an affidavit

How to Obtain Business Loans

from the Trustee stating the Trust is still active and that said Trustee is empowered to act on behalf of the Trust in all manners. Similar to other borrowing forms, the Trust must provide a minimum of two years balance sheet and income information.

The third area focuses on the information needed for specific types of credit.

SELECT TRANSACTIONS

LOANS AGAINST ACCOUNTS RECEIVABLE	LOANS AGAINST INVENTORY
Prefer 24-month history of volumes.	Prefer 24-month record of balances.
Listing of accounts (at least major ones).	Cost accounting summary of of holdings. LIFO[g] or FIFO[g] method of valuation?
Current aging of accounts.	
Bad debt history (breakdown of uncollected accounts).	
OWNER-USER REAL ESTATE LOANS	**LOANS AGAINST TENANT OCCUPIED FACILITIES**
Tax assessed value.	Tax assessed value.
If recent, an appraisal. [However, under FIRREA[g] the bank will still probably have to order another.]	Also recent appraisal if possible.
If construction: Plans and specs, survey, and cost breakdowns. Construction contract if available. Elevations[g].	Same. Large projects will require a bonded (insured) contract[g].
In some cases, environmental audit.	Same.
On public facilities, ADA certificate of compliance.	Ditto, and good luck getting tenants to reimburse you for compliance costs.
	If existing: Rent roll with copies of leases. Operating statements detailing expenses.

Chapter Four

**DEVELOPMENT LOANS
(CONDO PROJECTS,
SUBDIVISION LOT SALES)**

Typically, larger undertakings require a detailed pro forma; inclusive of all salient marketing information. If you're not experienced in this area, it's well worth your time and money to retain someone who is. Without a quality job done here, your project stands little chance of getting off the ground.

Market study/appraisal. The latter, of course, must be ordered by the bank. But the former will get the ball rolling for you.

Resume of previous projects.

Survey(s), comprehensive plans and specifications.

Cost breakdowns, and copy of construction contract.

Copies of payment and performance bonds. Index of all major subcontractors.

Example of sales contract to be used. Listing of presales to date.

Site and elevation drawings.*

Environmental audit.

* Note: Elevations are always beneficial when presenting an application which incorporates improved real estate. In situations where marketability is the pre-eminent question, they are compulsory material.

LOANS AGAINST EQUIPMENT

Listing of equipment to be pledged.

Purchase agreement(s) to establish value.

If to be housed in a leased facility, a landlord's waiver (to rights against equipment kept on premises).

UNSECURED LOANS

Four-leaf clover.

Rabbit's foot.

Horseshoe.

Prayer book.

Note from your mother.

Keep in mind, the lists provided do not encompass all of which may be sought by a given institution. Rather, they represent starting

How to Obtain Business Loans

points and entail the minimum to be furnished in order to secure an indication of interest. (More technically described as a *warm fuzzy*, which some banks actually issue in the form of a precommitment letter. However, most avoid this like the plague so they have the option of pulling out later without fear of lender liability. Instead, if everything looks acceptable, it's customary to receive a verbal "go ahead." Which, oh by the way, is in no way binding upon the bank. Stacks of case law support this. Just thought you'd like to know.)

Further, other loan categories weren't included as they represent fairly straightforward petitions for credit. You'll discover loans backed by liquid collateral like CDs, stocks, bonds, and mutual funds, to be well within the lending practices of most institutions. In a recent poll, 9 out of 10 credit policy officers preferred liquid security when contemplating a loan. (On average, 10% abstained in the absence of additional information.)

If you're **not** offering liquid collateral, let's just say you'll increase your odds immeasurably by supplying the listed information up front. Then stand ready to forward another batch of data after the initial bank review, and do so with a smile (no matter how ridiculous the request).

You **can** attempt to limit supplemental behests for statements, et al. After your opening consultation with the bank, follow up with a formal letter soliciting a breakdown of what else may be needed in order to reach a decision. A word of caution, be careful here, as you could paint yourself into a corner. If your contact officer drafts such a letter without concurrence on the part of the other individuals required to obtain an approval, you might force a "save face" rejection. This occurs every day.

Say the officer delivers an inventory of what else he expects to be necessary, but does so without consulting others in the approval process. Later, Darth Vader, the credit policy manager, asks to see deposit records for a checking account in order to verify the timely restitution of a loan receivable. Shortly thereafter, he inquires about an environmental audit which was completed on an unrelated piece of company property. Then he wants to verify the repayment ability of certain tenants the company has under lease, by requiring them to meet a "reasonable" burden of disclosure. (Don't laugh, this happens.)

And rest assured, somewhere along the line your contact officer is going to become more than a little embarrassed with what's taking

Chapter Four

place. Especially when you're telling him how asinine each ensuing demand is.

Soon human nature takes over. What's the easiest thing for your officer to do? Stop fighting the battle. In fact, within the bank, he probably will begin to voice reasons to reject the credit. Doubts he "had all along." He'll be doing so because he can't bear the thought of a fourth trip back to you seeking your dental records. If you feel this transpiring, you should **strongly** request an audience with higher authorities. The senior lender, and Darth Vader, would be a good place to start.

However, the goal is to prevent the necessity of this by asking for those folks to okay the letter listing other information needed. Ol' Darth comes back from the dark side of the force when he's held accountable in this manner. When queries for additional items cannot be made so esoterically by the credit policy manager, they tend to be more reasonable.

IF your loan is ultimately approved, the bank will continue to dictate full financial disclosure on an ongoing basis. Whether or not you comply depends on certain factors...

When Not to Kill Trees

Running in the face of the Paper Reduction Act^g, THE BURDEN OF PROOF obliges banks to obtain the same financial statements utilized to originally approve a credit... **annually**, at a minimum. So if your affairs have you dealing with a half dozen commercial banks, you'll be asked to supply each of them with piles of paper each year. Say your personal return is complex (maybe 30 pages in all), you control significant interests in three sizable firms (typical return 15 pages each), and your four rental facilities have detailed operating statements (10 pages a piece on average). If your friendly CSR handles the Xeroxing, you're going to be out $172.50. Don't think of it as a copy fee though, think of it as a delayed loan cost. Then you can feel like you got something for your money. (There, doesn't that feel better?)

Should you go along with this destruction of our national forests? Fact: Your compliance is a requirement in most loan documentation drawn today. Within the commitment letter, loan agreement, note, and/or mortgage, will be a paragraph calling for the submission of

How to Obtain Business Loans

financial statements. Some banks have chosen to leave the wording somewhat vague, as a hopeful "catch all" clause:

> ...the bank shall be provided with such financial information as may be requested from time to time. The borrower agrees that the failure to supply said information will be considered an event of default under the provisions as herein detailed within the loan document.

While other institutions have chosen to be more exacting:

> ...when requested by the bank, the borrower agrees to provide, within 30 days from the end of each fiscal quarter, financial information which shall include, but not be limited to: profit and loss statements for the period, as well as balance sheet information, listings/agings of accounts payable and receivable, along with a summary of current inventory holdings. The preceding information must be prepared in accordance with Generally Accepted Accounting Principles^g, and if requested by the bank, must be reviewed by an independent Certified Public Accountant of recognized standing and acceptable to the bank. In the event borrower fails to comply with any of the aforementioned quarterly reporting requirements, said failure shall constitute an event of default. In which case, bank may accelerate the indebtedness and seek any and all remedies available as provided for under the provisions of the loan documents.

Will this happen? Not a chance. These provisions outline circumstances of nonmonetary default. Bank counsel will almost never attempt to accelerate and/or foreclose based upon a "technical default." Why? Because judges rudely toss them out of court when they do. A typical hearing goes something like this...

The situation is explained, and the judge will bellow from above the courtroom, **"Is the loan current?"**

Bank counsel will shrink in his seat, "Yes, your honor, but..."

"Complaint dismissed, next case."

Happens so fast the bailiff hasn't sat down from the "Hear ye! Hear ye!"

So why is the clause in there? To bully debtors into supplying information. And what's the worst that can happen if you choose not to give up your homework? Obviously, you're burning a bridge with

Chapter Four

the given institution. Believe it or not, you're also creating a reputation for yourself. Word of mouth travels fast in banking circles. Without fail, every seminar and industry meeting I have ever attended has included informal discussion about troublesome borrowers. *You will be talked about.*

You see, many bankers find it difficult to impose the requirements of disclosure THE BURDEN OF PROOF coerces. So when they are refused by a customer, it sits hard. As a result, they find solace in discussing the problem with others. (Misery loves company.) No confidant will be in any hurry to do business with a customer who doesn't abide by the new rules. Especially if they're described as a/an _____ (pick your own expletive).

I recall a specific instance where a borrower violently balked at continuing disclosure. Another officer had repeatedly requested updated information from a Mr. Steve Watson. He was a particularly arrogant individual with little use for the bank unless he needed something at the moment. The officer, Milton Klein, was able to get him on the phone only by calling several days in a row, multiple times daily. It was apparent Mr. Watson had no desire to talk with him.

Milton set forth the type of statements the bank was currently in need of, and was explaining why, when Mr. Watson responded in a rage, **"I'm not sending you all that stuff, talk to your Winthrop Eddles (the bank President). He knows I'm good for the *blank* money."**

"Yes, we're sure of that. And we're not questioning your integrity. It's a matter of meeting THE BURDEN OF PROOF with regard to your cash flow..."

In top voice, Mr. Watson yelled, **"You tell Winthrop I resent your badgering me... and you can be sure I'll let him know about it personally when I see him."**

"Mr. Watson, it was Winthrop who asked me to contact you."

With a megaphone, **"Fine, you tell him he doesn't know what the *blank* he's doing. Tell him he can kiss my *blank*!"** Click.

This story was recounted to a dozen or so grim faced bankers at the most recent ABA meeting. The result? Mr. Watson became persona non grata as far as the local lending community is concerned. He couldn't get credit if he offered gold bullion as collateral. Which, I think, vividly portrays the downside to denying financial statements. Especially if your refusal is expressed in such an acrimonious

How to Obtain Business Loans

tête-à-tête. But you should recognize the upside to withholding — **LEVERAGE** — and the circumstances where it can be applied with success.

By now you're on the way to becoming an expert on all that THE BURDEN OF PROOF entails. You're aware of the internal battles waged at the bank daily and are cognizant it's the loan officer who is sandwiched between "credit policy" and the outside (real) world.

This knowledge can be used to your benefit in many situations. Perhaps you'd like a slight rate reduction... Maybe you're looking for a partial release... Or a new loan altogether... Possibly a better deposit rate... Or some special service... Whatever it is, you can use the submission of financial data as an attractive bargaining chip. Especially if you have a large loan amount outstanding ($500,000 or more). Because, as you now know, in the absence of current statements, the bank is presumably setting aside increased loan loss reserves. Which is "costing" them money, as funds are brought from the bottom line. It is, conceivably, superfluous to illustrate their fiscal interest in gaining your compliance, but let's compare it to the cost of a modest rate adjustment:

> Given... $500,000 at 8% interest only, with annual principal reductions. The bank will receive $40,000 in interest income in the coming year. The loan is graded substandard due to a lack of up-to-date information. As a result, a 10% reserve is set aside — $50,000 — for a "net forfeiture" of $10,000. While this is not a cash loss, it has the same effect on stated earnings for the period.
>
> As prime has dropped to 6%, you would like your loan rate to do the same. Consider the effect on the lender. Interest earned in the next twelve months would fall to $30,000. However, if the bank were able to return the credit to a nonclassified rating, it could "save" $45,000 [9% being the difference in reserve requirements]. Thus, the $10,000 reduction in interest income would be more than offset by the $45,000 swing in the loss provision. Net "gain" $35,000. Recognize, however, the discount in interest income is a cash loss, and the gain from reserve reallocation may not be immediate depending upon the bank's capital position, and budgeting policies (more in Chapter 16). Nevertheless, you can see the value of your bargaining chip.

Now you need to know how to play the hand. Start negotiations by responding to a request for updated financial statements. Express profound concern over the lack of confidentiality the matter affords you. Intimate a fear of pillow talk among bankers and other profes-

Chapter Four

sionals. Play this line out, and then drop the notion you are considering placing your debt with a private investor.

Assuming the loan has otherwise been a model credit for the bank (but of course), they'll want to keep the outstandings so long as they can resolve THE BURDEN OF PROOF without an annual hassle.

From here it's as easy as 1-2-3:

(1) **Assure the loan officer you'd gladly supply financial statements if you were sure they would remain confidential.** He'll chatter about the bank's no-talk policy, and the lengths they go in order to ensure privacy for their customers. Quietly assent to his testimony.

(2) **Mutter aloud that you may be better served rate-wise elsewhere, given that the private investor is satisfied with a return of 6%.** Now he's going to illuminate the various costs to remortgage (if applicable), or stammer something about the convenience factor of dealing with an institutional lender. He'll likely recount how important your business is to the bank. Which is the cue to vocalize how much you've enjoyed the relationship to date, and how you'd hate to see it end.

(3) **Ask if it might be possible for the bank to give consideration to a rate adjustment. After all, you've never missed a payment. And now that you've gotten this confidentiality problem satisfied in your mind, it seems a shame to move a mutually beneficial "relationship" just because of a small difference in rate.** Although you should add, "A couple percent on half a million means a lot more to me than it does the bank. Say... what are your CD rates now?" Pledging the timely submission of financial information, along with focusing on a banking "relationship" (major industry buzz word), will go a long ways towards getting your rate adjusted. Dropping the not so subtle hint of additional deposits — will guarantee success.

Let's consider a different set of parameters. You're still seeking a rate adjustment, but say you've been providing information all along. And although there has never been a delinquent payment, the bank carries your loan as substandard because your statements don't (in their opinion) depict an adequate repayment ability.

Two quick points. One, you're not going to know this unless you ask... so do. Simply inquire as to what your loan's risk classification

75

How to Obtain Business Loans

is, and get an understanding of how the bank's particular system is structured. Two, if you find out you're rated substandard, don't let your ego get involved. Resist the urge to take such a declaration as a personal affront. It's not. Instead, treat the news as the discovery of an opportunity.

Provided you have some liquidity (but of course), offer a 6 month interest reserve. Vow to keep making payments out of pocket, and reason that the reserve should afford the bank a higher comfort level. Ask your officer to see if he could get the loan upgraded based upon the scenario.

Let him test the waters before you toss in the money. This will take days, or even weeks. He won't be able to quickly confer with the powers that be. On the contrary, it will be necessary to complete several forms, and present the suggestion to some type of committee. He might even have to seek enlightenment from a Regional Credit Guru.

We'll assume he comes back with an affirmative answer. Now is the time to ask for a rate adjustment as consideration for what you're willing to do in an effort to help the bank. Remember to stress the give-and-take necessary in any good "relationship."

The numbers from the institution's perspective shake out the same as the other example. And what about from your end? Are you getting a good return for employing your money in this way? I hear you. "Not with the reserve being held in a money market account paying 2.5%. That's one poor application of funds." (Gong. Buzz. Aaaannnnnck. Thank you for playing. Don Pardo what's our parting gift?)

"Well, Addison, today we have a Hewlett Packard HP 12C financial calculator... which our departing contestant can use to better analyze rates of return."

I don't think you can find a better use for your cash, at least not yield-wise. Consider...

- $500,000 @ 6% = $30,000 in annual interest.

- A six month reserve would be $15,000

- Let's say the cash would yield a 15% return if employed through normal business operations.

- $15,000 @ 15% = an opportunity cost of $2,250

Chapter Four

- $15,000 @ 2.5% = $375 in interest earned.

- Which would mean a "loss" of $1,875. Right? (Hands off those buzzers.)

- Not quite. What the analysis ignores, to this point, are the savings enjoyed from the rate reduction reciprocated for fronting the reserve.

- $500,000 @ 1% = $5,000

- Which means your actual return on the $15,000 is:
  $ 5,000
  (1,875)
  $ 3,125 / $15,000 = 20.8%

- Not a bad yield, eh?

Under what circumstances should you become environmentally conscious, and completely disregard requests for information?

- You feel absolutely certain you will not need the bank's credit services again.

- You are confident there'll be no reason you'd require help from any lending institution in the immediate vicinity again, or you have kept your connection with the existing lender amicable even though you have declined to supply financial statements. And, as a result, you anticipate no damaging word-of-mouth.

So... basically, you should provide the darn information, curse the government regulators, and pledge to recycle. (Is it a coincidence that lumber prices reached an all time high not long ago?)

Character Loans

In March 1993, regulators of thrifts and commercial banks under the direction of President Clinton announced a plan to reduce documentation by strong and well-managed thrifts and banks for a *basket* of loans to smaller businesses. "This policy initiative is designed to reduce costs for both businesses and lenders, reduce the

How to Obtain Business Loans

time it takes to respond to credit applications, and clear the way for 'character loans' that give more weight to a borrower's reputation and standing in the community and less weight to a strict item-by-item financial evaluation of loans and borrowers." [6]

To many in the banking industry, this sounded like the reinstatement of CHARACTER LOANS. But let's look more closely at what some of the key parameters of the new program are:

- The government will require minimal documentation for loans made to small- and medium-sized businesses by "banks and thrifts with *strong* regulatory ratings, and with *adequate* capital." [7] (Strong and adequate being somewhat open for interpretation.)

- Banks cannot grant loans requiring minimal documentation loans in excess of 20% of the institution's total capital. (This basket of credits being the banking equivalent of the protected player rule professional sports leagues utilize during expansion. Institutions are able to choose which loans they wish to make "untouchable." These would not necessarily be the bank's best loans, just the ones they are having the toughest time documenting. Which sort of defeats the purpose, doesn't it? Now banks have a way to hide semi-problem credits from review, while THE BURDEN OF PROOF rages on for the balance of the portfolio.)

- There is a maximum limit on the amount of any individual minimal-documentation loan. The limit is the lesser of the following: $900,000 or 3% of the institution's capital. For multiple loans from a single borrower, the banking institution must total these loans before applying the maximum size limit.

"'The initiatives... will give the nation's strongest banks and thrifts increased flexibility to make loans to creditworthy customers by eliminating unnecessary documentation requirements,' said White House Communications Director George Stephanopoulus.

"'The banks and thrifts that are both highly rated and adequately capitalized will be able to devote a portion of their loan portfolios, based on the institution's capital, to making loans to small- and medium-sized businesses and farms, using their own best judgment as to the creditworthiness of the borrower and the necessary documentation,' he said."

The government's policy statement went on to say: "These

Chapter Four

loans will be evaluated solely on the basis of performance and will be exempt from examiner criticism of documentation... The agencies will continue to recognize the difficulty and cost of obtaining some documents from small- and medium-sized businesses and farms. These difficulties and costs could result in some deviations from an institution's own loan documentation policy.

"Such deviations are frequently based on past experience with the customer. In such cases, the loan will not be criticized if the examiner concurs that sufficient information exists to serve as a basis for an informed credit decision." [7]

Wait a minute. First we heard that the loans in the *basket* "will be evaluated solely on the basis of performance and will be exempt from examiner criticism of documentation." Then we heard, "if the examiner concurs that sufficient information exists to serve as a basis for an informed credit decision." Orwellian newspeak at its best.

This is the insipid message from Washington. "We understand the documentation burden is a heavy load, and we endorse described ways of easing the hardship, because the banking system needs to get money back on the streets... the regulators will look for 'adequate' levels of documentation, which would substantiate the credit decisions being made."

What's "adequate"? If this is supposed to be a return to CHARACTER LOANS, what would be an *adequate* proof of character? A clean credit report? A track record with the bank? Church attendance? Membership in civic organizations?

Definitive answers (from anyone) are conspicuously absent. A few years ago when the examiners began walking not so softly and commenced swinging their big stick, a lot of banks suffered when they were forced to set aside additional loan loss reserves as a result of regulatory reviews. In light of the contradicting banter coming from both governmental officials and regulators, line auditors and the banks they examine have chosen to err on the conservative side.

The field regulators remain hard on institutions. When auditors are judged on performance, how does it appear if they consistently have little or no negative comments about the banks they examine? They are trained to find problems. If they aren't discovering any, are they doing their job? Better yet, will they keep their job if they aren't finding problems? And as an agency, consider the downside if, after posting a solid review, the bank in question later trends toward insolvency.

How to Obtain Business Loans

From the bank's perspective, why invite possible criticism? With a lack of real direction from Washington, and the knowledge that the regulators continue to be tough in the field, institutions continue to play out THE BURDEN OF PROOF to the Nth degree... on all loans, not just those outside of some *basket*.

You want confirmation of the reticence to buy into the CHARACTER LOAN rhetoric disseminated from the capitol? Witness the memo I received from Lightning Lou, Credit Guru at Large, only two weeks after the issuance of the Interagency Policy Statement.

BANK MEMORANDUM

TO: Commercial Lending Departments
FROM: Lou Elmerton
DATE: April 16, 1993
RE: Credit Policy Statement/Obtaining Interim Financial Statements for Business Loans

As you undoubtedly know, maintaining our level of excellence in credit servicing rests on our ability to gather the most accurate, complete and timely financial information from all customers and prospects. This information is particularly essential in the servicing of our existing customer base.

Certainly, all of us have seen situations where companies began downward spirals which could not have been foretold without access to interim financial statements. Our documentation program must focus on the early identification of negative trends. Therefore, the following changes to our bank's credit policy will be effective immediately. (The orchestra hits a crescendo.)

1. In most cases, as practical, interim financial statements shall be required on a not less than quarterly basis. (Read: "Usually, but not always required." The ability to be vague is a necessity in this business.)

2. Before the loan is actually closed, but after the Commitment Letter has been accepted, we will need to obtain and analyze appropriate financial statements as may be necessary. (Lou's mother's maiden name was Stephanopolus.)

Chapter Four

About a week later, another memorandum followed which succinctly stated said: "CHARACTER LOANS... don't even think about it! No approval will be awarded in the absence of regularly required documentation." (Can't you just feel the flow of credit loosening as a result of the emphatic position taken by the government and the categorical alignment made by the regulatory agencies?)

Lightning Lou's negativism toward CHARACTER LOANS, and his assertions to step up THE BURDEN OF PROOF to quarterly analyses, proved outrageous in application.

A prospective customer had been seeking approval for a line of credit ($600,000) which he planned to use for the construction of some pre-sold duplex units. I labored for weeks to meet Lou's insatiable desire for additional information. Finally, the prospect was at the end of his rope.

"I'm running out of time here, I need to get these units started in order to meet the delivery clause on the contracts. What if I can convert one of my partnership holdings to cash, and pledge funds equal to the loan amount? Can you get your regional fella to sign off on this thing then?"

I nobly promised my efforts and approached Lou for the approval of a CD secured loan... albeit without some of the most recently requested information he'd wanted on the borrower.

"You don't understand what we're striving to attain here," he started. "We must show the borrower has the ability to produce the cash flows necessary to service and retire his existing and proposed obligations. Without complete information on his partnerships, as I requested, we cannot satisfy this objective."

Exhorting myself not to pass out, I offered, **"But Lou, we have LIQUID collateral. Unless the funds are lost from our vault, I know we're going to be repaid. Whatever happens with regard to his various partnerships is a moot point, it doesn't matter! We're lending him his own money!"**

(Came the rain.) "Addison, if we don't meet an "adequate" BURDEN OF PROOF, we could be forced to later downgrade this loan... regardless of what's being pledged. Remember now, we're not collateral lenders."

How to Obtain Business Loans

Actually, in this instance, we weren't lenders at all. Needless to say, the prospect moved on when I returned to him with Lou's illuminating comments on the indispensable need for additional data on his unrelated activities.

Later that same week, I was privy to a residential loan being extended to a Mr. Lloyd Tengstrom (in the sum of $500,000). The amount applied for not falling within Lightning Lou's approval net, the affiliate was able to offer this loan without his concurrence.

The credit was an 80% extension on the borrower's vacation residence. His supplied financial statement indicated a significant net worth, and liquid assets in the area of half-a-million dollars. The bank had not, however, obtained a copy of any tax filings. He had been in a hurry to close and confirmation of liquidity (a brokerage statement) was all that was required to meet THE BURDEN OF PROOF. These funds weren't even pledged as collateral. It was just verified he had them.

(Consistency, it's what you think of when banking comes to mind.)

---

[1] Smith, Ed: "Clear thinking in Florida," *Bankers News*, Volume 1, Issue 4, June 8, 1993, pg. 67.

[2] Smith, Ed: "Clear thinking in Florida," *Bankers News*, Volume 1, Issue 4, June 8, 1993, pg. 67.

[3] Smith, Ed: "Clear thinking in Florida," *Bankers News*, Volume 1, Issue 4, June 8, 1993, pg. 67.

[4] Smith, Ed: "Clear thinking in Florida," *Bankers News*, Volume 1, Issue 4, June 8, 1993, pg. 67.

[5] Smith, Ed: "Clear thinking in Florida," *Bankers News*, Volume 1, Issue 4, June 8, 1993, pg. 67.

[6] Seiders, David F.: "Economic Fundamentals Appear Sound," *Nation's Building News*, Vol. 9, Number 5, April 26, 1993, pg. 7.

[7] Ginovsky, John: "Character Loans," *ABA Bankers Weekly*, Vol. 12, Number 13, April 6, 1993, pg. 1.

CHAPTER 5:

THE LEGISLATIVE IMPACT

Milton Klein sat behind his gen-u-INE imitation wood desk in his less than spacious 7' X 9', windowless office. With a lanky 6'6" frame, not including a sporadically bushy hairstyle, he was better known as "Dinky" to most of the bank's staff.

Seeing him at his work-station was always painfully humorous. His desk was originally much too short to allow his knees beneath it. He had looked every bit like an adult attending tea time at a child's play table. In characteristic fashion, the bank had remedied the situation with a band-aid of sorts... setting the desk up on wooden blocks to allow freedom of movement. (Classy.) In the dim lighting, Dinky could have passed as Abe Lincoln toiling away in the corner of some log cabin of yesteryear.

On this particular morning, no abandoned car jokes cast in the direction of his desk or other aspersions about his surroundings

How to Obtain Business Loans

could dampen his spirits. "Have you talked to Esther today?" he questioned with a devilish smile.

"No, not yet. I've been out this morning... I had to meet with Pratt Development and break the news we aren't renewing their land loan," I answered in a monotone.

"I'm sure that was pleasant."

(Laden with sarcasm) **"Lovely. They understood perfectly why we no longer trusted their repayment ability after a six or seven year track record."**

Dinky glibly smirked at me (which I thought very un-Lincolnesque) and said, "Go see Esther. She's got one that's going to make your day." This made me instantly nervous, as he was enjoying something much too much... and I was sure it was at my expense.

Esther was a residential originator who had been married to the bank's previous senior lender, Reuben, who now sold real estate within a development to which the bank had just extended a $750,000 commitment^g. In his spare time, Reuben now dated Madeline who was the attorney which had handled most of the bank's loan closings over the past few years, while changing firms three or four times herself in the process. Meanwhile, Dottie (Reuben's past secretary) now worked for the bank's present senior lender, Mortie, though she had formerly been retained by Esther, when Esther, Reuben, Madeline, and Mortie all were employed elsewhere. Inasmuch as anyone could tell, this was all on the up-and-up and what not, because no one was more closely related than first cousins and they were all at least 21.

I joined this typically dysfunctional American "family" when I was semi-promoted to oversee the Residential Real Estate Division. Which left me responsible for approving all of Esther's loans, without fully being her supervisor... while still retaining my commercial "lending" responsibilities. (Banks like to ease you into positions. Give you the additional responsibilities on top of your current duties for awhile — with no raise — then after a year or so of "seasoning," you might get the title — with no raise — and finally a special salary review when they begin to surmise that your experience qualifies you for a jump to another institution... and they suspect you stand on the precipice.)

Honest Abe spoke the truth. Esther had one heck of a deal for me when I caught up with her around lunchtime. "Do you remember the

Chapter Five

loan the bank did for Mr. Tengstrom?" she began.

"The gentleman who couldn't supply tax filings from his accountant in time to meet a closing date... the credit was approved based upon his verified liquidity." (How could I forget?)

"Right. Well, now his wife wants a loan."

"Huh? You mean for a car or something?"

"No, for a condo."

"As an investment?"

"No, for her home."

"I'm confused. Didn't we just close a $500,000 loan for her and her husband to purchase their residence?"

"Yes, but now they're getting divorced."

"Divorced. Affably or otherwise?"

"Mostly otherwise."

"As my father would say, that's like being kinda pregnant. What's mostly otherwise?"

"Well, they knew they were going to divorce when they applied for the other loan, and..."

"They did, did they? Pray tell, were we privy to that tidbit of information?"

"No, Addison, of course not. I'd have told you or Mortie."

"Uh-huh. You'd have jeopardized your $2,500 commission solely to benefit our institution's credit quality."

"Y e s, I w o u l d h a v e."

"I'm sure. I bet you'd be happy to pay more taxes for President Clinton, too. Let's go back, though. What's *mostly* otherwise?"

"Well, Mr. Tengstrom has agreed to give Paulina money for the down payment... but they've both retained counsel to hammer out how much will be paid in alimony."

"Does she, by any chance, have any visible means of supporting herself in the meantime... say savings, or better yet... a job?"

"No, and Mr. Tengstrom moved all the funds from joint accounts into ones in his name only. But, Addison, she'll definitely receive part of his income when the divorce is finalized."

"Esther, we have no real idea what his income is! Remember, he didn't supply us any tax filings."

"Right, and actually, he's refused to allow Paulina any financial records, so we can't get them this time either. At least not until a settlement is reached."

"Well, then we'll have to wait for the final divorce decree."

How to Obtain Business Loans

"Can't. Paulina must close within two weeks, or the developer will sell the unit out from under her... and she'll lose the deposit Mr. Tengstrom put down."

No cash. No job. No income. No problem. THE BURDEN OF PROOF is not the same on the residential side of the bank. My stomach hurts. No lunch.

Uniform Application *Among* Institutions

Congress authors new legislation with the anticipation of homogeneous procedures falling in line at financial institutions nationwide. However, as is the case with many macro-economic approaches, application falls short of theory.

THE BURDEN OF PROOF varies somewhat between banks, dependent upon their size. Large institutions, especially those with sizable commercial real estate portfolios, are closely scrutinized in examination. They are expected to meet a high degree of proof in their analysis of new and existing credits, whereas smaller depositories appear to receive a break from their auditors. Perhaps this is because the smaller banks are not being required to demonstrate the same level of thoroughness.

Bankers are aware of who eventually finances the deals they decline. Finding out doesn't take much investigative work. If it's construction, the lending institution will always proudly display their sign, "Construction Financing Provided by X-Bank." If the loan were to purchase existing real estate, you might hear about the eventual financier via the agent whose commission you threatened by rejecting the request. Typically, they want you to know what you turned down, someone else approved "easily." And they like to remind you that you'll not be looking at the next opportunity as a result. The parting comment is often, "Let me know when things loosen up there, but for now I've got to go where I can get things done." Which, in actuality, must be a perpetually moving target.

Many times you'll receive feedback from the small business owner who had to seek credit elsewhere after being turned down. You may have an officer from the extending bank inform you they were "able to find a way to do the deal." Insinuating a puzzle your bank couldn't figure out had been solved. The point being, in most instances, you know who is doing what locally. Which becomes a source of amazement when the examiners make their rounds.

Chapter Five

One of the biggest stumbling blocks in the path of uniform regulation is that the governing bodies are not the same for all institutions. The Office of the Comptroller of the Currency audits nationally chartered banks (often the larger ones), and the Federal Deposit Insurance Corporation reviews state chartered banks (many times the smaller ones). Over the past few years, it has seemed as though these two groups did not possess the ability to communicate with one another and Congress. (Perhaps they all had unlisted phone numbers to thwart crank calls.) For there has been the appearance of small banks being spared some of the regulatory "intensity" unleased on their larger counterparts.

How would I have any idea what a review at another institution went like? (Come on, catch on would you!) By means of knowing what's in another bank's portfolio, and by word of mouth.

If my institution passed on a deal because there was no way to meet a reasonable BURDEN OF PROOF, the approving bank who followed did not discover additional statements within an Egyptian tomb. They just chose to accept the risk of criticism, and approved the loan. With uncanny accuracy, the gossip pipeline will let you know how an exam went (either directly, or in the form of a sudden evaporation of available credit at the given bank).

As a result, many times over the past few years, institutions known to have housed many *unpalatable* credits with regard to PROOF, have received solid reviews. While larger banks in the same area, who turn down a disproportionate amount of loans because of failure to meet THE BURDEN, receive deficiency notices identifying areas for improvement (or worse).

How can this be? I have heard, albeit third-person, that a regulator addressed the double standard in the following manner: "Larger institutions have the resources available to them, such as credit staff, to review borrowers more completely. So it is appropriate that they are expected to meet a higher level of diligence than smaller banks... who do not have the same resources at their disposal."

(Makes a lot of sense. The risk in a transaction is obviously different according to who does it. The borrower will certainly take into consideration the size of the bank which made the loan before defaulting. Without a doubt they will pay longer for a smaller institution, because they know there weren't sufficient means to analyze the undertaking more adequately.)

How to Obtain Business Loans

Although the playing field for examination can be leveled, another impediment to uniform application is, unfortunately, impossible to remedy. The individuality cannot be taken out of the reviewer. No matter how rigid the mandated guidelines, personality traits cannot be legislated out of the equation. The subject matter is simply too diverse for any functional "Go To" chart to be formulated.

However, it would help to have the same auditors review all banks within a given jurisdiction, rather than what transpired last year in my neck of the woods. Twelve OCC examiners set up camp at the local Ritz-Carlton, and divided themselves equally among three different caches.

The Ritz-Carlton. THE #*^%@=&+ RITZ mind you! This is the OCC's equivalent to NASA spending $25 per nut and bolt for the space shuttle. A dozen bureaucrats in seven rooms, which go for an average of $160 a night in the off-season, for roughly twenty days. Total lodging bill — $22,400. (THAT'S TWENTY-TWO THOUSAND, FOUR HUNDRED DOLLARS AND 00/100s if you're writing the check. And here's the joke... you are.) As opposed to a Holiday, or Days Inn averaging around $65 per night. Total bill — $9,100. (Care to guesstimate the annual cost to house these watchdogs across the country? Me neither, I already missed lunch.)

Oh well, I'm sure they get package deals. The room rates they expensed at the local Ritz are without a doubt much less than what the public pays. Or they probably at least received coupons for return visits to the beach. (Oh yeah, The Ritz is surfside.)

And I suppose they need their rest after hectic days spent interacting with files, and pontificating via esoteric memoranda. It's a stressful job being a hall monitor.

The Consequence of Uneven Regulation

An unexpected result of split regulatory enforcement has manifested itself in a shift in lending appetites by institutional size. Historically, large banks had always been the ones extending significant credit to finance commercial construction, leveraged buyouts[g], residential development, and the turnover of trading assets[g]. While smaller institutions specialized in personal loans, and mom-and-pop business financing.

In either case, the corresponding staffs displayed expertise in the

Chapter Five

areas in which their banks focused. However, eyes began to wander under the increasing pressure of regulation. Large banks found it difficult to book as many development loans as they had in the past and the same may be said for other forms of commercial credit. Applicants then turned to smaller institutions for help.

Previously, this had not been an avenue traveled by most as the process was more cumbersome than dealing with a big bank. Smaller institutions have much lower legal lending limits[g], which means they must "participate[g]" significant credits. In other words, they will take whatever outstandings they can by law, and then spread the balance between additional institutions who wish to be involved. Multiple approvals take time, and fundings are a veritable nightmare in many instances. However, borrowers will go where money is available.

Conversely, the giant institutions shifted their concentration elsewhere (to the imposition of fees wherever possible, home mortgages, and just riding the yield curve down).

The fallout from this flip-flop was the mismatch of loan types to expertise levels. Suddenly, the lender at the outlet bank in the mall was mulling over requests from the largest of commercial concerns and trying his hand at multimillion dollar development loans... two prospects he had no familiarity with.

Congress had pushed for tighter regulation in an effort to produce a more standardized methodology for lending. The regulators were given the task of monitoring banks to ensure proper policies were implemented and subsequently adhered to by experienced personnel. To a degree, unequal examination has made sure exactly the opposite transpired.

The designed methodology did not trickle down to the wee institutions in the same manner as which the hammer fell on mid- to large-size banks. This allowed the small institutions to seize a market opportunity by extending high dollar commercial credit via the creation of lending consortiums. Which were/are able to circumvent legal lending roadblocks by participating debt across regular confederations, if you will. The four to five diminutive banks in my area routinely evaluate and approve credits heretofore entertained only by their bigger brethren.

An officer at one of the tiniest banks led the succession of good ol' boy institutions into the commercial lending fray. A Branch Manager by job description, Parnell Redford became a folk hero of sorts.

How to Obtain Business Loans

If you found yourself with a deal the big guys were filibustering over, you could rest assured salvation was a phone call away. 1-800-EASY-YES. "Hello, Parnell speaking! What can I do you for?"

If Push-It-Thru Parnell couldn't cover you in-house, he'd convene his counterparts on your behalf posthaste. And before you knew it, you were the proud debtor of a participated loan. His feats were legendary. A likable individual, I found myself referring deals to him which I knew to be viable, but difficult to meet THE BURDEN OF PROOF on.

Parnell's bank mopped up. They generated more fee income than you can imagine and received a clean bill of health from the regulators in the process. All good things come to an end though... Parnell's institution was gobbled up by a mega-bank conglomerate. (Superman's cape got cut.)

Ironic, isn't it? The bank was acquired because it was so profitable. And the reason it had been a money-making machine was loan growth. So what did the purchaser do? Tightened credit, of course.

Uniform Application *Within* Institutions

Equating regulatory application between banks of differing sizes is akin to comparing apples and oranges. But... when you're gathering from beneath the same tree, shouldn't your bushel be filled with matching fruit? Much to the chagrin of those seeking to standardize procedures for the analysis and treatment of risk, banks assess and monitor loans very differently by department of origin.

The following is an abridged edition of how the lending function is typically broken down within an institution:

Bankcard Services	Mastercard and Visa
Commercial Real Estate	Development(s) and owner-user
Consumer Finance	Car, boat, other personal
Corporate Lending	Equipment and trading assets
Indirect Lending	Finance paper
Residential Real Estate	Home mortgages

There are areas of specialization within each department, but these are the basic divisions. And while you'd not be surprised each has some unique procedures, you would assume the assessment of risk is analogous throughout. It is not.

Chapter Five

The real BURDEN OF PROOF lies only within the commercial and commercial real estate departments. The justifying school of thought goes something like this:

> These areas have large dollar exposures and are where the biggest losses occurred within the S&L industry. Although many banks also extend major dollars for single residential credits, there is an axiom of unknown origin which says, "If everything goes bad, an individual will stop paying his home mortgage last, because he must have a place to live." Which is why residential lending is believed less risky than commercial credit. (While statistical data backs this up, if it's me, I stop paying for food last.)

Lending against someone's home requires much less analysis than extending the same dollar amount against a sole proprietor's[g] place of business. And the residential loan requires no mid-stream evaluation of continued credit worthiness.

In this case, the interest rates banks charge appear to distinguish commercial credit as a higher risk, and thus the additional labor seems rational.

(Current)	1 Yr.	3 Yr.	5 Yr.
Residential Rates	4.25%	5.75%	6.25%
Commercial Rates	6.55%	7.35%	8.00%

However, take two $250,000 loans to the same individual. The operation of his printing service is your ultimate repayment source in both instances. Should the 75% extension credit on his business property be treated so differently in its analysis than the 75% loan against his residence? The regulators would have you believe so. The approval package for the commercial credit might take as long as a month to complete, while the residential loan would often be *closed* in that time frame.

Arguments explaining the vast difference in work associated with credit type hinge on data confirming where past losses have occurred, and seem ratified by the banks' own decisions to charge more for commercial credit. Meaning, the greater the risk, the more in-depth the analysis.

How to Obtain Business Loans

If this logic held true, then which loan type would have the greatest BURDEN OF PROOF?

(Current)	1 Yr.	3 Yr.	5 Yr.
Residential Rates	4.25%	5.75%	6.25%
Commercial Rates	6.55%	7.35%	8.00%
Consumer Rates	6.75%	8.00%	9.25%
Bankcard Rates	14-18%	14-18%	14-18%

Looks like bankcard to me. Which no less than four dozen institutions qualified me for this year... without my even submitting an application. Admittedly, they're not approving me for $250,000.

Which brings us back to dollar exposure and collateral, large dollar loans against other than one's primary residence necessitating detailed evaluation. Then again. If that were factual, the same in-depth studies would be done for second home requests, and investor purchases of residential properties.

(Current)	1 Yr.	3 Yr.	5 Yr.
2nd Home Rates	4.25%	5.75%	6.25%
Investor Rates	5.50%	7.00%	7.75%
Commercial Rates	6.55%	7.35%	8.00%

Second home rates are the same as primary; and investor properties, although priced higher than primaries, are still below commercial terms. So any residential loan is actually considered less perilous than commercial credit.

A contention would be that commercial real estate values fluctuate more widely than residential ones. This statement has some validity in that commercial properties sell based upon the income streams they generate, while homes trade on market value. The latter is sometimes assumed to be less volatile.

Lightning Lou always said commercial real estate lending was the riskiest of credit extensions. Most regulators, and Congressmen, would agree. Although, if this is the case, why is it one of the areas that officers typically have the most individual authority in?

Banks set personal lending limits by category for all their officers.

Chapter Five

A typical line lender might have the following approval levels.

Unsecured	Secured Commercial	Commercial Real Estate	Consumer Real Estate	Residential
$ 50,000	$100,000	$250,000	$ 50,000	$300,000

So, according to approval authority, which for the bank is, perhaps, the ultimate judgment of risk, commercial real estate is the next to safest category.

For those of you scoring at home, let's recap apparent risk ratings within the three categories shown below. In descending order, they are...

Government	Interest Rate	Loan Authority
Commercial	Bankcard (Unsecured)	Bankcard (Unsecured)
Commercial	Consumer	Consumer
Commercial	Commercial	Commercial
Commercial	Any Residential	Any Residential
Other		

Notice any similarities? It appears banks estimate that the highest default risk is in the area of personal credit, while feeling that any type of residential mortgage is the safest extension of debt. Commercial rates of interest charged, and approval levels, lag only slightly behind residential.

Notice any differences? The government feels the biggest risks are in commercial lending (particularly commercial real estate).

So who is right? Are the examiners justified in requiring the level of analysis they do for commercial credit, when bank management appears to *assess the risk of real loss so differently*? **The answer has to be either the regulators have overreacted, or bankers are not correctly pricing their portfolio's risk/return relationship. Or, more likely, it is a combination of both.**

"May I Take Your Order?"

"Fine. That's nachos for you, ma'am. Black bean soup and the

How to Obtain Business Loans

Cajun chicken for you, sir. Would you like the soup brought out as an appetizer, or with your meal?"

An important question. If the soup is too filling, I might not have room for my Cajun delight (gaaronteee). On the other hand, it might be better not to mix everything at once. Decisions, decisions.

Sequence is so important. When ordering food, and when presenting multiple requests to a bank. (Hey, wouldn't it be great if bankers got 15% of the tab as a gratuity? After all, S&L administrators used to.)

All banks have loan limits. They have legal lending limits and often lower "house" limits. To explain, institutions found statewide or nationally are part of conglomerates. While customers often view X-Bank as the same no matter the location, this isn't typically the case. Huge banks found, in order to be more responsive within individual communities, it was advisable to decentralize front-line matters. Therefore, X-Bank in Smallville, is not exactly the same as the X-Bank in Metropolis.

Each have their own board of directors and, within holding company guidelines (very restraining ones mind you), set local policies and procedures.

One of the areas they have little leeway in is authority over "house" limits. Credits over certain amounts set by the holding company must be sent up the chain of command for approval on high. However, the affiliate itself will have its own policies as to what can be done beneath the ceiling

It is always important to ask what the "house" limit is. Regional folks are invariably a lot less motivated to close loans. Affiliate banks and their officers have budgets to meet; regional Gurus are not held directly accountable for production. Translation: If you can keep your loan amount under the "house" limit, you stand a much better chance of being approved.

For instance, say a bank's local threshold is only $500,000. You had the intention of requesting a loan in the amount of $800,000 to construct an eight-villa project, total cost $1,070,000. On the surface, a $500,000 extension would not appear to allow for completion of the development.

However, you could alter your request to ask for a $500,000 **revolving**^{g} construction loan (meaning the balance can go up, be slightly retired, and be redrawn again). Under this structure, your build-out might take place as follows:

Chapter Five

Cost for 5 villas	$668,750	($1,070,000/8 × 5)
Equity apportioned	168,750	(Land held free and clear is worth $270,000)
Loan necessary	$500,000	
Loan available	$500,000	

Then as units close, and the balance on the line is reduced, construction could commence on the last three villas. While you might anticipate this scenario being required by institutions, you may be happily surprised to find some using a more liberal approach.

Rather than build five homes, then have to wait for closings to reduce the revolver and enable construction to commence on the latter three villas, all eight could be begun under the same line:

Cost to complete 3 villas	$401,250	
Equity apportioned	101,250	
Loan proceeds used	$300,000	
Cost of next 5 villas	$668,750	
Equity apportioned	168,750	
Funds needed	$500,000	
Remaining availability	$200,000	($200,000/$500,000)

Which means 40% of the work on the remaining homes can be completed before the initial closing of the first villa set. Assuming an average sales price of $157,000, and a 90% of gross release provision[g], the first closing would provide another $141,300 of availability after reducing the line. And so on, as the rest of the completed homes closed:

Villa Closings	% of Work Which Could be Funded on Latter 5 Villas
One	68.3%
Two	96.5%
Three	Equity begins to return to developer

How to Obtain Business Loans

The advantages to you?

---

(1) **You get your deal approved easier.**

(2) Construction of the overall project can proceed on an even basis, even with a lower loan amount.

(3) The loan will cost you less. Note the differences:

	$800,000 Loan	$500,000 Revolver
Doc Stamps[s]	$ 2,800	$ 1,750
Title Insurance[s]	4,075	2,575
Bank Fee (1.5%)	12,000	7,500
Estimated Interest	36,000	30,000
Total	$54,875	$41,825

For a difference of $13,050. Real cash American. (As if easier approval wasn't beguiling enough for you to structure your next request a little differently!)

But from a regulator's perspective, is the treatment of risk the same under either arrangement? Or does the affiliate's willingness to extend a revolver circumvent steps to properly assess the breadth of the undertaking?

Lending authorities are set so ventures with higher exposures, and associated risks, are reviewed by senior personnel. In our example, structuring the debt as a $500,000 revolver sidesteps a guideline, which was implemented to help ensure a more thorough analysis of larger and riskier credits, and masks the true exposure. Which is much more than $500,000.

Say the disbursement process is not monitored correctly. The developer could attempt to bring completed units on line too fast, not staggering construction properly. For instance, if one villa is all that reaches CO[s], and the rest are in various degrees of completion:

Cost to complete 1 villa	$133,750
Equity apportioned	33,750
Loan proceeds used	$100,000

Chapter Five

Cost to complete project	
($1,070,000 - $133,750)	$936,250
Equity apportioned ($270,000 - $ 33,750)	236,250
Subtotal needed	$700,000
Available under revolving line	400,000
Funds needed	$300,000
Provided by only closing	141,300
Shortage	$158,700

$500,000 might be out the door, and only one villa could be closed. The bank might then have to fund an additional $158,700 to bring the rest of its collateral to a salable point. In this light, the true exposure is $658,700. Varying the use of proceeds and the construction timetable bring about other assorted examples of increased exposure when funding under a revolver.

What's more, additional games are played with "house" authorities. The limits are set based upon aggregate related debt. So if an individual has a $250,000 commercial loan on the books and will be the guarantor on a $300,000 request, then in the absence of some creative structuring the approval will have to come from outside the local bank. Which makes sense given the overall exposure of $550,000.

What doesn't track are the exceptions to the rule. At some banks, installment debts[g] aren't included when calculating the aggregate exposure, while almost all institutions exclude primary residence credit from totals. Which means the following can transpire:

Home mortgage	$ 525,000	(Residence)
Car loan	35,000	(Installment)
Car loan	33,000	(Installment)
Boat loan	47,000	(Installment)
Commercial loan	275,000	
Total existing debt	$ 915,000	
New request	225,000	
Apparent aggregate debt	$1,140,000	
Aggregate for approval purposes	$ 500,000	
($275,000 + $225,000)		

Although the bank is relying upon the borrower to repay over $1 million, they treat the risk as if the exposure were less than half that

97

How to Obtain Business Loans

amount. While these gyrations to bypass lending authorities are... colorful, they pale in comparison to the next illustration:

> A wealthy prospect has a need for several credit facilities, each of which is retiring an obligation at a rival institution with which he is disgruntled.
>
> (1) A $25,000 unsecured line of credit to his wife's business, Creekside Realty. Not to be accompanied by a personal guarantee.
>
> (2) A $40,000 unsecured line of credit to the individual's principal business, a building company. Personal guarantee included.
>
> (3) A $50,000 lot loan to Titan Ltd. Partnership. 50% pro-rata guarantees[g] to be offered along with a 65% position against the property.
>
> (4) $50,000 more for another lot under identical parameters.
>
> (5) A $400,000 personal line of credit collateralized by over $1,000,000 in marketable securities.
>
> That's $565,000 in total.

If all the related requests are to be approved simultaneously, the regional Guru would have to review the merits of each individual loan. Which might be a tough sell in that...

(A) Loans to closely held businesses without personal guarantees are **against policy**.

(B) Unsecured lines of credit to contractors are **against policy**.

(C) Pro-rata guarantees are **against policy**.

(D) And the lot loan requests are for terms which are **against policy**.

Conversely, the personal line supported by liquid assets is the proverbial "no-brainer." So here's where the art of ordering comes

Chapter Five

in. You definitely want your appetizers first. Approval of the smaller, "more difficult" requests should be sought to begin with. The bank can approve both the unsecured business lines and the lot loans in-house. *They should be closed.*

Then on to the main course. In this case, the $400,000 personal line. Even the surliest of regional nerds has a love for loans secured better than 2:1 by liquid collateral. And by that point, the other credits are often overlooked because they are already closed.

Remember, when ordering multiple "courses," go for the spicy stuff first. Save the bland for your main entrée. You'll sleep much better.

Farnham Humphrey was a banker of note within my hamlet. The Humphrey's were long-time residents and owned the city's landmark hotel, among other things. Farnham didn't need to work since his income was derived from family holdings and sufficient enough to allow him the luxury of living within the most affluent neighborhood in town.

Nevertheless, he was retained as an executive officer in charge of business development for the newest small bank to open in our community. The affluent market responded well to the institution's focus on upscale customer service. They furnished their offices in elegant decor, and invited "clients" to have a seat and be served rather than standing in some teller line. This was very well received, and as a result, they attracted a lot of lucrative trust[g] business.

But the grass was greener on the other side of the fence. They saw the opportunity to raise their loan volume in leaps and bounds by moving into commercial lending. Farnham was their man. Unfortunately, he wasn't an experienced lender.

Here was banking's example of The Peter Principle via regulatory influence. An outstanding community banker found himself thrust into the role of commercial financier due to market "opportunities" spawn from unequal examination. More than once, he approved deals which my institution had rejected (and not just over a lack of documentation... but because they were BAD loans).

Eventually, he would become frustrated and resign. His last act, getting approved a participation for a motel loan in an area of town with a half dozen other lodging facilities. One of them being his family's.

Chapter Six

CHAPTER 6:

TRICKLE-DOWN BANKING

Regulation DD. Mocking remedial math students, many bankers refer to the mandate as Reg Duh-Duh. Another in a long line of directives (A through Z, plus AA through DD) designed to not only solidify the industry... but protect consumers in the process.

Reg DD. How nondescript. Might as well identify them by serial numbers as done with convicts. "Regulation 084569864, please step forward." I think they should be christened like hurricanes. Reg Andrew, Reg Camille... Then we can track their path and report on the damages left in their wake. Reg Dee Dee. She was a doozy. Daughter of TISA (The Truth in Savings Act of 1991), she hit the states June 21, 1993. The date of required implementation nationwide.

Her focus was the standardization of deposit rate disclosures among banks and S&Ls (but not credit unions as their customers are more intelligent). You see, Congress felt the public was having a

How to Obtain Business Loans

difficult time comparing deposit opportunities in light of the varying methods of advertising rates.

So they invented APY. Which stands for Annual Percentage Yield. The calculation, of which, is straightforward and easy to use:

$$APY = 100 \{ [1 + I/P]^{(365/T)} - 1 \}$$

I = Interest Paid   P = Principal Invested   T = Days in Term

---

Prior to the passage of this *simplifying* regulation, it was thought consumers had a hard time determining who offered the best rates of return. Using APY as an industry standard has clarified things beyond measure. Witness the vast difference in this before and after shot of one bank's rate sheet:

	Stated Return Before Dee Dee	APY
Checking Plus Interest	1.50%	1.512%
Savings	1.85%	1.854%
Super Savings	2.25%	2.271%
Money Market	2.10%	2.122%
Super Money Market	2.66%	2.683%
3 Month CD	2.00%	2.021%
6 Month CD	2.25%	2.274%
1 Year CD	3.20%	3.242%

Astonishing. Truly astonishing. And monetarily, these deviations amount to big bucks for the small consumers who the reg protects. If you have:

$1,500 in Your Checking Account. .012% difference in interest. That's 1 1/2 cents a month, or 18 cents annually.

$5,000 in Your Super Savings Account. .021% variance. Which is 8 4/5 cents monthly, and $1.05 over a year.

$10,000 in a 1 Year CD. A disparity of .042%. That's 35 cents per month. $4.20 annually! Now you're talking some change!! (Literally.)

Chapter Six

FRANK & ERNEST reprinted permission of NEA, Inc.

FRANK & ERNEST ® by Bob Thaves

APY must be provided whenever a customer asks for information and is required in written form prior to opening an account. While disclosure forms vary (slightly) from bank to bank (until the next micromanaging Savings Act), at a minimum they must include:

- stated and APY rates of interest.
- information on method(s) of compounding.
- balance requirements.
- fee schedules.
- transaction limitations.
- and any other information which might be relative to yield.

Similar data must be included in periodic statements to the customer, and identical information is mandatory upon any change which adversely affects the depositor in any way. (There goes another forest.) Further, any and all commercial messages, appearing on or stated through any medium whatsoever, must disclose deposit rates in terms of APY.

Dee Dee packs some heavy duty damages for noncompliance. Class action penalties may award up to 1% of an institution's capital or $500,000, whichever is less. (Talk about devastation and destruction. Film at eleven.)

Who Qualifies?

THE BURDEN OF PROOF sure narrows the field. It has often been said, "You can only get money from bankers when you don't need it."

How to Obtain Business Loans

While always proponents of the Missouri state motto, regulators have taken pocket-watch conservatism from the ridiculous to the sublime. When looking to procure commercial credit, how many can show the ability to repay proposed debt without any cash flow from the enterprise behind the request? If borrowing to develop condominiums, how many can retire the debt without sales? If constructing office space to be leased, how many can make monthly mortgage payments without tenants? If expanding a new business line, how many can fund operations with no new revenues from the endeavor?

These are the questions asked by THE BURDEN OF PROOF. "Neither a project nor a collateral lender be," said banker-Polonius recently when discussing a participation to refurbish a castle in Denmark. Or so you'd think, emphasis on secondary repayment sources being such a focal point throughout the industry.

Who can amortize debt on the shorter and shorter bases set by the regulators? Who can play by these rules? One group comes immediately to mind. The exceedingly rich. Who else qualifies without credence given to a proposed undertaking? The question then becomes (for examiners), **why** do the wealthy want to borrow rather than use their own cash?

A recent visit from the OCC found them reviewing a $1,000,000 line of credit I got approved (somehow) for Gilligan's Beach Country Club, an exclusive waterfront community located on a coastal island. Its membership had voted to borrow monies for improvements to the club, choosing to retire the debt over time from operating revenues, rather than doing a one time assessment of the owners.

This bothered the auditors to no end (probably causing them to toss and turn each night at The Ritz). "**Why** would they want to borrow the money? **Why** wouldn't they just collect it from the members upfront?" I spent hours explaining how I, as a lender, liked to make loans. Particularly to affluent country clubs. Given that the debt represented a one-time assessment of $1,500 per member, and the members... being past presidents of major corporations... were capable of paying cash for $500,000 homes, I felt fairly secure. Especially since, in an abundance of caution, I filed a mortgage on $6.5 million worth of common area real estate. "Yeah, but **why**?..." Eventually, the objection would subside as they realized THE BURDEN OF PROOF had been met, and no legislation was (yet) in place to enforce THE BURDEN OF REASON.

The wealthy's reason to borrow? Return on equity. A concept

Chapter Six

bankers consistently ignore when analyzing a request from a prospect... the return to the investor.

$5,000,000 development request.	
Borrower putting 25% into project	$ 1,250,000
Profit from projected sales	$ 875,000
Apparent return on equity	70%
50% equity into project	$ 2,500,000
Apparent return on equity	35%
100% equity used	$ 5,000,000
Apparent return	17.5%

The more money borrowed, the higher the percentage return; the less financed, the smaller the yield. (I wonder if we should calculate this on an APY basis?)

So the very rich get richer. I mentioned shorter amortizations. In the past, commercial debt was usually amortized over 25 years. Currently the maximum available at most institutions is 20 years, and on a great many loan types it is only 15. Ask yourself this question, how many projects will work on 15-year amortizations with 20% equity positions? Not many.

Let's say an individual, Antonio Comusa owns a small auto repair business. He's always leased space and dreamed of the day he could convert to ownership. With his immediate market area showing an increase in rental rates, and he with an adjustable lease, Antonio decides the time is now.

He locates a nearby facility for sale. The purchase price is $250,000, and he has 20% to put down ($50,000). At current rates of interest, he estimates his monthly mortgage payment will be $1,823. That's $21,877 annually, which he feels is more than comfortable based upon historical cash flow:

	1991	1992
Net Income	$ 1,978	$ 396
Adding Back Lease Expense	24,500	26,950
Available for Debt Service	$26,478	$27,346
Anticipated Debt Service	21,876	21,876
Debt Service Coverage	1.21:1	1.25:1
(This after paying himself a modest annual salary of $45,000.)		

How to Obtain Business Loans

However, Antonio applies to a couple of banks and finds the maximum amortization term available for this type of property is 15 years... something about environmental concerns, and wanting to be paid off sooner as a precaution. Now the cash flow picture looks much different.

	1991	1992
Available for Debt Service	$26,478	$27,346
Available Terms	27,555	27,555
Debt Service Coverage	.96:1	.99:1

He doesn't qualify. Trying to put Junior through college next fall won't allow him to take less money out of the company to make the statements appear stronger. Looks like he'll have to keep paying the escalating rental rates. And who will be the landlord? The prosperous fellow who can put a little more down:

Purchase Price	$ 250,000
35% Equity	87,500
Loan Amount	$ 162,500
Lease Payments Received	$ 27,000
Annual Debt Service	17,911
Annual Cash Flow	$ 9,089
Annual Return on Equity	10.4%

(Sure as heck beats the CD rates Antonio invests at.)

We often speak in terms of the concentration of wealth in our society. That a certain small percentage of the populace owns far and away the largest percentage of the country's privately held assets. Politicians perennially campaign on platforms which feature improving the standard of living for the mid- and lower classes. One administration even devised a plan on a cocktail napkin, and coined the phrase, "trickle down economics." Supply money for the *haves*, and they will generate more for the *have nots*. <u>Unequivocally, they will create more jobs</u>. But what chance does someone of humble beginnings have to rise from them — without access to capital?

THE BURDEN OF PROOF means fewer people qualify. A smaller

Chapter Six

and smaller percentage of Americans are commercially bankable. Call it, "The land of limited opportunity." Projects used to be developed by limited partnerships of modest backing. The local dentist, retailer, and accountant, pooling funds for equity infusion. Then each signing a guarantee equal to their pro-rata share.

Not anymore. Banks now, almost universally, require joint and several guarantees as a matter of policy. Should a default occur, they want the option of going after whomever is liquid. If the dentist had his personal accounts at the given institution, the balance of those funds would be zapped. (Right of offset. Found buried in the small print of the note and/or mortgage, along with the guarantee.) Under the following scenarios, compare the disparity in the risk/return relationship for investors:

Total Project Cost	$ 1,000,000
Aggregate Equity Position	300,000
Per Person Contribution	100,000
Loan Amount	700,000
Anticipated Profit	175,000
Each	58,333
Individual Return on Equity	58.3%
Exposure Under Pro-Rata Guarantee:	
700,000/3 + 100,000 Contribution	$ 333,333
Return Against Possible Exposure	17.5%
Exposure Under Several Guarantee:	
700,000 + 100,000 Contribution	$ 800,000
Return Against Possible Exposure	7.3%

Why would a middle class businessman subject himself to that level of risk given the corresponding rate of return? More likely he'll consider a nice mutual fund. One might argue that banks should be more aware of this fact and take prudent positions on collateral in the first place so that a fire-sale of the mortgaged premises would retire associated debt without any real risk of loss. Failure to recognize this, and instead using more stringent personal guidelines in structuring, removes the conservative, middle-class participant from the commercial banking arena.

How to Obtain Business Loans

Legislative intent dealt with safeguarding the system against catastrophic loss. In practice, underwriting has not sought to properly address risk, but rather to *eliminate* it in its entirety. Witness the rejection of 50% extensions against recently appraised property. Certainly exceptions can be found, but how often would an institution lose principal when secured in such a manner? Yet, in the absence of secondary repayment sources, this type of request is routinely turned down.

"Neither a project nor a collateral lender be."

Ellis Island

I wonder how we'd describe the landscape of economic opportunities to arriving immigrants today? Store ownership? Perhaps after a lifetime of indentured servitude. Most probable occupational title? Laborer.

And how will those employment opportunities be made available? If you believe national statistics, over 80% of the country's jobs are currently supplied by small businesses. But they may not be in the future.

In an economy producing high levels of unemployment, government appears to cut off its nose to spite its face. It contrives to stifle entrepreneurial endeavors within a quagmire of legislation.

Success magazine recently ran an article about the obstacles facing entrepreneurs. The six areas they covered were:

Taxes
Described as a "hemorrhaging" of resources more valuably employed as investment capital.

Benefits (Workmen's Comp, Unemployment Insurance, etc.)
Social costs which "drives the price of coverage up, wages and profits down."

Affirmative Action and The Americans with Disability Act
Shouldn't entrepreneurs be able to hire the best and most qualified candidates? Operating efficiency suffers otherwise.

Unlimited Tort Liability
"The legal system is rigged in favor of Big Business.

Chapter Six

>Lawsuits are a devastating competitive weapon for those who can afford to use them.... Tort reform, say advocates, would spark an explosion of productivity in America."
>
>**Environmental Laws**
>Another system favoring big business who alone can pay for "costly 'environmental impact' studies." Continues to "forc[e] out entrepreneurial competitors."
>
>**Family Leave**
>Big business can better manage to shell out paychecks "for people who aren't working." Small businesses can't.[1]

Increased operating costs make it even tougher for small companies to compete. Corporate America, via economies of scale[g], can force modest sized concerns into bankruptcy with unfair, below cost pricing. The courts recently ruled against Wal-Mart for doing just that. Meanwhile, the manufacturing jobs go to individuals on the other side of U.S. borders, as it is cheaper for large American companies to fabricate product where cost-inflating restrictions do not apply.

Given the current economic and jobless figures, placing additional impediments before the sector providing the most jobs here at home is dangerous folly. How dire an act is a matter of semantics. The reported unemployment rate is alarming, but, if announced, the percentage of Americans actually without work could cause a panic. Thankfully, Big Brother massages the data before disseminating anything too inflammatory.

Published unemployment rates do not take into account the "habitually unemployed." These are individuals who have been without work for extended periods of time. They are dropped from the unemployment calculation. They do not count. Rather, they often go into another statistical category... the homeless. One hopes we don't come up with a term like "habitually homeless" in order to put a better face on this "classification."

So the next time you come across data dealing with the jobless rate, remember the numbers have been "adjusted." The dis-information machine just makes it impossible to tell how much. But jobs aren't the only issue. Entrepreneurial spirit creates more than just employment... it built a country. Without venture capital

How to Obtain Business Loans

funding the undertakings of those with vision, where would our nation be today? Where will it be in the future?

The evening news recounts how we are being "colonized" by the Japanese. The velocity with which U.S. businesses and real estate are being purchased is well documented. I know their personal savings rate has been significantly higher than ours over the last decade, but the friendly takeover isn't being accomplished out of cash! Japanese banks are eager participants.

Good business means the proper assessment of risk, not a total aversion of any. Ideas are formulated into plans, and plans are put into action. That's how a capitalist society moves forward.

There will always be failures, and with those failures, some losses. Government cannot legislate setbacks out of an economic system which is cyclical by nature. Extreme efforts to do so should stir up thoughts of McCarthyism in the minds of the most zealous protectors of "The American Way."

Yes, the biggest portion of new businesses close their doors after a relatively short period of operation. What's not given credence is the jobs created during their existence, and the fact that, if allowed, another entrepreneur will immediately fill the void if demand so dictates.

No, banking institutions are not appendages of public finance. Under suffocating regulation, neither are they unbound participants of the private sector. For my (deposited) money, if the government

Chapter Six

wishes to *protect* me with various legislation, they can ensure banks finance growth. Ultimately, that may *protect* the jobs of all Americans.

The economy cannot prosper with the acceptable commercial borrowing base being so small. Banks must temperately, but with common sense, assess the risks and merits of undertakings, take prudent collateral positions, and extend the pooled savings of our society for growth. And they must not just make funds available to those at the very tip of the pyramid.

Community Reinvestment

The process of financial intermediation deals with the channeling of monies from net saving units to net spending units. Traditionally, households have (in aggregate) been surplus-spending units, while business concerns as well as governments (and how) have been deficit-spending units. The transference of surplus funds to productive investment is a vital function in a capitalist economy. This is often referred to as indirect finance. It is termed such because the parties involved do not meet directly, but indirectly through a financial intermediary of some sort.

When the intermediary issues a loan, the money supply increases as some of the same dollars on deposit are put in circulation. Thus, money is "created," and the loan proceeds eventually work their way through the marketplace to become income to another entity. Subsequently, this unit deposits the money into an institution of choice, and so on. This is known in economic texts as the deposit-expansion process.

In other words, the monies of a community are reinvested through the banking medium. If financial institutions do a poor job of distributing funds, the local economy will run at some smaller fraction of what is possible. In this book, we'll call it the *divisional effect*. The more loanable funds are divided into other forms of earning assets, the more meager the expansion from the multiplier effect.

Many bankers would argue it is almost impossible to efficiently distribute loans in an environment so dictated by THE BURDEN OF PROOF, their ability to recirculate money severely hampered by an "inadequate commercial borrowing base." (Read: Not enough borrowers who meet required levels of PROOF.) Sadly, while it is

How to Obtain Business Loans

undeniably true regulation has narrowed the list of bankable commercial applicants, the argument also serves as justification for noncompliance with The Community Reinvestment Act (CRA).

Some time ago, Congress took steps to ensure banks were granting loans to further develop the communities they were intended to serve. Which is why a bank in West Virginia cannot collect all the deposits of local coal miners, and lend them to Las Vegas developers. The money has to stay at home (unless a miner wishes to do a project out west, but there at least has to be a link to the area). CRA's passage meant money also had to be filtered to all levels of the community... not just the wealthy.

Which was a great idea, except that it is in direct conflict with subsequent regulation requiring higher levels of PROOF. The result is a ready-made excuse for not lending in underprivileged zones or to lower-income individuals.

From the bank's perspective, it can be a no-win situation. First off, without being able to meet an adequate BURDEN OF PROOF as to repayment, the loan will most certainly be rated right out of the gate. Which, as you know, for the bank means money is taken from income and placed into reserves. Secondly, the loans themselves **do** carry a higher degree of risk in many instances and the surrounding property values often have declining trends.

Nevertheless, although reserves are set aside (reducing income), risks are elevated (increasing the chance of loss), and property values are dropping (increasing the chance of loss), banks cannot charge higher rates of interest to compensate themselves for these factors. Quite the contrary. They are generally asked to offer below-market rates of interest, as the applicant's cash flow is tight. Charging more would be counterproductive to being repaid on a timely basis and could be considered discriminatory if compared to similar financing offered to parties who, from the bank's viewpoint, had a more palatable level of risk associated with their requests.

So THE BURDEN OF PROOF appears to be trumped by CRA regs. Auditors apply a stinging double standard and require CRA compliance in the face of conflicting requirements. The result is that banks carefully orchestrate their own reinvestment programs to show the examiners their *hearts are in the right place*. (Unfortunately the programs they supply usually aren't.)

Banks are allowed to identify primary zones of service. They can say they intended to do business within the confines of the city of

Chapter Six

Smallville. Conversely, institutions in major cities may have to be more specific, stating they operate in all of Metropolis south of Winter Avenue. Everywhere within this delineated community must then be provided with all services the institution offers. The bank can't decide not to serve a certain district within its delineated area, simply because it is an underprivileged zone. Doing so is called "redlining" and is against the law.

This keeps institutions from discriminating against neighborhoods. For example, the bank couldn't operate in the area shown, exempting only the Bay Vista Park vicinity.

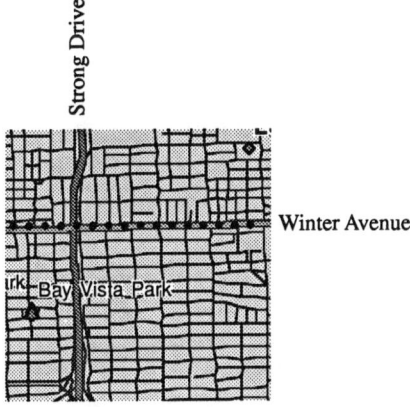

However, there is nothing to stop a bank from drawing its delineated business zone short of an underprivileged area. For instance, the same map could show the bank only servicing the area south of Winter Avenue and east of Strong Drive. They would just need to show they don't do business *west* of Strong Drive.

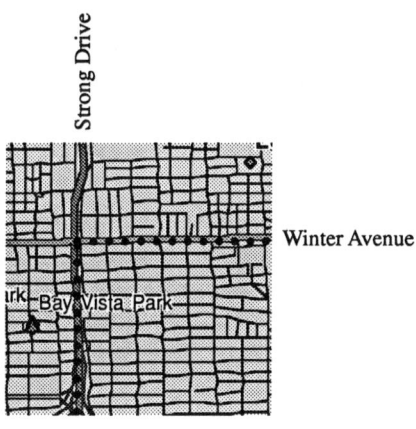

113

How to Obtain Business Loans

Does it really happen? My experience has been yes. To cite a specific case, my bank received a request from a Mr. Sugino. He owned a motel northeast of the city, in a community primarily comprised of migrant farm workers. The area certainly qualified as an underprivileged zone under anyone's criteria.

Mr. Sugino wished to refinance the outstanding debt on the motel, his rate of interest being 3% above current market terms. His existing balance was $525,000, and the property had been appraised at $1,200,000. The only lodging facility in town, The Inn ran 80% occupied year round as sellers of pesticides and buyers of farm crops filled the rooms. Apparent debt service coverage was better than 3:1! Additionally, Mr. Sugino offered a strong secondary source of repayment with liquidity in the low six-figure range.

I submitted the request to Senior Loan Committee, feeling it had strong merit, and knowing, due to location, it would qualify as a CRA loan... giving the bank (I thought) much needed help in its level of compliance.

The decision was made quickly and communicated succinctly by the bank president. "The credit looks good, but I don't want to start lending there. We've always said that area wasn't in our delineated business zone... so I don't want to do something there and then have to entertain other requests from the same vicinity." (Maybe it wasn't "redlining," but the crayon had a burgundy tint. Bloodlining?)

So you're thinking, "Your institution just had a terrible record." Depends on where one is standing. Almost two months later to the day, the newspaper ran an article praising the bank's work in the area of CRA. The piece started by saying The State Bankers Association honored the bank with its Community Reinvestment Award for adherence to fair lending practices, above and beyond the call. The president of the association went so far as to openly praise the bank for its efforts in the area of community involvement. The article went on to say the association president was also chairman and president of the recipient bank's parent company. (What a coincidence!)

A few days after the piece ran, I received a phone call from a banker at a competing institution who was trying to find out how we received the award. He inquired as to the programs we offered the underprivileged. Did we do anything special in the consumer or residential lending areas? Did we offer more lenient terms on the commercial side... what?

"Well, we don't have anything which would really qualify

Chapter Six

itself as a special program... we're maybe just more aggressive when entertaining requests in that sector."

"But you guys were one of the only banks not involved in the CRA loans participated earlier this year."

"Well, yeah... but we're active in a lot of community affairs."

"Like what?"

"Well, we do financing seminars for those in underprivileged zones, our officers are involved in a lot of volunteer efforts for revitalization, and we attend minority business meetings..."

"But no loans, right?"

(Boy, my office is hot. I gotta get the air checked.)

Not only could I not recall any special programs, I could only think of all the unacceptable loans by transaction and collateral type which often fell into the area of CRA, and were listed as "undesirable" in the policy manual.

- Loans to new businesses where repayment is based upon future operation alone.
- Loans for strip shopping centers.
- Loans for mobile home parks.
- Loans for mini-warehouse facilities.
- Loans for lodging facilities.
- Loans for restaurants.
- Loans for lounges.
- Loans for bowling alleys, and other entertainment facilities.

Noting that "undesirable" credit types were then further listed as against policy itself, I remembered that next to none of these got done. What's more, the bank even had categories for collateral quality which seemed to impugn CRA.

Type A	Located within the highest end of the market.
Type B	Located in an above average area of the market.
Type C	Located in what might currently be a successful area, but a "poor mix of occupants" may result in deteriorating values.
Type D	Deficiencies in "the tenant base," **and other areas**, result in an unacceptable level of risk being associated with this type of property.

How to Obtain Business Loans

It was the stated policy of the bank to finance properties which fell within Type A alone. Type B would *occasionally be entertained if valid compensating factors were involved*, and the other types were considered "undesirable," and not to be extended against.

(Sweating) **"Listen, it's good talking to you, but I've gotta go. I have an appointment waiting."**

"Uh-huh. I bet it's not for a CRA loan." Click.

After a shower, I continued to contemplate my bank's record on CRA. Good or bad? I concluded we were average. All the institutions go about putting on the appearance of being active within underprivileged zones, but no one really does much more than keep up a good front.

This was even affirmed at a Latino business meeting attended to show CRA involvement. Standing in the back of the meeting room, several bankers from different institutions stood talking while the assembly was in process. The speaker was discussing how to raise capital and extolling the virtues of pooling the money within the Latino community... for Latino businesses only. "After all, you're not going to get the money from the bankers, they're only here to eat the food and comply with their CRA guidelines." (Man, air conditioner units are going out all over the place.)

In truth, banks all have similar policies as to what's been described. The lending manuals of the institutions I have worked for are almost identical. As a result, not a whole lot of CRA loans get done. When they do, the characteristic composition is a credit to a wealthy developer who intends to build or revitalize within an underprivileged zone. The facility is usually participated among several banks to further spread the risk of lending in the area.

Profits flow to the wealthy developer, interest to the prosperous banks, and the benefits are to be felt by those in the surrounding neighborhood of the project. Community reinvestment, or trickle down banking?

Just when it appeared safe to come outside after Reg Dee Dee hit, controversy kicked up surrounding the yield calculations. Apparently they don't always work as intended.

Take, for instance, using the formula on a multiyear certificate of deposit that does not compound interest. As an article in *Bankers*

Chapter Six

News points out, you "get an annual percentage yield that is less than the interest rate."

During a recent meeting, several governors of the Fed Board "lamented the 'flawed regulation' but cited the law's requirement to produce an industrywide rule with 'hardwired standards.'"

The board issued an either/or solution, offering a new method of calculating APY, and granting the option of doing nothing.

The first approach "would factor into the calculation the time value of money, which the current formula ignores for noncompounding accounts." Unfortunately, this would require banks to make all new disclosures available at each transaction. (Timber!!)

As for the second method, institutions would be able to state yields equal to interest rates "so long as interest is paid out at least annually." [2]

Stated Return Before Dee Dee	APY
2.25%	2.25%

There, that should clarify things for consumers. We want to make sure the little guy in our society gets a fair shake.

---

[1] Poe, Richard: "Generation E," *Success*, Vol. 40, Number 9, November 1993, pg. 30.

[2] Smith, Ed: "Reg DD Formula Woes," *Bankers News*, July 20, 1993, pg. 8.

Chapter Seven

CHAPTER 7:

TURMOIL ON THE HOME FRONT

The friction caused when THE BURDEN OF PROOF meets Community Reinvestment is evidence that legislative action does not always render its desired result when applied at the institutional level.

Think of the banking system in terms of a tranquil pond. Each time Congress tosses in a regulation carved in stone, ripples go off in all directions. The more stones they throw, the more waters crest against each other.

The bombardment of rules has management making decisions all over the map. Courses are clearly defined only from moment to moment. Witness BankAmerica's announcement of record profits... half a billion dollars! Followed immediately with the news of a 4% reduction in its work force... over 37,000 jobs. (Let the good times roll.)

How to Obtain Business Loans

Policy Pigeons spend their days reading the *Wall Street Journal* and dreaming up procedures to effect wide-scale change. Boards rubber stamp the resolutions with little grass-root input.

Ever serve as a director of anything? Whether a charity or a for-profit organization, boards are big on overall guidance. However, have you ever asked a board member **exactly** how operations are designed? **Specifically** how things work? If you did, you probably got a long-winded response highlighting goals and objectives, with a mix of policy statements added for good measure. If you really want to know what's going on, you've got to ask someone on the front lines.

Policy Pigeons? Regional types who make decisions in a vacuum. Basing judgments on slides, graphs, etc., rather than outside interaction. They fly in from company headquarters, drop their newly penned policies and procedures, and fly back to roost. Which leaves line personnel to decipher spirit from literal intent within volumes of manuals and reams of memorandums. Preferred loan types, undesirable collateral categories, structural exceptions... the inundation of constantly changing guidelines is confusing at best... paralyzing at worst.

Loans for restaurants, lounges, and entertainment facilities are eschewed due to their high rates of turnover. Successful lodging operations are avoided based on the premise of inevitable competition driving vacancy rates up, and room rates down. Mobile home parks experience value fluctuations too great to be considered palatable. Strip centers and office space are thought to be over-built. And raw land is out of the question because it isn't readily marketable. (If you have a request forthcoming in one of these categories, run, don't walk, to your nearest mortgage broker.)

Again, liquid collateral is acceptable, but big board stocks are to be margined at very low percentages of current value (50-60% according to an exceedingly bearish Lightning Lou)... as the market is thought to be overdue for a major correction. (This is the feeling on the lending side of the bank, but not one dispensed from the brokerage department.)

Emphasis on cash flow is celebrated as paramount ("...nor a collateral lender be"), but lottery winners are to be forsaken because their annuity payments are unattachable by law. (Besides, who knows if the winnings will ever be paid out. People might stop buying tickets, and the whole Ponzi scheme could collapse.)

Chapter Seven

Banks agree to disagree, as much of the externally caused debates take place internally...

Harmony and Discord

As has already been demonstrated, regulators seek uniformity. They look for stated policies on everything under the sun, and test to see if an institution practices what it preaches.

Mandated by the FDIC Improvement Act, banks are asked to set tolerance levels by percentage for loans which fall outside of expressed procedures. As an institution approaches its limit, policy becomes less and less flexible. In other words, the bank can't justify an exception for your loan, if they've already got a boat full of deviations for the year.

Officer adherence to policy is also tracked. Care is taken to ensure no individual shows a particular propensity to waive certain requirements. Under some circumstances, this practice can directly affect your loan request.

Generally speaking, experience levels allow officers to entertain different types of transactions. Newer lenders handle modest applications as a rule. And as small business loans don't come in anything close to cookie cutter form, these credits tend to have the most inherent exceptions. Thus, the new kid on the block will have more departures from accepted practice. So if you draw the junior man on the totem pole late in the year, his basket of allowable irregularities may be full. This will add some rigidity to the handling of your request and will be compounded by the lack of latitude afforded to a lower ranking individual.

At most banks, some standard exceptions to policy include the following:

1) Incomplete, or stale-dated personal/business financial statements.

2) Insufficient supporting financial information.

3) Loans to individuals with poor credit histories.

4) Loans outside of lending area.

5) No personal guarantees on loans to closely-held companies.

How to Obtain Business Loans

6) Pro-rata guarantees.

7) No parent company guarantee in the case of a subsidiary borrower.

8) Loans for less than desirable collateral types.

9) Loans for properties falling outside of Type B collateral ratings.

10) Loans to undesirable borrowing types, such as non-regionally affiliated clubs, organizations, and religious orders.

11) Loans with less than 20% cash equity.

12) Extensions of credit made outside of the following loan-to-value guidelines:

Certificate of Deposit	90%
U.S. Government Securities	90%
General Obligation Municipal Bonds	90%
AAA-AA Rated Corporate Bonds	85%
Industrial Revenue Bonds	80%
Owner-User Real Estate	75%
NYSE and AMEX Stocks	70%
Nonowner-User Real Estate	70%
Regionally Traded OTC Stocks	65%
Housing Authority Bonds	65%
BB-CC Corporate Bonds	65%
Locally Traded OTC Stocks	50%

13) Loans for raw land not intended for immediate development.

14) Development loans with land shortfalls[g].

15) Development loans accelerated[g] at less than 125%.

16) Loans to unseasoned builders and developers.

17) Unsecured lines of credit to builders or developers.

Chapter Seven

18) No clean-up requirement on lines of credit.

19) No bonded contracts for construction in excess of $500,000.

20) No environmental audit for loans in excess of $500,000.

21) Presales with less than 20% down.

22) Presales in an amount less than necessary to retire proposed borrowing.

23) Pre-leasing insufficient to service proposed obligation.

24) Loans amortizing over more than 20 years.

25) Loans ballooning outside of 5 years.

26) Real estate loans that do not meet target debt service coverage requirements (see page 162).

So obedient to policy are banks that it requires the next highest authority to okay exceptions on any approved loan. For instance, if an individual officer's authority is sufficient to sanction a request, but the loan carries an exception to policy; he must seek approval from the next highest authority... say a department manager. If the department manager had originally approved the request, he would have to pursue the senior lender's concurrence. If it was the senior lender's credit, he would look for absolution from loan committee. Had loan committee been the one to stray from the path of righteousness, the president could offer a pardon. Should the president have been the initial culprit of nonconformity, the regional credit officer would have to sign off. And, in the case of a divine intervention itself, where the regional credit officer had actually ventured out of the monastery to meet with a customer and thereafter approved a deviant loan...the Pope himself would be sought for forgiveness.

Compliance to such a *literal* framework while harmoniously applying the *spiritual* resolve of policy is as likely as our government sticking to a deficit reduction plan. *There just **have** to be exceptions*.

Besides, individual banks within a holding company can't even reach accord over the guidelines set by the parent company.

How to Obtain Business Loans

Oftentimes, conflicts arise among inter-company loan participants of larger transactions. Even though the overall risk to the holding company is the same in aggregate, each affiliate involved is asked to do its own separate credit analysis of the undertaking. Both initially and on an annual review basis. This is another illustration of regulator logic, although in recent months, the OCC has softened its approach to independent evaluation. However, in typical, *better-safe-than-sorry* fashion, parent company's require documented files at each participant's address. This is an effort to meet the *spirit* of application, and not the more temperate *literal* guideline.

In an attempt to comply, Dinky Klein, recently inquired from Lightning Lou as to what **exactly** constitutes a documented file. Ever the Freudian thinker, Lightning asked Dinky to write him a memo expressing what *he* thought comprised an adequate file.

Dazed, and submissive, Dinky forwarded an answer to his own question for approval. It was returned with the notation, "Your list of what constitutes a well documented file seems appropriate, and will be considered so... except in those situations when other information is needed, and should be obtained." (Read: You're right and it's okay, accept when you're not and it isn't.)

Later, when further pressed on the matter, Lou said he "could do no better to specify what and when other information might be necessary to meet the documented file requirement, as no decision could be reasonably made without being privy to all the salient data within respective lead bank records."

This basically forced affiliates to reproduce page for page everything the lead bank had on a borrower. With many participations spread between 3 or 4 affiliates, and files made up of several hundred items, the copying time alone calls for additional fees.

However, in the eyes of some individuals, this allows bankers to better identify and reduce risk. Which is downright hilarious. In 9 out of 10 cases, only the lead bank has EVER had any contact with the borrower. In 9 out of 10 cases, only the lead officer has EVER visited the borrower's project site or place of business. The only separate analysis done is prepared by a first year management associate who writes the equivalent of a book report on information supplied by the lead. Which is then promptly filed away without further review.

Although, interestingly enough, there have been **rare** occasions where an affiliate bank differs in the assessment of a participated loan's risk. The lead bank rates the credit a Class 'C', but the

Chapter Seven

participant wishes to grade the loan a 'D'. The participant may not actually rate the credit differently, but must note nonconcurrence within its own (completely documented) file. Call this a secretly dissenting downgrade.

What's Taking So Long?

A few days after Christmas, a mother was working in the kitchen while listening to her son play with his new electric train in the next room. She heard the train stop, and her boy say; "All you SOBs who want off, get the *blank* off and be quick about it. All you SOBs getting on, move your *blankes* cause we're trying to keep a *blanking* schedule around here."

The mother was astonished, and immediately went in and reprimanded her child. "Don't use that verbiage in this house! Now go to your room for a couple of hours and think about what you did. When you come out, you may play with the train again, but I want you to use different language."

Two hours later, the child came out of his bedroom and resumed playing with his train. Soon it stopped and the mother heard her boy say, "All disembarking passengers, please remember to take all your belongings with you. Thank you for riding with us today, we trust your trip was a pleasant one. Travel with us again soon... For those of you boarding, we ask you to stow all hand luggage under your seat. And for the safety of all passengers, please remember there is no smoking except within the club car. We hope you will have a comfortable and relaxing journey... For those of you who are ticked off about the two-hour delay, please see the old nag in the kitchen."

You watch your phraseology. Because in banking, that's everything. Use of the wrong words can severely delay your loan's departure from the vault.

I recall a Super Senior Regional Executive Double-Dog Credit Policy Officer's visit from the home office. We had been having great difficulty getting any sizable construction loans approved through Lightning Lou. The SSREDDCPO visited in an effort to help unearth the problem.

Armed with loads of pre-visit reading material on our marketplace, and given a day long tour of the community upon arrival, the SSREDDCPO felt prepared to offer comment as to the origin of the

How to Obtain Business Loans

predicament. "You all have been calling these credits, 'project loans.' Which carries with it a negative connotation. You should refer to them as 'development loans' and you'll have much better luck." (Shazam! Can it be this easy?)

Other than bankers being ridiculous, one of the biggest complaints prospective borrowers have is the amount of time necessary to obtain an answer. Decisions seem to take forever in the making. Accordingly, this has become the advertising focus for many an institution.

Most recently, my bank had initiated a state-wide campaign directed at the small- to mid-sized business owner. TV and radio slots portrayed fast response time as an asset to the everyday businessman and spot-lighted the holding company's decentralized structure which "makes local approvals possible."

"Local" being a relative term. My affiliate's lending authority was only $500,000. Anything above that amount headed to Lou, 150 miles to the north. Above his limit, approval had to be sought from HQ... some 300 miles, and a zillion light years away.

"Small- to mid-sized business" was vague at best. The ad's target market were companies with between one and five million in sales. Although the lending authorities were better suited to firms with a few hundred thousand in revenues. (Like those untouchable ventures still in their infancy.)

A time delay caused by sheer distance takes away some responsiveness. Which is compounded when absentee authorities have a deficiency in local market know-how. Imagine trying to convince someone the sky, where you live, is green when above their head every day it's blue. The realities before them belie what you represent. You're placed in the position of proving the earth is round and that the bank won't sail off the edge if it proceeds in a given direction.

In my own case, the surrounding community (delineated area) was very affluent. More so than anywhere else in the state. Homes routinely sold upward of $2,500,000, and costs to construct regularly ran $100/SF and above. The sky may as well have been green. Regional folks were aghast. Their own markets saw higher-end residences going for over a million... but two-and-a-half!? And they always choked on the cost per square foot figures, builder estimates in their vicinity running 25-30% less in most cases.

These, and other dissimilarities, added another tier to THE BURDEN OF PROOF for area lenders. Even when the borrower was

Chapter Seven

readily bankable, collateral questions came into play as no one believed reported values. Especially Irwin Ashton. Irwin's position was in the stratosphere somewhere above Lightning Lou. Getting a high-end property past him was akin to sneaking a hanging curve past Hank Aaron.

In an effort to substantiate a spec loan request which called for construction costs in the $120/SF range, I compiled two dozen examples which we had been able to approve locally due to lower loan amounts. In each case, the cost per square foot was in excess of $120. I further attempted to justify the figures by forwarding the following memo:

BANK MEMORANDUM

TO: Irwin Ashton
FROM: Addison Parker
RE: Builder Costs on High End Homes

In our immediate marketplace, we experience costs and corresponding values far in excess of those for comparable properties in other parts of the state.

Specialized construction characterizes the homes of Gull Harbor, Green Pines, Colonial Preserve, etc. Extravagant materials such as solid oak doors, Travertine marble flooring, custom pickled cabinetry, Corian counter tops, Espana tile roofs, and interlocking cobblestone pavers are often incorporated in their design.

Many times, features like elaborate security systems, wall-vacs, wine cellars, oversized in-home saunas and Jacuzzis, as well as intercom systems are then added by the owners. Some have even been known to tile their garages and build up to three wet bars within their house.

When these features are combined with distinctive craftsmanship, they drive the cost per square foot well beyond what appears "reasonable." The extras, however, should not be considered over-improvements. A great number of homes within our market, which are similarly built and equipped, routinely resell at premiums.

I found out later much of this fell on deaf ears, not just because of

How to Obtain Business Loans

a lack of local knowledge, but due to a general prejudice against contractors. Apparently, Irwin got taken pretty good by a builder when he bought his last home.

However, distance, lack of market knowledge, and individual prejudice, can all be overcome if you know the magic words. The problem is, the words aren't the same every time. Which means your loan officer may be sent to his room for fresh, blunt, or graphic language as he communicates your loan request and pushes for an answer.

Consort memos (or something analogously named) have become all the rage at vogue banking centers. They are written by your account officer early on and addressed to ultimate approval authorities. They are not put together for purposes of approval, although they contain all salient data about the request. Rather, they are intended to be simpler versions of the same information to be later regurgitated into a larger, more formal, credit package to be reviewed by loan committee. The stated purpose of these memorandums is to gain an "indication of preliminary interest" from above. Without which, further work on an application will cease.

You cannot be approved, but you can be denied during *The Consort Stage*. Accordingly, affiliates put an incredible amount of emphasis on the "writing styles" these packages contain. So much so that anyone thinking of a career in banking today should consider an undergraduate degree that includes a minor in journalism.

Officers pen their consort summaries as soon as they feel they have information of sufficient scope to prompt an opinion. The task is tricky, in that SSREDDCPO types don't want to be led to a conclusion. The details must be stated in such a manner as to be read in colorless blips of raw data.

Steering the reader by focusing on attributes, and mitigating risks, will most assuredly precipitate an "edit" by the local credit policy officer prior to being routed for an indication. Meaningful rewrites include changes like:

- **"is expected to"** to **"could result in"**

- **"will mean"** to **"might cause"**

- **"vast holdings"** to **"considerable assets"** (One credit officer even set guidelines as to what fell in adequate, sizable, signifi-

Chapter Seven

cant, and substantial categories. For example, if someone had $999,000 in total assets, they were said to have "sizable" holdings. Had they had $1,000,000 worth, they would've been said to have "significant" holdings.)

- "market niche" to "novel approach"

- "long track record in" to "having related experience"

- "entrepreneur" to "businessperson"

Overly strong adjectives and adverbs are also to be avoided, lest they meet the red X of the proof department. Like... scrupulous, above reproach, esteemed, accomplished, seasoned, weathered, steadfast, enlightened, wise, discerning, calculated, proficient, expert, tenacious, comprehensive, prosperous, impressive, affluent, grand, and **qualified** to name a few.

But most importantly, it is absolutely forbidden to write in a manner which makes adverse commentary seem... well... silly. The following stanza would never be permitted:

> Given the conservative 50% LTV position contemplated, and considering the primary repayment source would cover the proposed obligation at a rate of better than 2:1, the guarantor's substantial liquidity serves only as additional justification for this credit's extension. Approval is recommended.

Turning this loan down for some peripheral reason now would appear ludicrous. So, in order to keep negative options (sans an egg-covered face) alive, SSREDDCPOs insist consort writers keep the material bland.

Remember the ABC credit? The guarantors posting a letter of credit equal to one year's principal and interest payments? Considering our loan could have been repaid for 12 months after any cash flow problem took place, and the borrowing contingent had that period of time to right its problems before the difficulties directly affected the bank, I made "wantonly brash" comments in my consort memo for the renewal.

I suggested the bank "should always be so lucky as to get 12 months notice prior to default." I went on to add, "given the supporting strength of the guarantors, and the lack of real alternatives since

How to Obtain Business Loans

the loan is already on the books, approval is only rational."

It was noted on the returned copy that, "while this is undoubtedly true, such language is not appropriate for memoranda. Please address suggested changes and resubmit."

So the next time you're awaiting a response from the bank and you feel the old nag in the credit department is holding things up, you might ask your officer if he'd like to borrow your thesaurus.

"May I See Your Palm, Please?"

Long after the last rewrite is finished for the day, officers toil over their existing portfolios. Countless hours are spent gathering and dissecting financial information on performing borrowers. But you already knew this. What you didn't know was your officer actually holds down a second job on the carnival midway. The morning's stuffy gray suit and somberly striped tie giving way to a flowing robe and turban in the late afternoon, as Carnac the banker appears.

As you are aware, lending officers are held directly accountable for the timely identification of problem loans. One institution I worked for saw the need to develop its own early warning system. Senior management intensely wanted to guard against unexpected changes in loan classification, so they called for monthly forecast meetings to be held.

This meant officers had to take the time to predict, on an individual loan basis, what might occur in the future. After plotting all projected migrations for the next two years, by quarter, a meeting would take place once a month to profile the differences envisioned for the entire bank's portfolio. The president led the loan-by-loan witch hunt.

The opportunity cost of this exercise was staggering, especially given its impracticality:

7 Line Officers x 3 Hours/Month Individually	21 Hours
21 Hours x an Average $19/Hour	$ 399
$399 x 12 Months	$ 4,788
10 Total Officers x 3 Hours/Month Meeting as a Group	30 Hours
30 Hours x an Average of $26/Hour	$ 780
$780 x 12 Months	$ 9,360
Total Annual Salary Cost of Swami Program	$ 14,148

Chapter Seven

Multiplying this by 60-odd affiliates meant the company was investing well over $800,000 in these seances. And to do what? Sit around and guess what's going to happen over the next two years? We've already said you can't predict more than 12 months in the future based on submitted financial data. Well, at least you can't substantiate continued repayment, although you can speculate to the contrary.

The forms used to chart credit migration looked something like this:

Year	1992				1993			
Quarter	1	2	3	4	1	2	3	4
Mountain Farms	C	C	D	E	D	D	C	C

Comments:
Predict farm will be ravaged by locust in the third quarter of this year. As a result, Pa Walton will collapse near year's end. First quarter 1993 will see insurance proceeds flow to the family, and Pa Walton will recover in time for fall harvest.

Year	1992				1993			
Quarter	1	2	3	4	1	2	3	4
Inc. Chemicals	C	D	E	E	D	D	C	C

Comments:
See liability suit in second quarter arising from rash attributed to baby powder product. Cash settlement will drastically affect operations. Business returning to some semblance of normalcy by third quarter 1993.

Year	1992				1993			
Quarter	1	2	3	4	1	2	3	4
Adams Retail	C	C	C	D	E	F	F	F

Comments:
The holiday blues will hit Mr. Adams hard this year. In a dramatic mid-life crisis, he will run off with Madonna after meeting her backstage at a concert. Without his knack for inventory control, the business will plummet into bankruptcy.

This process, concocted as a means of "staying on top of trends in the bank's portfolio," was outrageous. I wondered if anyone else thought the program was as mindless as I did. Each month I'd listen

How to Obtain Business Loans

to six other officers detail their predictions as if they were based upon something factual, rather than what they saw in their crystal balls. It was laughable how prophesized migration almost always was to take place well in the future.

You had to foresee *some* movement; sitting with a pat hand wasn't an option. But you didn't want to predict movement and then not have it occur. Big-time negative reinforcement was received when you were wrong on a prognostication. Each time a loan changed categories without being foreseen, the failing officer would be severely reprimanded for not anticipating what transpired. "How could you have missed that? Aren't you familiar with your customers?" Being incorrect carried a price. So everyone saw changes happening... only later, much later.

As has been said, most of the internal fuss is either a direct or indirect result of external regulation. The application of well-meaning legislation often touches off a chain reaction of events, many of which cause banks severe operating difficulties.

Rarely does anything shake out in practice as it was composed. Remember that game you played as a kid? (Not the one with the train.) The one where a short story was whispered from person to person around a circle? By the time it returned, the tale was always hilariously different. Something similar transpires with the dissemination of performance expectations.

In a effort to combat over-regulation, and standardize methods of interpretation and use, banks gear up their Political Action Committee. The industry's large, well-capitalized, but under-effective lobbying group.

An officer's individual membership in the PAC is not a matter of personal choice. Large banks are notorious for "influencing" worker participation in areas serving the institution. A previous employer orchestrated the leverage process without peer. Once, they declared the company's intention to be a major sponsor of the United Way, which was in dire need of support in the wake of a misappropriation scandal. The announcement focused on the bank's wish to be "community oriented" and its desire to "give something back."

Shortly after the public relations bit was over, a staff meeting was (curiously) scheduled to coincide with the next pay day. Employees

Chapter Seven

were amassed in the central lobby area of the main branch and shown a film containing very emotional pleas for money. At its conclusion, the bank president communicated his "fervent hope" all those in attendance would donate their "fair share." Which he then thoughtfully defined to be 1.5-2% of one's annual gross earnings. (Between $600-$800 for your typical lender.)

The president called on everyone to fill out the payroll deduction forms they were handed on their way in and return them to one of the senior management members stationed at each of the exits. (No pressure, of course.)

The means by which officer PAC contributions were collected were only slightly more subtle, but actually even more mandatory. Mailers were sent out "calling bankers to action." They focused on the PAC's central role of effecting necessary change within the financial services industry.

I... ahem... misplaced the original correspondence.

About a week or so later, I received a call from one of the branch managers. She informed me she was the bank's PAC captain, and asked, "When will you be forwarding your payroll deduction form?"

Audaciously, I inquired, **"What exactly does the PAC do with the money?"**

"You *are* aware our president is a huge proponent of this program? And the bank always has 100% participation from its officers!"

"Right, I understand. I was just curious who the PAC supported. Do you know?" (Oh captain, my captain.)

(Long pause.) "The PAC sponsors politicians and causes that are in the best interests of banking."

"Uh-huh. Like who? What causes?"

(Longer pause.) "I don't have any specifics. I'll have to call you back."

A few days later, I received an inter-office package from the president. With it came a hastily scribbled note:

> "...understand you had interest in whom PAC supports... attached is list. As you may not know, this affiliate has always had 100% participation from its officers. (I had heard that.) It's in your, and the bank's, best interests this continues."

Oohhhhh K. Happy to be involved, sir.

Chapter Eight

CHAPTER 8:

FOR WHAT IT'S WORTH

It's public knowledge, all third Tuesdays falling in the second month of each calendar quarter are designated red letter days. They are the internally prescribed meeting dates for another kind of PAC. The acronym, in this instance, standing for problem asset committee.

For this, I as well as other line lenders prepared discussion reports (DR) on substandard credits. As the following indicates, their format reveals them to be a not-too-distant cousin of onsort memorandums:

How to Obtain Business Loans

Date
May 18, 1993

Primary Debtor(s)   Guarantor(s)
Art and Vivienne Sullivan   Harbor House Restaurant, Inc.

Original Balance	Currently Funded	Additional Availability
$500,000	$454,481	$ 0

Present Classification	Accrual Status
E	Non-

History
First mortgage on 2.06 acres of harbor-front property, and a 7,000 SF restaurant improved thereon. Total cost, including furniture, fixtures, and equipment — $2,000,000.

Repayment Structure
Construction loan flipped to permanent basis in April of 1991. Funded balance amortized over 25 years, ballooning in 5. Monthly principal payments of $1,667 plus accrued interest at a floating rate of Prime + 1%.

Collateral Valuation
Real estate appraised in June of 1990 to a Value Upon Completion of $1,500,000. Initial loan-to-value 33.3%. Current exposure (against real estate alone) 30.3%.

Advance/Reduction Since Last Report
($5,091)

Reason for Inflated Risk
Loan originated as construction/mini-perm in October of 1990. First classified by Loan Review in April of 1991 due to:

    (A) A lack of disposable income, on the part of the primary debtor, in an amount sufficient to allow for deviations from proforma.
    (B) Illiquid personal and business financial statements.

        (I wasn't the originating officer, but I assume these details were known going in. I'm not sure why the loan was cited after the fact.)

Chapter Eight

<u>Actions Taken to Reduce Risk</u>
Real estate taxes and insurance are current. Payments to bank have always been made on a timely basis.

Strategy is to continue monitoring financial statements quarterly, in order to stay abreast of trends in cash flow.

> (The "strategy" was added by the credit policy officer during the crucial DR editing stage. I had found it tough to come up with a risk reducing artifice for an amortizing obligation being handled perfectly by the borrower.)

<u>Progress Toward Risk Reduction This Period</u>
Payments continue to be made in a satisfactory manner.

<u>Summarize Trend in Latest Financial Statements</u>

3/31/92 to 3/31/93

Net Sales		$	2,150,070
Change in Accounts Receivable		(	23,310)
Cash Collected from Sales		$	2,126,760
Cost of Sales	(791,430)		
Change in Inventory	(14,430)		
Change in Payables	(1,110)		
Cash Paid Suppliers		(	806,970)
Cash from Trading Activities		$	1,319,790
Sales, General & Administrative Expenses			
(less non-cash items)		(	1,099,912)
Cash after Operations		$	219,878
Other Income			3,345
Net Cash from Operations		$	223,223
*Interest Expense		(	135,261)
Net Cash Income		$	87,962
Current Portion of Long Term Debt		(	98,496)
*Cash after Debt Amortization		(	10,534)

(* At first glance, the restaurant does not appear to be keeping its head above water. However, a large portion of the interest expense is discretionary as it is paid to Mr. Sullivan's father-in-law, who is an investor in the venture. Accordingly, this service could be reduced, or temporarily suspended, if necessary. During the most recent 12 months, operations were able to cover all other obligations at a rate of 1.34:1)

137

Breaking the Bank

In addition, Mr. Sullivan indicates liquidity of better than $157,000 on his 3/31/93 personal financial statement.

> (This is interesting given the figure is a significant improvement from last year and Mr. Sullivan's only income is reportedly derived from the restaurant, which he did not disclose taking monies from at an advanced rate over the last twelve months. Could some undisclosed cash be funneling through the restaurant? I've heard that sort of thing happens. But this, of course, isn't appropriate for discussion.)

Exposure Summary/Justification for No Specific Reserve
Bank holds real estate collateral valued at $1,500,000; and is in first position against all furniture, fixtures, and equipment whose original cost totalled over $500,000. Using $0.50 on the dollar to arrive at a new value yields a conservative $250,000 figure for FFE^g. Therefore, the bank's aggregate exposure is somewhere in the area of 26%.

Based upon this, no specific reserve allocation is warranted. Ten percent will continue to be set aside according to policy.

A Parker	*Mortie* Fabian Faulkner	*Winthrop Eddles*
Relationship Mgr.	Senior Lender Credit Policy	President

> (*Quarterly monitoring statements.* Perhaps not enough to know what's really taking place. Why not require on-line computer hookup with the restaurant's registers? Then the bank could review receipts on a meal-by-meal basis. Now there's a "strategy" to reduce risk.)

The PAC meeting where this report was submitted saw the attending loan review member, Brice Abernathy, focus on another matter.

The loan's E classification and nonaccrual status brought the bank's method of collateral valuation under great scrutiny. Brice got radar lock on my exposure summary and a long debate followed, punctuated by this exchange.

"Mr. Parker, how can you substantiate the $250,000 value assigned to furniture, fixtures, and equipment?"

Chapter Eight

"I just used 50% of the total cost to purchase."

"Can you use that in good conscience? How can you be sure that figure is altogether reliable?"

"I can't, I suppose. But 50 cents on the dollar would seem fairly conservative. A lot of the decor would actually sell at a much better percentage of its original purchase price."

"Have you any way to estimate the remaining useful life on the equipment?"

"No, Brice, I can't say I do. Nor can I say I actually considered trying to make such an evaluation."

"Then how can you be comfortable assigning any value to the equipment?"

"Okay. Let's say we give no consideration to any furniture, fixtures, or equipment. I'm at 30% loan-to-value on the real estate alone, which I have an appraisal for, so I'm pretty comfortable with our position."

"Well... that's true. But for the sake of presenting an accurate form, some method to better account for the FF&E's current value must be obtained."

Why bother?

Who Needs Collateral Anyway?

Banks are to base loans on a borrower's ability to repay. The fact that you have a request representing a 50% extension against collateral value means very little. Banks are not in the foreclosure and sale business, as are some mortgage companies. Remember the ads? "If you have equity in your home, we'll get you the money you need... and without a lot of hassle." Fade to a smiling elderly couple who just signed on the dotted line.

No, banks are different. Particularly on the commercial side. Loan-to-value doesn't mean a whole lot in the rate and reserve game. THE BURDEN OF PROOF surrounding cash flow overshadows consideration given to a lack of probable loss based upon collateral position. With qualifying requirements so stringent, you might suggest security interests are taken in an abundance of caution. An important, but quite ambiguous principle.

Valuations are necessary for any collateral taken. With many items (such as equipment), some fraction of original cost is (generally) acceptable. In the case of real estate, formal appraisals are

How to Obtain Business Loans

required by law... unless the loan is exceedingly small, or the property is taken in "an abundance of caution." According to regulators, the phrase is defined as follows:

> If the bank would normally extended the loan in question on an unsecured basis, but takes collateral as a safeguard against unforeseeable events, then it is said to be taking a security interest in "an abundance of caution."

A most favorable translation would allow a great many loans to fall within the terminology. However, an examiner's interpretation poses a rhetorical question to each circumstance in which the bank has liberally read and applied the definition. "If you would've done the loan unsecured, why didn't you?"

Next to no explanation satisfactorily establishes why the bank would take real estate collateral without an outside appraisal being completed. The passage of a regulation called the Financial Institution Reform Recovery & Enforcement Act, and the characteristically more restrictive internal controls adopted in its wake, made certain the practice would all but cease. As a result, the ensuing guidelines now exist:

> Credits in excess of $100,000, collateralized solely or partially by real estate, must be documented by an **independent** appraisal under all circumstances except the following:
>
> - when the proposed extension is as a result of a maturing obligation already on the books and, (1) the borrower has performed according to the terms of the existing loan, (2) the worthiness of the debtor has not deteriorated, (3) the value of the property in question is not anticipated to have declined, and (4) no additional funds will be advanced.

Independent means being completed in accordance with specific regulatory standards (too numerous and dull to list), and done by a party other than the extending account officer. For loans less than $250,000, the valuation may be done by other bank personnel. However, loans in excess of $250,000 require **outside independent** appraisal, done by professionals who must meet specific regulatory standards in their own qualification (also too numerous and dull to list).

Chapter Eight

There are many who believe the appraisal issue was the primary culprit of the S&L fiasco. Overly optimistic, poor, and downright fraudulent property valuations necessitated the write-off of millions of dollars. Accordingly, the regulating bodies stepped forward with new guidelines on report preparation.

Banking Circular 225, set forth by the OCC, stated no credit decision shall be made without an appropriate appraisal. And while I understand *shall* has been softened to *should*, or something of the like, banks are still implored not to issue commitments without complete appraisals in hand.

While this may seem only prudent, the elimination of contingent approvals is actually another blow to small business. Take the entrepreneur who has operated his concern out of a leased site for the past several years. Sales growth and consistent margins have made expansion desirable and he wishes to purchase a larger facility. Submitted financial information looks good, and would well support the amount of debt contemplated. However, the bank can no longer approve his request "subject to" an appraised value indicating a 70% extension, and a DSC^g via the income approach^g of 1.25:1.

Instead, the individual must pay for a commercial appraisal (running between $1,500-$5,000)... without knowing whether or not the loan will go through. Sure, business is good, but we're talking about small business. It's tough for the modest sized concern to lay out money without assurances of some kind. Unfortunately, as a result of the circular, banks have become very reluctant to offer contingent commitments.

To compensate, someone came up with "interest letters." If everything about your request appeared satisfactory, the bank would forward a note (with a dozen disclaimers) indicating it would "strongly contemplate extending credit should the appraisal come back at such and such a value." Which is, of course, in no way a contingent approval.

However, there are numerous times no double-secret interest letter is issued. The bank simply accepts an application with minimal commentary and orders the appraisal. Only to subsequently reject the request down the road. How can this happen? With banks generally adopting a position of avoidance with regard to contingent approvals, your initial offering might receive only a quick going-over until the appraisal is ready. This is prone to happen when the lender in question has an exceptionally large portfolio. (<u>So ask about</u>

141

How to Obtain Business Loans

your account officer's work load! Anything in the area of $50 million and/or more than 50 accounts is unmanageable.) In a situation where the individual can't adequately service what he has, other items are addressed only on a priority basis.

Given that no approval can be put in place until an appraisal arrives anyway, a derivative of time management has your application tabled until that juncture. Request a letter summarizing perceived weaknesses to the credit at the initial review. You'll make sure the loan is fully analyzed at that time, and have longer to overcome any objections.

By law, outside valuations must be ordered directly by the bank. In reality though, almost all appraisers will complete a report upon the request of a borrower, and then readdress it to the bank once the institution forwards its "letter of engagement" formally requesting the report.

Is this woeful disregard for the law? Suppose an individual applies for a development loan at Institution A. The bank has the prospect either pay for the appraisal up front or sign an agreement indicating they will bear all related costs incurred in valuing the project.

The institution then orders the appraisal and weeks, or months, later the report is received. A copy is given to the prospective borrower (so long as payment has been made).

Institution A subsequently rejects the loan request. Now the prospect must apply at the next corner, and possibly elsewhere thereafter. If the legislation were strictly interpreted, on each occasion the individual would have to allow the respective bank to order its own appraisal. At a cost between $1,500 and $5,000 a piece, depending upon the breadth of the project and the scope of the requested analysis. Which would lengthen the process immeasurably.

Sticking to the letter of the law would grind development to a near standstill, with more than a few other folks being added to the list of "habitually unemployed."

Lawmakers felt that requiring banks to order their own appraisals would put an end to MAI^g (made as instructed) reports; valuations contrived to meet the numbers necessary to make a deal work. In reality, however, it does nothing of the sort. The very day I was writing this piece I received an appalling residential appraisal. The market approach to value looked like this:

Chapter Eight

	Subject	Comparable 1	Comparable 2	Comparable 3
Address	345 Ocean Blvd.	886 Sand Castle Ln.	1491 Starfish Pt.	473 Salty Way
Proximity		2 blocks West	3 miles South	2 miles East
Sales Price		$ 1,400,000	$ 1,625,000	$ 800,000
Price/Gross Living Area		$ 379.71	$ 340.74	$ 290.07
Date of Sale		12/92	03/93	05/93
Location	Beach Front	Beach Front (715,000)	Beach Front (520,000)	River Front (210,000)
Site	12,500 SF	12,500 SF	22,000 SF (265,000)	15,000 SF (80,000)
Age	Proposed	6 Years $ 10,000	1 Year	3 Years $ 5,000
Condition		Good $ 10,000	Good	Good $ 5,000
Rooms	4 Bd/4 Bth	5 Bd/4 Bth	4 Bd/5 Bth	3 Bd/3.5 Bth
Living Area	3,391 SF	3,687 SF $ 24,000	4,769 SF (83,000)	2,758 SF $ 241,000
Pool	No Pool No Dock	No Pool No Dock	Pool Dock (30,000)	Pool Dock (30,000)
Net Adjustments		(671,000)	(898,000)	(69,000)
Value of Subject		$ 729,000	$ 727,000	$ 731,000

Comments on Sales Comparables:
The sales selected are the best available at the time of this appraisal. They are the most recent sales that are in this market area and are the most similar to subject in size, age and physical characteristics.

INDICATED VALUE BY SALES APPROACH $ 730,000

(appraisal continued on next page)

How to Obtain Business Loans

Additional Comments:
This appraisal represents a resume of data collected. Supporting documentations is (sic) retained in our files. Additional comments and conditions are attached.

Final Reconciliation:
Greatest weight was given to the market approach. It was well supported (HA). The cost approach adds support. The high percentage of owner occupied single family dwellings precludes rental data, therefor (sic) the income approach was omitted.

I ESTIMATE THE MARKET VALUE,
AS DEFINED, OF THE SUBJECT
PROPERTY AS OF 11/2/93 TO BE $ 730,000

Dale Mathews
_____
Dale Mathews (MAI)

Notice anything interesting? You may not have had occasion to review too many appraisals, but I'm sure a few items jump out at you nonetheless. Working from the top down, the first issue is whether or not an $800,000 home is directly comparable to ones of $1,400,000 and $1,625,000. Further, the price/gross living area has a pretty wide range for supposedly similar properties ($290.07--$379.71). With those two points in mind, in order to make the residences comparable, you'd expect large adjustments in the areas of property size and location.

Comp 1	(715,000)
Comp 2	(785,000)
Comp 3	(290,000)

In each case, the "comparable" sites are considered far superior to the subject. Conversely, Comp 3, whose sale price turns out to be the closest to the subject's final appraised value, requires a $241,000 adjustment in the other direction, as the home itself is much smaller (1,173 SF) than the proposed Ocean Blvd. residence.

Other modifications (which are minute in comparison) are made, leaving final net adjustments of:

Chapter Eight

Comp 1	(671,000)	(47.9%)
Comp 2	(898,000)	(55.3%)
Comp 3	(69,000)	(8.6%)

You don't have to be an expert in property valuation to see the first two are as comparable to the subject as the White House is to an outhouse. And the seemingly reasonable third comp? Consider: How similar are the residences if the subject's location is $290,000 inferior to the comp, but the home itself is $241,000 superior? (As alike as a 10,000 SF mansion in Death Valley and a shack along Pebble Beach.) Undoubtedly, this is a bad appraisal. Real bad. How could something like this be put together by a licensed professional?

More than a bit disgruntled with the blatant dissimilarity of the "comparables," I required the appraiser to readdress his work. He did so and quickly forwarded the following:

	Subject	Comparable 1	Comparable 2	Comparable 3
Address	345 Ocean Blvd.	790 Douglas Ln.	1641 Cris Ct.	473 Salty Way
Proximity		3 miles East	3 miles East	2 miles East
Sales Price		$ 725,000	$ 720,000	$ 800,000
Price/Gross Living Area		$ 241.67	$ 245.99	$ 290.07
Date of Sale		12/92	03/93	05/93
Location	Beach Front	Bay Front (50,000)	Bay Front (50,000)	River Front (100,000)
Site	12,500 SF	22,000 SF	12,500 SF	15,000 SF
Age	Proposed	18 Years $ 50,000	10 Years $ 25,000	3 Years $ 5,000
Condition		Updated	Good $ 15,000	Good $ 5,000

(appraisal continued on next page)

How to Obtain Business Loans

Rooms	4 Bd/4 Bth	4 Bd/3 Bth	3 Bd/3 Bth	3 Bd/3.5 Bth
Living Area	3,391 SF	3,000 SF	2,927 SF	2,758 SF
		$ 47,000	$ 50,000	$ 59,000
Pool	No Pool No Dock	Pool Pool Dock Dock (30,000)	Pool Dock (30,000)	(30,000)
Net Adjustments		$ 17,000	$ 10,000	(61,000)
Value of Subject		$ 742,000	$ 730,000	$ 739,000

Comments on Sales Comparables:
The sales selected are the best available at the time of this appraisal. They are the most recent sales that are in this market area and are the most similar to subject in size, age and physical characteristics.

INDICATED VALUE BY SALES APPROACH $ 730,000

Additional Comments:
This appraisal represents a resume of data collected. Supporting documentations is (sic) retained in our files. Additional comments and conditions are attached.

Final Reconciliation:
Greatest weight was given to the market approach. It was well supported. (uh-huh) The cost approach adds support. The high percentage of owner occupied single family dwellings precludes rental data, therefor (sic) the income approach was omitted.

I ESTIMATE THE MARKET VALUE, AS DEFINED, OF THE SUBJECT PROPERTY AS OF 11/12/93 TO BE $ 730,000

Dale Mathews
_____
Dale Mathews (MAI)

Let's see... two new comps, but the third one is the same. Sales prices are closer in range, as are the prices/gross living area. Hmmm...

Chapter Eight

here's something interesting... Comp 3 now requires only a $100,000 adjustment due to location (versus $210,000 a few days earlier)... and no adjustment for lot size (which had been previously altered by $80,000). Plus a modification of just $59,000 for the home's smaller size (as opposed to a $241,000 adjustment when last we looked.)

Comp 1's site is 9,500 SF larger, but no downward compensation was made for the subject property. Further, Comp 1's structure is 18 years old. How similar is *this* residence to the property being appraised?

The other distinctions made are relatively modest, and the Net Adjustments appear much more reasonable.

Comp 1	$17,000	2.3%
Comp 2	$10,000	1.4%
Comp 3	(61,000)	(7.6%)

Looks great, eh? And, miraculously enough, the subject property once again appraises at $730,000... AMAZING.

The comments are intriguing. Although a bit redundant when you read them for the second time. They are exactly the same as in the first report. Undoubtedly, this is a bad appraisal. Real bad. How could something like this be put together by a licensed professional?

Allow me to set the stage. The bank only extends residential loans (without private mortgage insurance[g]) at a maximum of 80% loan-to-value. The builder has proffered a construction contract of $560,000, and the land cost is $170,000. Total $730,000.

If the appraised value comes in less, then the borrower has to put up the difference. In a situation where this is not possible, the deal could fall through if the valuation doesn't come in at cost. Who would lose then?

- The realtor who listed the property site wouldn't collect any commission.
- The realtor who brought the prospect to the property wouldn't either.
- The builder wouldn't sell a home.
- The subdivision wouldn't gain another dues-paying resident for it's association.
- And the bank wouldn't receive fees and interest by making a loan.

How to Obtain Business Loans

As you can see, there are several parties with a vested stake in that appraisal coming back at $730,000. Regardless of whether or not the bank orders the report, the appraiser will certainly be informed (by an *interested party*) of the number needed to make the deal work. The result is an astonishing propensity for reports to come in right at contract prices. Even if one has to adjust half a "comp's" value to do so.

Excluding the buyer who would've paid too much, what other party is damaged under the described set of circumstances? The answer, of course, is the bank... should they have to foreclose on an over-extended position. And yet, witnessing the S&L disaster, it seems apparent some institutions need to be protected from themselves. Or so the government would debate.

As a result, regulations restricting the way (is it me, or is this a recurring phrase?) outside appraisals are ordered and reviewed have been put in place. Additionally, most institutions allow their officers to complete their own property reports on only the smallest of loans, and even then there are specific guidelines for how to gather comps, extrapolate from tax assessed values, and compile the data for file submission. These parameters, set in a desperate attempt to guarantee precise values, are obtained on real estate taken as collateral.

Is one appraisal enough to ensure this?

Thank You Sir, May I Have Another?

In a situation similar to the Ocean Boulevard appraisal, where the report isn't worth the paper it's written on and the value of the subject property is still anybody's guess, a revised estimation or second opinion is obviously necessary. But there are other instances as well.

Large banks now often retain staff appraisers. Their primary function is the review of outside valuations and the compilation of internal reports. These individuals represent a significant investment on the part of an institution. Although we know banks are not collateral lenders, it is interesting to note staff appraisers are paid roughly twice the salary of cash-flow-conscious line lenders. (How odd.)

At any rate, staff appraisers spend their days sitting in supreme judgment over those who would set forth values. However, few reports are sent back to be readdressed and a second opinion is

Chapter Eight

sought even less often. Instead, a lot of requests for elaboration are sent to the original preparers and volumes of commentary are added to already bulging files. Most often, reports are ultimately acceptable after some artful, but inconsequential, internal debate and memoranda have been throw into demonstrate a generous measure of due diligence. That is, they are acceptable in substance so long as the preparer was acceptable from the outset.

Banks have approved appraiser lists. If you submit a personally ordered report with the intention of having it readdressed to the bank, you might be disappointed to find the appraiser himself unsatisfactory to the institution which would necessitate a second valuation. So, if you intend to shop a deal, or anticipate it will take a few presentations to gain approval, it's in your best interests to contact those you would petition... for a list of approved appraisers. A few individuals will meet everyone's standards. They'll be the most expensive, but the additional cost will certainly be less than that of two (or more) reports.

This business of sanctioned appraisers can also be a problem for consumers on the residential side of the bank. I recall one instance where an applicant was seeking to procure credit for 90% of a property's purchase price. As is customary in such a situation, the bank required private mortgage insurance (PMI) as a condition of the loan.

PMI companies basically ensure the bank's extension beyond the point of 80% LTV and receive a "premium" for doing so, which is factored into the borrower's monthly mortgage payment. As a prerequisite of this coverage, the issuing company controls property valuations. Here, *they* have the approved appraiser list.

In this implausible example, the bank contacted the PMI firm to inquire as to who was approved for work in the property's area. (The endorsement of appraisers is territorial. Just because Mr. Val Ewe (MAI) is approved, doesn't necessarily mean he's acceptable for all segments within the bank's delineated market, nor does it indicate his work is always admissible on every **type** of property.) The bank, informed of three suitable appraisers, passed the information along to the prospective borrower so he could shop for the best price. After which, the bank formally ordered the report from the applicant's preference.

Upon receipt, the institution reviewed the appraisal and found it satisfactory in form and content. They then forwarded a

How to Obtain Business Loans

copy to the PMI firm, who said, "You know, we told you wrong. We've taken this guy off of our approved list. We'll need another appraisal." (True story.)

At this point, the bank had three choices. (1) Eat the cost of a second report in an effort to ward off an irate customer. (2) "Portfolio," or keep the loan on its own books, without insuring the 10% above policy. Or, (3) have the customer pay for another appraisal. Hey, we're taking about an institution who lowered its light wattage to save a few nickels, and who balked at a CD-secured credit without proper financial disclosure. You **know** option #3 was selected. And an infuriated applicant paid for a second report.

Now this sort of communication breakdown is not commonplace, but things like this happen more often than anyone would like to admit. To safeguard yourself, ask your officer to forward you short letters to you indicating so and so firm is approved for appraisals, and this or that title company is satisfactory, etc. You'll be told it's unnecessary... but it's your money being spent... and, besides, who's working for who?

In small communities, that can become a question of real importance on the commercial side of things. Say you contemplate undertaking the construction of a relatively large-sized condominium project and, during your decision making process, you contract the local appraisal firm to complete a feasibility study on your behalf. Once received, you're convinced the endeavor makes perfect sense and you proceed to the corner bank for some financing.

Their first agenda item: "We'll need an appraisal."

"I have a feasibility study just completed by Bart Haywood, which sets forth values for the land and completed units. He uses both cost and market approaches to arrive at the estimates."

"Yes, but we'll need to order another report."

"Why? I checked to see that he was on your approved list. I thought Bart was well respected here."

"He is. However, how can we get an unbiased valuation from him... if he's already done a feasibility study for you stating what a great opportunity the venture is."

"Wait a minute, isn't that GOOD news?"

"Well, it's encouraging. But, under FIRREA, the bank must order its own report. I can't use the feasibility study Bart prepared for you."

"What if he readdresses the report to the bank? I know you guys allow that sort of thing sometimes."

Chapter Eight

"Yes, but that's on *appraisals* not *feasibility studies*. They're two different things."

"Look, you're concerned with the value of your collateral at different stages of development... which the report indicates. And you want to know how fast the units will be liquidated upon completion... which the report also estimates. What's the difference?"

"Under the regulations, appraisals and feasibility studies are two vastly separate things. We'll have to require an appraisal."

"The feasibility study cost me $4,500, now this additional report is going to run about the same again... and it's not going to tell you anything more than you already have before you!"

"Nevertheless..." (Welcome to another edition of "Jam It to the Applicant." With your host, Ira Banquer.)

The real zinger comes once the institution has you on the hook. Within the finer print of the multitude of documents you'll sign at closing is an expensive little clause born out of paranoia. It's called, The Reappraisal Provision. (Contestants, hold on to your wallets, we're moving into the bonus expense round.)

FIRREA requires banks to have collateralized properties reappraised at any time in which their corresponding values are presumed to have declined. Whether or not the bank's loan position is in jeopardy from a repayment standpoint, or on a collateral basis, is immaterial under the regulations. If the institution feels the worth of its collateral has deteriorated, it is compelled to order another valuation. And guess what The Reappraisal Provision calls for? You to pay the freight!

> The bank can conclude, at any time and for any reason, that the value of its collateralized subject property has declined or the value is less than originally anticipated at a particular stage of development and/or within a particular time frame. At which point, upon written request from the bank, the borrower must provide, at their expense, an updated appraisal report. The bank shall designate an appraiser to be used, and the form and content the report itself must have. The bank, at its sole discretion, may ask for reappraisal an unlimited number of times.

Remember, however, that failure to comply with a provision such as this would constitute only a *technical* default, provided all

How to Obtain Business Loans

payments have been kept current. Your decision involving restitution for any reappraisal should be based upon your relationship with the institution, and other items as discussed in Chapter 4. Just keep in mind, the documents will call for your compliance in footing the bill, and the bank's occasion to call for revaluation happens with increasing regularity these days.

For example, say you received a loan two years ago for the construction of a 15,000 SF office building. Your own company was to occupy 5,000 SF, and the rest was pre-leased to unrelated tenants. The original appraisal's income approach to value might have looked something like this:

15,000 @ $15/SF	$ 225,000
Vacancy and Collection Loss (5%)	11,250
Effective Gross Income	$ 213,750
Estimated Operating Expenses (20%)	42,750
Net Operating Income	$ 171,000
Capped at 9.75%	$ 1,753,846
Rounded to	$ 1,750,000
Bank's Original Loan	$ 1,100,000
LTV	62.9%

Suppose a major tenant went out of business 18 months into the loan and you were unable to re-lease the 3,000 SF vacated, primarily because of additional office space coming on line in the area. The bank could feel the building's value had deteriorated because a recalculated income approach to value shows:

12,000 @ $15/SF	$ 180,000
Estimated Operating Expenses	42,750
Net Operating Income	$ 137,250
Capped at 10%	$ 1,372,250
Rounded to	$ 1,375,000
Existing Balance	$ 1,085,029
Apparent LTV	78.9%

And so a new appraisal would be ordered, probably indicating something close to the following upon receipt:

Chapter Eight

15,000 @ $14.50/SF	$	217,500
Vacancy and Collection Loss (7%)		15,225
Effective Gross Income	$	202,275
Estimated Operating Expenses (22%)		44,501
Net Operating Income	$	157,774
Capped at 10.25%	$	1,539,263
Rounded to	$	1,550,000
Existing Balance	$	1,085,029
Apparent LTV		70.0%

The updated report reflects a reduction in value, though not as severe a drop as recalculated in-house. Gross Income is a reflection of currently leased space, and vacated space rented at diminished rates (needed to attract tenants when an over-supply of space is on the market).

12,000 @ $15.00/SF	$	180,000
3,000 @ $12.50/SF		37,500
Gross Income	$	217,500

Note that the following were adversely altered, causing the decline in value:

Vacancy and Collection Loss	From 5% of Gross to 7%
Estimated Operating Expenses	From 20% of Effective Gross to 22%
Capitalization Rate	From 9.75% to 10.25%

Had these items remained the same as in the original report, the property (even given a drop in rental rates) would have reappraised accordingly:

15,000 @ $14.50/SF	$	217,500
Vacancy and Collection Loss (5%)		10,875
Effective Gross Income	$	206,625
Estimated Operating Expenses (20%)		41,325
Net Operating Income	$	165,300
Capped at 9.75%	$	1,695,384
Rounded to	$	1,700,000
Existing Balance	$	1,085,029
Apparent LTV		63.8%

How to Obtain Business Loans

Reflecting a difference of only $50,000 from the initial report, and mocking the dire $375,000 deterioration approximated at the institutional level.

So why did the actual reappraisal indicate a much more conservative value of $1,550,000, $200,000 less than was first set forth? Two reasons are probable.

(1) The original report might have been prior to MAIs tightening their practices at the insistence of their ultimate customers... the banks.

At the height of the credit crunch, conservatism overflowed to all those providing services to lending institutions. In the case of appraisers, the banks nudged acceptable vacancy rates from the 3-5% range to 5-10%, operating expense estimates from 15-20% to 20-25%, and capitalization rates (whether derived by comparables, band of investment, or voodoo) from 9-10% to 10-11%. And while the latter doesn't seem like much, consider the values stemming from the varying cap rates used upon a property's income stream:

Net Operating Income — $157,774	
9.0%	$1,750,000
9.5%	$1,650,000
10.0%	$1,575,000
10.5%	$1,500,000
11.0%	$1,450,000

A difference of $300,00, or 21%! With the OCC's auditors using 12% cap rates to estimate collateral positions on graded credits, banks wanted analogously right-wing approaches applied by MAIs.

(2) Similarly, when an appraiser became aware that a report was being ordered to revalue an already collateralized property (and believe me, they were **always** made aware), they buckled down. Made as instructed really applies when your #1 customer is placing the order.

In practice, updated valuations are often requested from the original appraiser who, of course, wants to know why another

Chapter Eight

report is necessary having previously completed one. The bank's answer, "We feel the value has been impaired." And upon reappraisal, (alacazam) so it would have!

When reports are ordered from a party other than the original appraiser, the individual will typically inquire as to the reason for valuation: purchase, refinance, foreclosure... or update. The bank's answer, "We feel the value has been impaired." And upon reappraisal, (alacazam) so it would have!

Regardless, material differences in bank exposure are not characteristically found. Take, for example, our 15,000 SF office building. Original appraisal $1,750,000, reappraisal $1,550,000. LTV from 63% to 70%. The value might be impaired, but the collateral position? Hardly. The 7% change is immaterial.

I once had a $275,000 maturing loan collateralized by vacant, commercially zoned, river-front property. The last appraisal, only a few years old, indicated a value of $1,150,000. Contemplating a straight renewal, I was told by the credit policy manager that "a reappraisal might be in order." Justification: no parcels within the site had sold over the last couple of years.

At this juncture, FIRREA did not mandate an updated valuation from a *time* standpoint, the owner's decision to wait for higher offers determined the property must be reappraised... *no sales having occurred*. "Addison, without a reappraisal, how can you justify the project's continued viability?" Of course, there was no satisfactory answer.

Needless to say, it was a tough sell to the borrowers.

"You're at less than 25% LTV, and you have all of us guaranteeing...

	Net Worth	Liquidity
Joseph Crawford	$2,618,600	$1,021,254
Charles Birch, Sr.	$4,296,500	$1,161,500
Charles Birch, Jr.	$1,613,000	$ 831,387

...What's the problem?"

"Internal personnel feel the value of the property has deteriorated, given that belief, under FIRREA we must now order a new report."

How to Obtain Business Loans

"Hell, if the value had dropped $300,000, you'd still be at about 50% LTV. Besides, we've never been late on a payment! *What's the problem?*"

I found myself hard pressed to offer any rational explanation. There wasn't one.

At our next problem asset committee meeting, I was instructed by senior management to either (a) get the loan paid down below the $100,000 threshold, or (b) get a new appraisal.

I forced the borrower to reduce the outstanding balance, negotiating a $200,000 reduction by releasing the individual guarantors and retaining only an illiquid real estate holding company as the debtor. I then went directly to an in-house sales seminar on how to bolster loan volume. (Apparently the bank was experiencing significant run-off.)

A hallway discussion in the not too distant past.

"**Hey, Thurston... wanna catch lunch today?**"
"Can't buddy, gotta take Brian Harris to Pierre's La Cuisine."
"**Oooouuhh. I'm impressed. Say, isn't Brian the new residential appraiser in town?**"
"Yep, and he's hungry for business."
"**Well then, shouldn't he be taking you to lunch?**"
"Today's on the bank. I'm doing this for Radcliffe (a departing senior officer being transferred to another affiliate). You know how the holding company purchases the big boy's homes once they've reassigned them outside of their existing area... well they do so at the current market value. Radcliffe wants me to make sure we get the *right* appraised value from someone."
"**You're kidding.**"
"Nope. Fourth appraiser I've had lunch with this week. I'm sort of entertaining bids."

Good thing made as instructed reports have been legislated out of the system.

CHAPTER 9:

SELF-INFLICTED WOUNDS

Run-off: A decline in aggregate outstandings. Liken it to a medieval bloodletting. Intended to be good for the patient... up to a point. Thereafter, bleeding to death becomes a real possibility.

Banks follow the same archaic approach in purging impurities from their portfolios. Performing loans which no longer fit the mold of *a proper credit facility*, either because of structure or transaction type, are pushed from earning asset totals... and a mad dash ensues to replace the lost volume. Having nonperforming debtors drained away is good for the patient, dropping clockwork interest payments from the income statement is opening the jugular vein.

Large bureaucratic bodies often cut off their noses to spite their own face. Realizing that image is everything for major public concerns, witness the recent headline...

How to Obtain Business Loans

> "Salvation Army plays Scrooge, fires
> bell ringer with near-empty kettle" [1]

The story told of a disabled laborer and four-year, bell-ringing veteran who was fired for not bringing in enough donations this past Christmas season. The Salvation Army said that they were not in the practice of imposing minimums for their donation collectors. However, a spokesperson for the charity did proclaim, "People have got to do a good job."[2]

The bell-toller estimated that he had brought in $450 over the five-day period immediately before his termination. He went on to lament how it would now be difficult for him to pay for his own outstanding bills, like the one for electricity, let alone afford any type of Christmas for him and his family.

I guess I never realized bell ringing was such a high pressure sales position. I thought we were basically talking about **donations**, but then I'm unfamiliar with the industry. Much like the average person might say a good loan is one that's being repaid on a timely basis, and be surprised to learn differently. They wouldn't be familiar with the industry... now would they?

In One's Best Interest

In a capitalist economy, all business decisions primarily come down to an analysis of risk and return. The operating mode of banks should be no different. On the contrary, given the preponderance of time spent fretting over default risk, you'd expect a well-informed institution to vary its pricing widely on a loan by loan basis... fashioning terms around the specifics of risk associated with each credit.

So why, at an average community-sized institution, would you find ninety-odd percent of the commercial portfolio priced between Prime + 1% (ADOC) and 325 basis points above the corresponding treasury indexes (rounded up to the nearest eighth).

Pricing Option	Standard	Current Rate
Floating	Prime + 1.00%	7.00%
1 Year Adjustable	3.71% + 3.25%	7.00%
3 Year Adjustable	4.66% + 3.25%	8.00%
5 Year Fixed	5.23% + 3.25%	8.50%

Chapter Nine

(From the public's perspective, the stringent parameters now defining bankable deals make 7-8.5% the prevailing riskless range of return.)

If banks did a better job of spreading loan pricing according to the risks they discern through lengthy analysis, more credit could be extended. In aggregate, higher rates of return would compensate for any losses experienced as a byproduct of more lenient approval standards.

Instead, rate hikes are applied, not at the outset, but after a loan has shown itself to be a "problem" in one form or another. Perhaps by becoming a graded credit. From the loan documents...

> ...The Borrower agrees that the Bank, in its sole discretion, may apply an interest penalty in response to any nonmonetary default as provided for in the provisions of the loan documents. Upon written notice of any such default, the bank may impose a 3% rate increase to the note's rate of interest. The advanced rate will remain in full force and effect until the Borrower has cured any precipitating item of default. Monthly restitution required to the Bank will reflect any and all changes to the stated rate of interest borne on the note.

For instance, perhaps you've failed to supply financial statements in accordance to the loan agreement...

> ...Should the borrower fail to meet the terms and conditions as set forth in the loan documents, with particular reference to the quarterly submission of operating statements, the Bank, in its sole discretion, may choose either to (a) advance the note rate as previously stipulated, or (b) seek other such remedies as set forth elsewhere within the loan documents.
>
> The Borrower shall not construe the substitution of note rates as an act of forbearance^g with regard to any other terms and conditions. Furthermore, such action does not invalidate the Bank's right to seek other such remedies as provided in the event of any default.

The bark of the straight technical default remedy is, **of course**, worse than its bite, but the option to advance the note rate has teeth. If the institution chooses to do this, and adjusts scheduled payments accordingly, any failure to make monthly remittance is now a monetary issue. Which means, **of course**, the matter is no longer just a

How to Obtain Business Loans

technical default. Suddenly, when this provision is included in the documents, neglecting to supply financial information becomes a whole new ball game. In this circumstance, either forward the statements or pay the freight.

Other scenarios will also call for intrepid acts on the part of your checkbook... even when the bank holds, as part of the loan structure, a reserve for interest payment.

> ...the Bank may, in its sole discretion, decide that its position has come into peril. At which point, it will be under no obligation whatsoever to continue funding interest payments from any established reserve. If this should transpire, the Borrower agrees to begin interest carry immediately...

And may be asked to supply its own reserve, *for the bank to hold...*

> If, at any juncture, the Bank, in its sole discretion, arrives at the conclusion that the undisbursed portion of loan proceeds allocated as an interest reserve is insufficient to cover the total aggregate amount of interest which the Bank estimates as necessary for the balance of the construction period, then the Bank may (a) require additional security, (b) require the Borrower to reduce the outstanding loan amount as a means of lowering the interest burden anticipated for the remainder of the construction term, or (c) demand that the Borrower deposit funds, in an amount satisfactory according to the Bank's sole estimation, to carry the funded balance's interest expense through the completion of the project's development phase, or longer if deemed appropriate.

A dicey little point to remember: Almost all loan documents include the Right of Offset. Which means that any funds of the borrower's which the bank has control over can be used to offset (read: reduce) outstanding balances should the bank deem itself in some way insecure (at guess whose sole discretion?). This not only includes monies placed in interest reserves, but funds in regular deposit accounts.

So when the bank suggests they will look more favorably on your loan request should you become a major depositor, go ahead and move in your accounts. Then, immediately after closing, transfer the bulk of your funds right back out. That is, unless it's in *your* best interest to leave the funds there...

> ...this loan carries a pricing schedule based upon compensating balance requirements.

Chapter Nine

Interest Rate	Conditions
Prime + .50% (ADOC)	Borrower has balances in a demand deposit (noninterest bearing) account or accounts with the Bank which total not less than 15% of the loan's funded balance.
Prime + 1.00% (ADOC)	Borrower has collected balances in an interest bearing account or accounts with the Bank which total not less than 15% of the loan's funded balance.
Prime + 1.35% (ADOC)	Borrower has compensating balances which total less than 15% of the funded balance.
Prime + 1.50% (ADOC)	Borrower has compensating balances which total less than 10% of the funded balance.
Prime + 2.00% (ADOC)	Borrower has compensating balances which total less than 5% of the funded balance.

Dangerous Standards

An alarming code of officer conduct is indoctrinated at problem asset committee meetings. In discussing a recently approved, or past performing loan, which has migrated into a sub-standard category, someone in senior management will always bellow at the *responsible* line lender, "You've lost control of YOUR customer." To which, the true (but inappropriate, should you need your paycheck) rebuttal would be... "I never *had* control."

In truth, banks aren't supposed to exhibit control over their borrowers. Actually doing so, puts them in a libelous position should a default occur. The debtor then has cause to argue the bank's constraints effectually managed the operation in question and were a major factor contributing to eventual insolvency. When courts have found for the flesh-and-blood borrower (versus the cold, anonymous, deep-pocketed institution), they have vacated repossessions, foreclosures, etc. and added damages to boot.

How to Obtain Business Loans

Still, THE BURDEN OF PROOF places strenuous trials on an institution, requiring it to properly demonstrate its loans are "good" (and not just paying to prescribed terms). As an operating response, banks flirt with disaster in their day to day loan structuring in an effort to gain a foothold in the rate and reserve tug-of-war.

Deposit minimums aren't the only targets now set. A host of other clever covenants are now often thrown in which frequently add little more than aesthetic value to the documents, although at times they become self-scaring in the end analysis. Call them **The Neutron Pledges**... they leave the debt in place, but destroy the collateral and decimate the probability of repayment. (However, they do drum up work for destitute litigators. And, hey, there are more lawyers in law school than in practice... so more work is needed. To help, call 1-800-LETS-SUE.)

One of my favorite radioactive covenants is the ever popular: *Required debt service coverage level.* By policy, banks set satisfactory cash flow coverages by transaction type:

1.15:1   "Institutional Grade" Class A properties (as defined earlier) with values in excess of $2,000,000, and underwritable in the secondary market for permanent takeout. For example, general warehouse or office buildings occupied by owners. Any lease period would have to be in excess of the loan term.

1.20:1   "Next to Institutional Grade" complexes. Generally multi-tenant facilities with longer-term leases and good tenant mixes. For example, medical office space adjacent to a regional medical facilities.

1.25:1   "Lower Grade" office facilities, apartments, etc. Guarantor support required.

1.30:1   Nationally, or regionally anchored, *Retail Space.*

1.35:1   All other acceptable collateral types.

These criteria are predominately used to internally assess a loan for credit rating after-the-fact. However, the standards are aggressively applied at renewal in certain circumstances. Take, for example, the situation where a borrower is passing excessive

Chapter Nine

nonbusiness related costs through the company income statement. Let's face it, whether appropriate for discussion or not, individuals sometimes beef up expenses to lower tax incidence. (Gasp.) In which case, coverage of the bank's annual obligation appears less than actually endurable, sometimes prompting an adverse credit classification and the resulting loan loss provision.

Often, this problem manifests itself with regard to real estate transactions. To illustrate, suppose the bank notes, from its in-file appraisal (which is based upon existing rental rates), that a property's debt service coverage should be in the area of 1.15:1. However, each year the debtor passes through expenses only peripherally related to the site (travel, entertainment, etc.). Without which, the coverage ratio would more closely approximate the appraiser's estimate.

Lightning Lou was always particularly enamored with the following clause (It looks great on an internal credit package):

> The Bank retains the option of accelerating the indebtedness, in the event the Borrower doesn't keep a DSC of 1.15:1.

A story comes to mind, which properly exemplifies the uselessness of this type of technical default provision. Hibernation Rental Space was a self-storage facility of relatively new construction. It was brought on line in response to high existing occupancy levels in the market (85% to 90%), and the anticipation of even greater demand given the housing coming on line in surrounding subdivisions. Baggins Store-All was directly adjacent to the site, and it had **historically** operated with less than 10% vacancy.

Hibernation Rental Space didn't fare so well. In the two years after the bank completed construction funding, the facility had remained half empty. In each year a real cash loss was incurred, which was funded out-of-pocket by the guarantor, Denton Goddard. Mr. Goddard was able to accomplish this via the successful operation of his national advertising company. Although one to overdo the negotiation of small details, the bank had had no real difficulty with Mr. Goddard since closing. And his advertising concern appeared to have the wherewithal to continue its timely support of the debt.

Under the heading of <u>BEAT THE DEAD HORSE</u>, Lightning Lou required a full funds flow analysis documenting sources and uses of cash among the advertising firm, the storage facility, Mr. Goddard's various other business interests, and he and his wife individually...

How to Obtain Business Loans

right down to allotting for personal living expenses. Although the analysis bore out the capacity for continued solvency, Lou rated the credit substandard and mused over the accrual issue.

After a fortnight firing supporting memoranda, I won the battle to keep interest accruing (subject to quarterly review), but lost the war on restrictive covenants. Lightning insisted upon the renewal's inclusion of annual debt service coverage targets. Given half of the facility's units sat empty, the addition of annually increasing coverage goals would only have made sense if (a) the borrower had been attempting to lease the units at exorbitant rates, or (b) he wasn't seeking to rent the units at all... or at least not very hard. **Because, he certainly wasn't passing through excessive expenses.** Nevertheless, the standards were added.

The following year... they weren't met. A technical default occurred. And nothing was done. I did subsequently find out why this particular facility significantly lagged all others in the area in terms of occupancy. Ever worrisome, Mr. Goddard was demanding renters sign *The Magna Carta* in order to enter into a measly six-month lease. (At least this helped support local members of the BAR.)

So then the bank elected (surprise) not to enforce the technical default. Forgoing, but not forbearing, its right to foreclose; the choice was made to adjust interest terms instead. Sure... experiencing poor cash flow?... let me raise that rate for you! (Drowning?... how about an anchor?)

Widening the gap between expected and reasonably attainable debt service coverage does not bode well for the future. Follow me on this, it *could* lead to monetary (read: *real*) default, foreclosure, and loss. Fledgling bankers, take heed; here are a few easy steps which can be used to create your own catastrophe:

Current Loan Status

Net Operating Income	$ 47,823
Existing Debt Service	$ 85,398
1st Year Debt Coverage Target	.75:1
Actual DSC	.56:1
Service Supported by Guarantor	$ 37,575

Step One: In an attempt to offset the effect of loan loss reserves allocated in response to the project's lack of success, bump the rate 3%.

Chapter Nine

Resulting Status

Net Operating Income	$ 47,823
Adjusted Debt Service	$ 108,510
2nd Year Debt Coverage Target	1.00:1
Actual DSC	.44:1
To be Supported by Guarantor	$ 60,687

Step Two: Without an increase in operating efficiency, the necessary support level expands. The rallying cry of Credit Administrators, "Let them pay out-of-pocket!"... becomes unrealistic after a point. Wells run dry.

I mean, an increase of $23,000 requires pretty deep pockets. That amount could make a real difference to some folks... enough to cause an *actual* default.

Step Three: Okay, now payments are no longer being made. The strategy, of course, is to foreclose. But first FIRREA requires a reappraisal prior to taking property into the Real Estate Owned category. As we discussed, due to the manner in which it will be ordered, you know the value's coming back lower than originally appraised. What you may not yet understand is how easy it now is for the appraiser to justify the reduction.

Over time, unit rentals ranged between a low of $5/SF for larger non-air conditioned space to a high of $10/SF for smaller air conditioned units. When the bank pushes the out-of-pocket burden over $5,000 per month, what happens to those rental terms? They become as fixed as hotel room rates at 2 A.M. (Let's make a deal.)

So the borrower, attempting to keep his head above water, starts leasing units for less and less in a desperate attempt to bring in as many dollars as possible. What's happening? "Market rates" are being reset. Thus, the appraiser looks at a future income stream based upon the trends in rental terms and, guess what, the property's Income Approach to Value plummets.

Step Four: Assume, after spirited legal wranglings, the bank gets

(steps continued on next page)

How to Obtain Business Loans

the property back in foreclosure. Suppose the original loan had been $975,000 against $1,220,000. 80% LTV.

Renewal was approved at $963,000.

Foreclosure took place at $953,000 and a reappraised value came in at $1,000,000. After interest, and (oh-by-the-way) a few attorney fees, the institution would be lucky to offset at 1:1.

Step Five: (Internal panic. "We've taken a piece of property back. Sound battle stations. We must liquidate immediately.") Most institutions hate to keep anything in REO for any length of time. Mumbling something about the "down time of money," Special Asset Coordinators are anxious to dump foreclosed properties. Which is why there is a whole group of real estate investors specializing in the purchase of bank retained assets. (Let's make a deal.)

"Bottom feeders," as they are called by bankers, are low-ball specialists. In our example, an offer of $800,000 might come in. After a few committee meetings, the bank might counter with $950,000.

"$850,000"

Committee meeting. "$925,000"

"$900,000 final."

Committee meeting. "Done."

Now you see why maximum loan-to-value positions are mandated. After denigrating the property's worth during the described process, a $100,000 charge-off becomes necessary.

Meanwhile, "The Catfish" picked up a property appraised a few years ago at $1,220,000 for $900,000. With proper management, the income stream can be repaired... shifting the value back into the area initially estimated.

FISH   + $320,000   FISHERMAN   - $100,000

Chapter Nine

> And I guess the original borrower was "The Worm." Of course, the bank exhibited no "managerial" control... they merely set targets.

A similar course is set on other loan types. Consider, for instance, construction financing for a shopping center. The difficulty here is magnified by a third party, the takeout (or permanent) lender. Traditionally, banks have provided construction dollars and monitored disbursements for large projects like this. Then, after a predetermined period, the debt was taken out by an insurance company or pension group.

The requirements to provide the permanent loan based upon project completion and a stabilized income stream are as follows:

- Bank to provide two-year loan; twelve months construction, interest only on funded balance. And twelve months principal and interest based upon a twenty-year amortization.

- Bank loan subject to SuperCity Grocery and Corner Drugs as anchor tenants, along with a small portion of remaining space pre-leased to local tenants.

- Takeout not to occur until stabilized income stream of 1.15:1 is attained. Failure to do so, vacating takeout, and with it the bank's ultimate repayment mechanism.

What targets does the bank set?

- 'X' amount of local tenant space leased through construction.
- 'X' amount in each of the next three quarters.

Then covenants are set to *ensure* final coverage will be in excess of the 1.15:1 required by the takeout commitment.

12 months from closing	1.00:1
15 months from closing	1.05:1
18 months from closing	1.10:1
21 months from closing	1.15:1

Should these standards not be realized, the bank retains the right

How to Obtain Business Loans

to stop funding tenant improvements (via a loan reserve account). In which case, leases fall out, coverage ratios drop farther, and no takeout occurs. Assuming a second clause can't be met... the one requiring the borrower to reduce the loan balance so the target coverage ratios are maintained by available cash flow.

The end result? The bank helps cause the fall-out of its ultimate repayment source. Recapping:

(1) Rental rates are dropped to help meet coverage requirements.

(2) Resulting in poor tenant mix, if not the loss of an anchor (whose lease would still be paid, but departure would drastically effect the site's attractiveness as a shopping destination).

(3) Together necessitating eventual foreclosure, and reappraisal prior to that action.

(4) After movement into REO, anxious sale takes place at reduced price.

(5) Partial charge-off.

At the community bank level, this has happened enough to require holding companies to set up centralized departments to entertain this type of request.

ATTENTION INSTITUTIONAL INVESTORS:

(Insurance companies, pension groups, universities, etc.)

...beat the bureaucracy out of one of its highest yielding product lines. Become active in construction lending.

You've been placing long term rates into your portfolio(s) at 9%, a decent yield for what you regard as a relatively secure investment. (How is real estate safe in the eyes of institutional investors, but high risk from the view point of bank administrators?) **However, today's decent rate of return is at the bottom end of the yield cycle. Why not do the same type of lending, repricing your investment balances as rates start to go back up?**

Chapter Nine

$5,000,000 Loan to Construct Shopping Center

<u>First Year</u>
1.5% Fee	$ 75,000
Balance 60% Funded During the First Year	
Interest Cost (Prime + 1.5%, 7.5% Currently)	<u>225,000</u>
Total First Year Earnings	$300,000
$300,000/$3,000,000 (Avg. Funded Bal.)	10% Return

<u>Second Year</u>
$375,000/$5,000,000	7.5% Return

<u>Combined</u>
<u>$675,000/2</u>	
$4,000,000 (Avg. Funded Bal.)	8.4%

Decent low risk return, eh? Or would you rather post funds in a certificate of deposit at 2.5%? (Hmmm... when banks used to do these they had pretty good spreads.) And remember, *the yields only get better the shorter the construction term is.*

Another example of banks' masochistic behavior occurs with loans scheduled to be repaid by the sale of units (either lots, condominiums, or single-family residences). Consider an acquisition and development loan for the build-out and sale of stacked condominiums. Of course, issue number one is the appraisal. ("How fast will these units sell? Tell us O Keeper of the Crystal Ball... tell us... tell us...")

Appraiser says 4 per month, Novelty Eight Ball says 2. Appraiser readdresses findings, decides to go with 3 as a compromise. Okay, now we're ready to structure the credit. In the future, loan review will check to see if the loan is being retired in accordance with initially projected target balances, which are based upon expected absorption. This is known as "curtailing[g]" a loan.

$5,500,000 Loan to Develop Condominiums
- Average sales price per unit $85,000
- Releases set at 90% of gross ($76,500)

(continued on next page)

How to Obtain Business Loans

- Meaning 72 of the 96 units must be sold to retire debt.
- First certificates of occupancy expected 9 months from commencement.
- Curtailments based upon 3 sales per month. (Making the very large assumption the bank didn't require all units to be presold prior to construction. It happens.)

Period from Closing	Number Closed	Target Balance
9 months	27	$3,434,500
12 months	36	$2,746,000
15 months	45	$2,057,500
18 months	54	$1,369,000
21 months	63	$ 680,500
24 months	72	$ 0

Heard in loan committee: "Looks alright."
"We'll be paid out in two years."
"Decent yield. Motion."
"Second."
"Any opposed? So approved." (Okay, so the Credit Guru would have drug it out a bit... humor me.)

Now what if, just what if, the appraiser is wrong? Say absorption runs at 2 per month. The borrower must curtail (read: pay down) the difference between the target and actual balances.

Period	Closed	Reduction	Target	Actual	Carry
9 months	18 units	$1,377,000	$3,434,500	$4,123,000	$688,500

If this out-of-pocket amount can't be met (and only the wealthiest contingent could possibly do so), the loan's in default. Real default, this (irrational as it seems) being a monetary issue.

In a case where not all the money has been disbursed, phasing being required, the bank could stop funding for construction if absorption targets are not attained. (And you thought not continuing to fund interest carry was severe.)

Say the bank funded $1,100,000 up front to take down all the land. The loan was then structured so as to fund construction in four equal phases.

Chapter Nine

Land Cost					$1,100,000	
Disbursed to Construct 24 Units					1,100,000	
					$2,200,000	
Release Value of Finished Units					1,836,000	
Shortfall					$ 364,000	
Period	Closed	Reduction	Target	Actual	Carry	
9 months	18 units	$1,377,000	$364,000	$823,000	$459,000	

The bank stops disbursing. Choosing instead to face a bulk sale of the property after foreclosure, rather than finishing funding to complete and sell units even though a wholesale approach is infinitely less marketable. And remember, the targets will have undone the property value by serving to push sale prices down.

The project doesn't appear to have failed by any stretch of the imagination, absorption is just slower than expected. Yet, the bank effectually shuts things down if the curtailments (based upon tarot cards) aren't kept.

I recall one loan where sales fell behind. The first three phases, financed by another institution, sold out at a clip of 8 per month. After the original institution inexplicably turned down the last phase after 3 highly successful ones, my bank had the remainder of the project appraised. Being conservative, the MAI returned an absorption estimate of 6 per month.

The loan was approved and funding began. Shortly thereafter, the city decided to rip up the site's access road to repair water lines. Work dragged on for almost a year. As one might expect, traffic through the project's model center fell off drastically, as did absorption. Was this a failed project worthy of shutting down, reappraising, foreclosing, and fire selling?

You may have a loan in place, but ultimately the bank controls when the money is due and payable... and that may not coincide with maturity.

It's Due... Now What?

Several years ago, I was putting together a CD loan for a customer. I remember the whole experience as quite odd. And not just

How to Obtain Business Loans

because I had a hard time understanding why anyone would pay an institution interest for the use of their own money. It was the way in which I was instructed to handle the transaction.

I had, naively, drawn documents without requiring the submission of **any** financial information from the "borrower." I deemed the exercise unnecessary, as the bank held much more than the loan amount in its collateral vault. Discovering my actions, the boss sat me down to explain the ways of the world.

"I wish things were as straightforward and easy as you make them out to be... but the fact is, you can't just lend money like you're doing."

"Why?"

"Because it's up to the bank to show the customer can repay the loan we're giving him."

"Why?"

"Because it is..."

"I think holding a $10,000 CD for a $9,000 one-year loan sufficiently demonstrates repayment ability."

"Ah, but you're looking at this wrong. You can't base repayment on your collateral... even if it is liquid."

"Why?"

"The bank has a BURDEN OF PROOF to meet on this type of consumer credit. Worst case, if we can't show a judge we did our due diligence... indicating repayment from other sources was likely... he could nullify our security interest in the CD."

"On what basis?"

"The big bad bank rule. If he feels the loan was extended solely with the intention of liquidating the borrower's CD, he won't let us take away the consumer's savings."

"So I have to make the loan as if there is no collateral."

"Now you're getting it!"

Contagious as *IT* might be, not everyone gets *IT*. Like so many banking rules, this one isn't universally applied. Application in the commercial arena contradicts the premise behind the sage's advice. There, regulators have insisted it's in an institution's best interest to "turn the portfolio" as often as possible. Doing so doesn't hurt earnings any either. Allow me to explain. Banks used to provide the type of permanent mortgages we've spoken of previously. Credit was extended with the intention of being repaid over a long period of time. Often over 25 years.

Chapter Nine

Regulators felt this could be hiding problems which would eventually surface at a later date. They theorized institutions would be better served to address any difficulties head on... perhaps before they even arose. (Like bandaging a knee before a fall?) So they suggested banks begin the practice of ballooning commercial credit.
Definition...

>   **balloon**   1: a bag of hot air or lighter-than-air gas which can float in the atmosphere. 2: an inflatable toy. 3: the outline around words in a comic strip. 4: to swell up. 5: a final loan installment bigger than the preceding ones.

Most everyone at all experienced in affairs of commerce is now familiar with the term in its small print capacity. (Street translation: The money's due, pay up or speak to Mr. Knuckles.)

(Alright, so its not that bad unless you borrowed at the corner pool hall and not the corner bank.) Ballooning notes at 3 and 5 years, the bank will usually renew your obligation when due. Ask your officer and he will tell you:

"Well now, Mr. Trusting, I can't actually guarantee you the loan will be renewed at its balloon... but I can say there's little to worry about. Maturing notes not yet paid in full are almost always rolled over. Unless there's been some 'problem'."

Previously, you would have heard, "As long as payments are made on time, its okay." But now you know better. Such a conclusion ignores the rate and reserve game taking place in the board room.

In reality, the bank can choose not to re-up your loan for another 3 or 5 years based upon its internal rating system. Which makes you wonder how an institution can call a loan due knowing the debtor is unable to retire the balance in one colossal payment. Double standard #974,449. You can't make a consumer CD loan without verifying the "debtor" can pay the credit back, but you can make a loan to the same person on the commercial side of the bank and balloon the obligation... knowing the balance can't be retired in full at the maturity.

When approaching an upcoming balloon, it's **in your best interest** to know what your loan is rated. You might need to start shopping another home for the credit. After all, that's generally what not offering to extend a renewal does. It forces the borrower to place the loan elsewhere.

How to Obtain Business Loans

Regardless, whether the facility is renewed at Bank 'A' or on the next corner (bank, not pool hall), "turning the portfolio" costs you money.

$200,000 Maturing Balance

Bank A:

Recording Costs	$ 19.50
Title Search	75.00
Credit Investigation	50.00
Attorney Fees	350.00
Photo copies, Fax, etc.	35.00
Reappraisal	1,500.00
Bank Fee (.5%)	1,000.00
Total Costs to Renew	$ 3,029.50

Next Corner:

Doc & Intangible Tax	$ 1,100.00
Recording Costs, Mortgage	69.00
UCC-1 County	15.00
UCC-1 State	19.25
Title Insurance	1,075.00
Endorsements	100.00
Tax Service	72.00
Credit Investigation	50.00
Attorney Fees	725.00
Photo copies, Fax, etc.	65.00
Appraisal	1,500.00
Bank Fee (1.5%)	3,000.00
Total Cost to Place Elsewhere	$ 7,790.25

It just costs you a lot more at Bank 'B' because they're starting from scratch, so-to-speak. Institution A will frequently use this difference in expense to improve its covenant position(s) at renewal. It works something like this:

> Say the bank wants to raise its rate of interest, or wishes to acquire additional collateral, shore up a guarantee, or step up reporting requirements. It conveys this information to you while "negotiating" the continuation of the credit.
> You recoil. **"I'll just take my business to another bank!"**

Chapter Nine

"Well, that's certainly your option... but are you aware of the additional costs you will incur in doing so? On your $200,000 balance, out-of-pocket expense will be about $3,000 more... if you're approved."

You have but one possible card to play. If your mortgage is for 20 years and does not contain balloon language (rather it is your note which has the balloon provision), you might be able to force a renewal at the original terms. Some ground has been gained in arguing the following: by ballooning only the note and not the mortgage, the bank has tacitly approved the continual renewal of debt through the term of the mortgage maturity... not just through the note's balloon. Success with this approach varies. For the most part, the institution has you by the BALLoonS.

Early morning scene in my office last December. I've got my genuine imitation wood chair thrown upside down on the floor, and I'm tying it's "hooves" with duct tape. (No the stress didn't finally get to me.)

Sure enough, in walks Myron. "What in the world are you doing with that chair?" (Obviously concerned with bank item #09709573, so marked on the leg.)

"I'm taping the sharp edges where the wheels attach. They scrape up your shoes something awful, and I just got new ones for Christmas." (You'd have thought he caught me playing rodeo with the family cat.)

"But.. wha.. why..?"

"I'm just tired of ruining my shoes." (Since they're worth a couple times the value of this kindling I'm working with.)

"But... taping the... is that necessary?"

"Yeah. I'm sick of self-inflicted wounds." Maybe others wouldn't see it that way.

---

[1] Associated Press. "Salvation Army plays Scrooge, fires bell ringer with near-empty kettle," December 5, 1993

[2] Associated Press. "Salvation Army plays Scrooge, fires bell ringer with near-empty kettle," December 5, 1993

Chapter Ten

CHAPTER 10:

ADJUDICATING COMMERCIAL CREDIT

Judgments are always biased by one's state of mind... by what slant your brain puts on things. Is the glass half full or half empty?... optimism versus pessimism... (good versus evil?).

Bankers tend to believe it's partly cloudy, with a *probable* chance of rain. Which reminds me of a story about an agricultural lender I knew, Sam Ploughman.

"Hey Sam, beautiful day today, huh? Not a cloud in the sky."

"Yeah... but if this sunshine keeps up, it's gonna dry everything out. A drought's all we need."

Days later. "Hey Sammy boy, we're sure getting the rain you were hoping for! Good thing, eh?"

How to Obtain Business Loans

"Yeah... I just hope it doesn't go on too long. A flash flood's all we need."

Months later. A mutual customer asked the both of us to go duck hunting. Norman Donaldson was a farmer who dabbled in real estate development, and was successful *in both fields*.

When we arrived at his spread, Norman was excited to introduce us to his new dog, Shep. "He's fantastic! He can do things no other hunting dog in the world can. And just look at his coat! Isn't he great, Sam?"

"Yeah... he's scratching at something though. He doesn't have fleas does he?"

Before long we were out on the water, the three of us and Shep poised in a boat among some reeds. "Quack, quack, quack."

"Here they come!"

"Blam. Blam." (Sam didn't take a shot.)

"Got one! Go get 'em Shep!"

To my amazement, Shep jumped out of the boat and ran *on top of* the water until he reached where the duck had gone down. Then, gently grasping it in his mouth, he returned to the boat and climbed back in. I was dumbfounded, but Sam wasn't at a loss for words.

"Norman, that dog can't swim, can he?"

Sometimes, even the most miraculous facts have no effect on a banker's outlook. They roll off like water on a duck's back...

Sittin' On the Dock of the Bay

Winthrop Eddles, the bank's president, is not what you'd call an accomplished golfer. Those who believe all bankers are on the course by 4:15 will find this hard to believe, but it's true. Actually, he's what you might refer to as a hacker, thrasher, or divot specialist. To his credit, he does get out there with some regularity, remaining congenial no matter how quickly his score mounts. Because of this, people enjoy his company on the course... choosing to overlook the amount of time he spends in the woods. In fact, he has a long-standing weekly outing with the same group of guys he's hit 'em with for years.

Mark Jacobs was one of the boys. Winthrop asked me to meet with him to discuss financing a venture he had undertaken... the development of dockominiums. As indigenous to coastal regions as sea shells, sand castles, and sunburns; dockominiums probably aren't as well known throughout the rest of the country.

Chapter Ten

Similar to condominiums, you're purchasing a boat dock and a percentage share in the surrounding common areas — pier, service station, dry storage, parking, etc. The proposed project was known as the Bimini Beach Yacht Club, and Mark Jacobs had been working to realize its creation for years.

Back in 1988, five individuals formed a partnership. Together they purchased waterfront property and the rights to develop a marina upon it. Later, in order to raise capital, additional investors were brought on board and the partnership was converted into a corporation... Breakwater Ventures, Inc. Mark Jacobs owned a 25% stake.

Fast forward four years. Mr. Jacobs purchased, from Breakwater, the right to develop 96 boat slips on a submerged land lease[g] in place with the state. At the time his request for financing was presented to the bank (on the 5th hole), 23 years remained on the lease. Which, by the way, allowed for renewal (I hear you, "as long as there's not a 'problem'.").

Mr. Jacobs subsequently procured permits to construct a dockmaster's station and provide additional parking on the site. No doubt his expertise as an engineer allowed him to accomplish this, he being the founder and president of Pelican Engineering, Inc., a large firm specializing in coastal construction.

What Mr. Jacobs hadn't been able to obtain was financing. Eventually, we sat down and he laid out his request. "The project will be constructed in two phases. The first has 52 docks on 4 floating piers and 20 parking places. The second phase will have a total of 44 slips on two piers and additional parking for 20. Here, look at the site map:

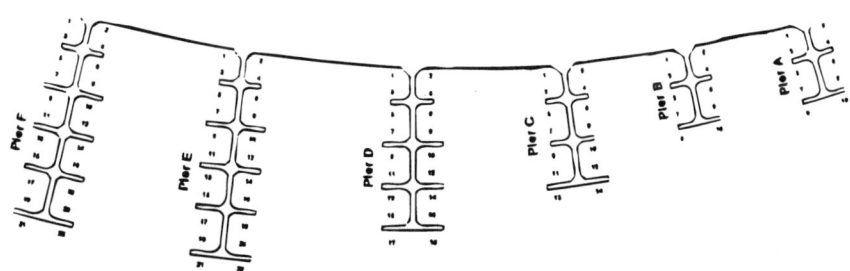

How to Obtain Business Loans

"The docks themselves will range from 35'-50', and will sell for between $30,000 and $45,000. Which, as you know, is very reasonable for slips with immediate deep water access."

"Uh-huh. **I know Palm Strand markets theirs in the $80,000 range.**"

"Sure. Of course, that **is** in the heart of town. Bimini Beach is certainly rural."

Mr. Jacobs went on to explain all the virtues of the marina, its site and the amenities to be included. Ultimately, we shook out the numbers for the first phase:

Requested Loan Amount — $960,600

Average Dock Price	$ 35,492
Closing Costs, Commissions (10%)	3,549
Net Proceeds From Sales (Available to Reduce Debt)	$ 31,943

$960,600/$31,943 = 30 docks, or only 57.7% of the phase.

I put together a consort memorandum, focusing on the meat of the deal... how the bank would be repaid. Which was, of course, from the sale of docks. I asked for a quorum to discuss the credit as soon as possible.

"Nice try," was the message filtered back down the approval chain. It was conveyed that, perhaps, it was premature to convene and deliberate over the matter. Any meeting should be postponed until the "sponsorship" portion of the loan had been more formally addressed.

My next memorandum supplied the following financial summaries:

Personal Financial Statement — Mark Jacobs

ASSETS		LIABILITIES	
Cash	$ 273,902	Breakwater (%)	$ 115,109
Notes Receivable	143,592	Mortgages Payable	1,039,076
Real Estate	2,071,800	Capital Gains Provision	395,768
Personal Property	24,000	TOTAL	$ 1,549,953
Cash Value of Ins.	19,200		
IRAs	194,196		
Pelican Eng.	900,000		
TOTAL	$ 3,626,690	NET WORTH	$ 2,076,737

Chapter Ten

Hmm. A *sizable* net worth, with *significant* liquidity. In a real pinch, those IRA monies could be made available, too. After tax and penalty, over $110,000 would still be at the individual's disposal in a worst case situation.

Personal Tax Filing Analysis — Mark Jacobs

	1990	1991
Wages	$ 249,838	$ 181,820
Interest Income	24,082	27,385
Business Income	140,196	80,414
Adding Back Noncash Expenses	10,240	2,689
Gross Income	$ 424,356	$ 292,308
Income Tax	(118,682)	(81,131)
Real Estate Taxes	(5,750)	(4,586)
Social Security/FICA	(6,148)	(6,148)
Net Income	$ 293,776	$ 200,443
Home Mortgage Interest	(19,100)	(14,798)
Other Interest	(7,668)	(1,700)
Consumer Debt	(17,014)	(16,968)
Total Debt Service	(43,782)	(33,466)
Cash Flow	$ 249,994	$ 166,977
Apparent Debt Ratio	14.9%	16.7%

I'm thinking... not bad, not bad at all! Keep in mind, an acceptable debt ratio based upon FANNIE MAE guidelines (used to qualify consumers for residential credit) is 36%. And that's 36% of gross income. Taxes aren't accounted for as they are in the analysis provided. Under FANNIE's method, Mr. Jacob's debt ratios for the past two years were 10.3% and 11.4% respectively. I'd say the "sponsorship" portion of the credit looked just fine.

Within the memo, I requested Lightning Lou come down and meet with our applicant. Given the highly technical permitting necessary, dealing with wetlands, gopher tortoises and all, I thought a face-to-face discussion would be appropriate.

Days went by and I received no response from Lightning. I followed up with a phone call. "Gee Addison, I'd really like to. I've

How to Obtain Business Loans

just got so much going on right now... (long pause) ....and I'd really like to zero in on the other aspects of the deal before we get to that point. Could you get me something on how funds have been disbursed on the project to date? Where do we stand on a loan-to-cost basis? Is there any equity in this thing?"

"Lou, our loan to sale price is going to be in the 50% range. An appraisal will bear this out. Obviously there's equity in the project."

"Well, right. We just need to match up the sources and uses."

Consort #3. A statement of funds allocation looks like this:

	COST	DEBT	EQUITY
SOFT COSTS			
Architectural/Eng.	$ 109,200	$ 0	$ 109,200
Legal/Accounting	36,000	0	36,000
Other Professional	36,000	0	36,000
Interest Reserve	36,000	36,000	0
Contingency	24,000	24,000	0
TOTAL	$ 241,200	$ 60,000	$ 181,200
HARD COSTS			
Land	$ 80,400	$ 0	$ 80,400
Site Development	124,800	124,800	0
Utilities	126,000	65,400	60,600
Construction	624,000	624,000	0
Landscaping	24,000	24,000	0
Contingency	62,400	62,400	0
TOTAL	$1,041,600	$ 900,600	$ 141,000
Closing Costs	$ 19,693	0	$ 19,693
GRAND TOTALS	$1,302,493	$ 960,600	$ 341,893

All except the land acquisition money was up-front equity. Thus, loan-to-cost is 73.8%. Well within policy.

Days passed. I finally reached Lou for a response. "Okay, so there's 20% in upfront, and roughly 26% overall. But, now he's allocated funds to engineering costs. I thought he was an engineer. You're saying someone else is doing the work in that area..."

"Not at all. Costs are incurred by Bimini Beach Yacht Club. Pelican Engineering is paid by Bimini Beach."

Chapter Ten

"Yeah... but Mr. Jacobs is really the party behind both, so you can't include those dollars as equity... they're really not funds out-of-pocket."

"Perhaps not, but if we're looking at a loan-to-cost analysis to see if there is a cushion to the project, those figures need to be included. Certainly, the costs are real. If a third party were acting as the developer, they'd have to be paid."

"True, but we also want to see that the borrower has a real vested interest in the project... we need to be confident he'll stay with it should any problems occur."

"He's been working on this thing for over four years now. That's a lot of time invested to simply walk away, plus he's spent monies of his own not included in the presented breakdown."

"I don't understand."

"Dollars were expended as part of his investment in the Breakers Venture."

"Yeah... but you can't count that as equity."

"Lou, you're making me work with a double-edged sword. I can't count engineering monies because they aren't out-of-pocket. And I can't count out-of-pocket investment funds because they aren't specifically allocated to the current portion of the project. You've got me coming and going."

"Well... how can we verify the dollars invested to date?"

Consort memo #4. As discussed, the loan-to-cost and simultaneous out-of-pocket expense analysis are somewhat skewed against the prospective borrower. Please note, the funds allocation provided in previous memoranda does not include monies expended by Breakwater Ventures. Of which, Mr. Jacob is a 25% owner and contributor.

Costs Incurred by Breakwater

Planning, surveying, environmental	$ 322,800
Fees to county	62,400
Clearing, excavating, fill	386,400
	$ 771,600
Funded via a loan by Seaside Bank & Trust	347,220
Out-Of-Pocket	$ 424,380

Which shows, Mr. Jacob's proportional investment to this point

How to Obtain Business Loans

is $106,095. Which more than offsets the strictly engineering costs credited in the earlier funds allocation.

Days passed. (Again) This time, my follow-up calls weren't returned. Mortie finally came to me with the latest wisdom from high above. "Lou wants us to look at whether or not Mr. Jacobs could cash flow the proposed debt over five or ten years... *without the benefit of any dock sales.*"

"You've got to be kidding."

"Nope. Put something together in a memo."

Numero 5.

Personal Tax Filing Analysis — Mark Jacobs

	1990	1991
Wages	$ 249,838	$ 181,820
Interest Income	24,082	27,385
Business Income	140,196	80,414
Adding Back Noncash Expenses	10,240	2,689
Gross Income	$ 424,356	$ 292,308
Income Tax	(118,682)	(81,131)
Real Estate Taxes	(5,750)	(4,586)
Social Security/FICA	(6,148)	(6,148)
Net Income	$ 293,776	$ 200,443
Home Mortgage Interest	(19,100)	(14,798)
Other Interest	(7,668)	(1,700)
Consumer Debt	(17,014)	(16,968)
Proposed Loan Service (5 yrs)	(239,286)	(239,286)
Total Debt Service	(283,068)	(272,752)
Cash Flow	$ 10,708	(72,309)
Apparent Debt Ratio	96.4%	136.1%
Proposed Loan Service (10 yrs)	(146,022)	(146,022)
Total Debt Service	(189,804)	(179,488)
Cash Flow	103,972	20,955
Apparent Debt Ratio	64.6%	89.5%

Days passed. (Once again.) I was definitely removed from the loop. Mortie kept calling Lightning for a response. Eventually, he got

Chapter Ten

one and passed it along to me. "He feels, since Jacobs can't cash flow the debt without sales, it's a collateral dependant loan."

"Under that whacked-out definition, I guess it is. Who can cash flow development debt without sales from the corresponding development?"

"Maybe we should try and look at lowering the loan amount... try and keep it inside our house limit so Lou doesn't have to approve it."

"What a tough option for Mr. Jacobs. The more you down phase this thing, the higher you'll drive his construction costs. There is some synergy gained by not building something like this one brick at a time, you know.

"What if I showed Thunder how much docks could be discounted, with the bank still being orderly repaid?"

"Give it a shot."

Tree number six, if you're still counting.

Worst-Case Repayment Analysis	
Average Dock Price	$ 35,492
Closing Costs, commissions (10%)	3,549
Average Net Proceeds	$ 31,943

Policy calls for the bank to be out within 75% of the salable units within a phase. Meaning $960,600 must be retired in 39 units. This requires net proceeds of $24,631 per dock. Resulting in an average sales price of:

$$\$24,631 / .90 = \$27,368$$

Which represents a 23% discount. And seems to indicate sufficient pricing latitude is available.

Further, nowhere in our discussions have we accounted for Mr. Jacobs' capacity to carry the debt via existing holdings. His $273,902 in cash, less the $89,400 in land acquisition costs, would pay interest on the fully funded amount for 27 months. To say nothing of his ongoing income's ability to support the project until sales take place.

Some more days passed. (I was starting to wonder if erosion could end up being an issue before a final decision was made.) When

How to Obtain Business Loans

the response came, I felt I should have foreseen it. "How can the bank be sure he can generate the solid presales we need in order to offer any commitment?"

"He's got 9 already, with very little activity taking place on the property, and no sales center set up. I've checked and there's no similar dockage available for 15-20 miles. Demand should be good. Besides, we wouldn't be disbursing until he got the sales in place. What's our risk if we require 75% of the project to be presold prior to funding?"

"Well, presales could fall out. Have you looked at the effect fall-out would have on repayment?"

Lucky number 7. (At this rate, renewal of the submerged land lease will soon be an issue.)

Average Release Proceeds $31,943 (39) =	$ 1,245,777
Loan Amount	960,600
Excess Revenue from Sales	$ 285,177
$285,177/$31,943 =	8.93

Illustrating that nine contracts could drop out and the bank would still be systematically repaid. However, this scenario does not take into consideration deposits on hand which would be made available to the bank from buyer nonperformance.

39 Presales with 25% Down	
$35,493 (25%) =	$ 8,873
$ 8,873 (39) =	$ 346,047

Say 12 of the 39 presales fall out.....

$ 8,873 (12) =	$ 106,476
$31,943 (27) =	862,461
Total Generated	$ 968,937

Thus, almost a third of the required presales could go south, and the debt would *still* be retired. What's more, consider no sales are consummated... as was suggested in earlier discussion.

Chapter Ten

Loan Amount	$ 960,600
Deposit Monies	346,047
	$ 614,553

Say 75% of Mr. Jacobs' cash remaining after land acquisition is used to offset the balance at that point.

$193,501 (75%)	=	$ 145,126
$614,553 - $145,126	=	$ 469,427

Amortizing the remainder straight over 10 years results in the following personal cash flow summary:

Proposed Debt Service	(71,571)	(71,571)
Total Debt Service	(115,353)	(105,037)
Cash Flow	178,423	95,406
Apparent Debt Service Coverage	39.3%	52.4%

Under the scenario, if done on FANNIE MAE'S gross basis, the average debt ratio for the two years would be 23%. Meaning, if he were a residential applicant at this juncture, Mr. Jacobs would qualify for another $238,231 in debt according to policy. (Of course, that would only apply to residential debt. Repaid from entirely different sources.)

Fact overload. Lightning skipped right over my boss, and phoned Winthrop. In turn, Winthrop called a meeting with Mortie and I.

"Let Mark know we can't look at this *until* he gets the presales... something in excess of 40 docks."

Silence. (So much for golfing cronyism.) I at least had to ask... **"So we wouldn't offer a commitment *subject to*, perhaps, 80 - 90% presales?"**

"No. Let him get them first. Then we'll look at the deal."

(What have we been doing for a month and a half?) **"Okay, but had he a commitment for financing, he would be able to undertake some aggressive advertising, and move some dirt around to create interest."**

"No. Let him get the sales first. Then we'll look at the deal."

How to Obtain Business Loans

From Docks to Doctors

Sometimes pessimism, or rather, *pessimists*, wrap themselves up in policy... as, say, protesters do with the First Amendment. It is their shroud of almost-holy protection.

Dr. Arturous Nostraissaut, an Internist with a local practice of more than 15 years, had been a long-standing customer of the bank. He was extremely well thought of in the community. So much so, that when I moved to town, one of the first things Myron said to me (after "Be sure to cover your computer at night, I check for that.") was "Try Dr. No as your family physician." (He must be tried and true to gain Mindful Myron's endorsement.)

The doctor routinely maintained deposits in the $500,000-$700,000 range. He had a residential mortgage of slightly more than $800,000 and an outstanding equipment loan whose balance was inside $100,000.

With Myron's referrals drumming up so much business, Dr. No needed additional office space. He decided to build, rather than purchase or lease an existing facility.

Also one to be quite careful, the doctor liked to keep a lot of cash on hand. And I mean a lot. He requested the bank finance 100% of the cost to construct ($630,000), so he might maintain his existing deposit balances. (Battle stations, battle stations... good customer requests loan outside of policy. To the war room.)

I prepared a consort which recommended extending the all-inclusive amount necessary to bring about the proposed clinic. To me, Dr. No appeared to be an ideal candidate for sizable credit as his personal financial statement on the top of the next page shows.

A quick glance at his last three personal tax filings found him paying himself over $630,000 in wages each of the past three years. What's more, the PA itself looked very healthy. Even after paying such a huge salary, it posted modest profits and maintained good liquidity with a solid retained earnings position.

As you can see on the next page, a formal analysis of the doctor's cash flow for the past couple of years looked quite good.

Chapter Ten

Personal Financial Statement — Arturous Nostraissaut

ASSETS			LIABILITIES		
Cash	$	520,000	Residence Mortgage	$	809,329
Cash Value Ins.		169,265	Goodrich Mortgage		135,600
Vested Pension		642,548	Total Health Note Guar.		92,840
Def. Compensation		102,000	Total Debt	$	1,037,769
Walt Disney Stock		36,000			
Ready Cash	$	1,469,813	Estimated Tax Liability	$	546,000
PA Ownership		872,404			
% Bus. Interests		169,178			
Real Estate:					
Residence		1,440,000			
Lots		382,800			
Penn Circle		30,000			
Goodrich Bldg.		360,000			
Hancock Plains		7,670			
South Office Park		36,000			
Westwood Plaza		42,000			
Total Real Estate	$	2,298,470	Total Liabilities	$	1,583,769
TOTAL	$	4,809,865	**NET WORTH**	$	3,226,096

Personal Tax Filing Analysis — Arturous Nostraissaut

Wages	$ 642,000	$ 632,400
Interest Income	25,510	50,401
Business Income	30,983	87,635
Pensions and Annuities	2,514	2,720
Rents/Nonpassive Income	1,296	4,320
Passive Loss	(44,094)	(26,999)
Adding Back Noncash Expenses	3,024	1,440
Gross Income	$ 661,233	$ 751,917
Income Tax	(186,292)	(176,017)
Real Estate Taxes	(10,313)	(9,060)
Social Security/FICA	(3,825)	(3,825)
Net Income	$ 460,803	$ 563,015
Home Mortgage Interest	(16,200)	(65,093)
Principal Reduction in Mortgage	(0)	(21,509)
Other Interest	(27,147)	(0)
Cash Contributions	(0)	(12,642)
Consumer Debt	(9,000)	(9,000)
Total Debt Service	(52,347)	(108,244)
Cash Flow	$ 408,456	$ 454,771
Apparent Debt Ratio	11.4%	19.2%

How to Obtain Business Loans

Including the proposed obligation at 9.75% over 20 years yields the following figures:

Net Income	$ 460,803	$ 563,015
Existing Debt Service	(52,347)	(108,244)
This Loan	(71,708)	(71,708)
Total	(124,055)	(179,952)
Cash Flow	$ 336,748	$ 383,063
Apparent Debt Ratio	26.9%	32.0%

Great. I'm thinking this is truly a "no-brainer." Seasoned practice, good reputation, long-standing customer, cash resources almost equivalent to existing and proposed debts combined, along with ongoing cash flow to service all obligations at better than 3:1.

Not to mention the fact we'd be loaning him his own money to a certain extent, compensating balances totaling 34% of the aggregate anticipated obligations.

$$\$520,000/\$809,329 + \$92,840 + \$630,000$$

The retort from the local credit administrator was a no-brainer. After reading my consort, he penned a memorandum and circulated it to those in the approval chain. At the heart of his commentary was this nonsensical hyperbole:

> "I am concerned that with each incremental credit facility we extend to the good doctor, we are taking on a marginally disproportionate level of risk due to our inadherence to policy guidelines."

Which, I believe, meant:

> "You know, we have a policy exception here. And, hey guys, we started out lending Doc money against his home — which was okay — but then we made him a equipment loan — for gosh sakes — and now we're talking about 100% loan-to-cost on a commercial facility. Policy calls for a maximum of 80%, and... frankly... I'm worried about reprisal. "(Yikes.)

The remainder of the memo contained more of the same. **Never**

Chapter Ten

once was Dr. No's ability to repay the debt questioned. Only the conflict with policy was expounded upon. In the end, the memo declared:

> "Due to the excessive position the bank is asked to take, I cannot, in good conscience, support the request as presented. I recommend the account officer sell the borrower on putting 20-25% cash into the deal."

When instead I tried to sell internal folks on the credit quality of the loan, I received a "My hands are tied" response. Only President Winthrop offered any other input.

"Tell him we'll do up to 80% loan-to-value on his home, then lend him the rest of the money against the office."

Home Value	$ 1,440,000
80%	$ 1,152,000
Existing Debt	809,329
Availability	$ 342,671
Construction Costs	$ 630,000
Advance on Home	342,671
Office Loan	$ 287,329

"**Winthrop, I'm not very confident he'll agree to our gerrymandering. He's mentioned his intention to begin significantly reducing debt on his home. More conservatism, if you will. Moreover, what do we gain that's not available under a cross-default provision?**" (Covenant in loan docs providing for all bank loans of a borrower to be in default if <u>one</u> is. Remedy becomes available against all securitized^g assets. Typically used when the newest loan to be extended is at a reasonably high LTV, but earlier extensions are at lesser positions. The clause ties up any remaining equity in otherwise pledged holdings.)

"Collateral isn't necessarily the issue. We just can't be doing 100% of cost. You've got to make him understand. Anyway, lending to physicians is becoming inherently fraught with risk. Who knows what will transpire with health care reform on the horizon! Besides, he's not going to get a no-equity deal any place else."

How to Obtain Business Loans

"Actually, he is. The contractor involved, Newland-Oswell, is a good customer of Independent Savings (who falls under FDIC examination). Apparently, they shopped the deal there. They've already offered Dr. No 100% financing. The only reason we got a call was due to his loyalty to this institution."

(Pregnant pause. A hush, moving into dead quiet... quiet as a church. Shhhhh! Could've heard a pin drop. No noise.) Then finally, "Well, we will just have to lose the loan. Tell him we're just looking out for his best interests. With all the cash he has, it just doesn't make sense to borrow all that money. And if he's going to, he should spread more on his home to gain the deductibility of interest."

"Valid points, however, the doctor wants to do something else. And he, like most accomplished physicians, isn't entirely flexible once he makes up his mind."

"Addison, you can't just be an *order taker*. You've got to convince the customer what's right for the bank is in his best interests. We can't just disregard policy. Now can we?"

Even if it means letting an excellent customer, and outstanding credit risk, proceed directly to the next corner. Maybe for good.

Don't cloud the issue with facts. Just because you qualify for "x" amount of debt, doesn't mean you qualify for a loan in the amount of "x." No sir. The bank may have to spread things around a bit in order to feel warm and fuzzy.

Happened to me from the other end of the stick, a while back. I was looking to finance the purchase of a used Lexus 250. And I didn't want to put any money down. I called *my* bank and laid out the request. (Officers, where I was employed, being unable to obtain personal credit, other than home mortgages.)

"Mr. Parker, we wouldn't be able to do 100% financing for you. You see, we need to have some equity in the purchase in order to create a cushion... so... in the unlikely event... we had to repossess the vehicle... we could readily sell it... and retire any outstanding balance."

"Yes, believe me, I understand. But I have two unsecured credit lines with your bank. One for $8,000, and the other for $6,000. If you'll check, you'll see they've been handled perfectly. (Momen-

Chapter Ten

tarily forgetting track record doesn't mean squat.) **Just reduce the availability on one of the lines, and finance 100% of the car."**

"We can't do that, it's against policy."

"You understand I can simply write a convenience check (drawing on the line) **for my 'equity' and have you loan me the balance in a conventional car loan."**

"Yes sir, that's your prerogative."

Just don't cloud the issue.

Chapter Eleven

CHAPTER 11:

WHAT'S *ADJUDICATING*?

    Mildren Connelly was depressed. *This is a nasty business,* he thought to himself. *A nasty business, indeed.* He stood gazing through the dirt-smeared window on the 30th floor of Commerce National Bank's office tower.
    Mildren felt he was a good worker, meticulous in his efforts to be as error free as possible. He'd handled the day-to-day drudgery of his job, with few complaints, for over 15 years now. And without a word of thanks from the endless number of people who benefitted from his attention to detail. They expected him only to do that for which he was paid. He knew their minds. "Just do your job," they seemed to say when looking at him, "Just do your job."
    His superiors were much the same. "Mind your work Mildren. One mistake could be your last!" What a wonderful work environment.

How to Obtain Business Loans

But what else could he do? His supervisor had often said as much to him, "You've been doing this so long, Mildren, I'm not sure you're qualified to move into a different profession. It's a question of how well the skills transfer."

*And the money. Oh the money. Each year a pittance of a raise, **if he was lucky**. Maybe 3 or 4 percent, at the most. Barely enough to keep pace with the cost of living. Heck, if inflation were to heat up, he'd lose ground in a hurry. "How in the world was he going to put two kids through college?" he asked himself without an answer.*

Mildren became awash with despondency. There was an air of finality to it all. Only one thing to do. Only one path to take. He'd thought about it for a long time. Now was the moment. The money he'd pumped into that insurance policy over the years would finally pay off.

Overcome with emotion, Mildren slowly opened the window and in one swift move... leapt through. It was a sheer drop outside the building all the way to the concrete pavement... 30 floors below.

Miraculously he landed completely uninjured. And how, you might ask, did this happen? Mildren Connelly was a high-rise window washer. Sick and tired of his career, he opened the window and stepped in to the 30th floor. He then proceeded directly to his insurance agent to cash in his whole life policy and start his own business.

Sometimes, the place from which you view something causes you to see it altogether differently from someone with another vantage point. Which is why bankers tend to lend in areas where they feel they have some expertise... in industries they are familiar with. Where they don't believe they're on the outside looking in.

Can You See Alright?

Anything blocking your view? Everyone comfortable? Let's see... popcorn, Junior Mints, Milk Duds, licorice, and a gallon and a half of Pepsi. Okay, looks like we're all set. Roll 'em!

Americans know what we like *with* our films. Concession stands have offered the same "health foods" for as long as anyone can remember. It's *where we watch* the show that's changed over time.

Chapter Eleven

Hollywood still puts out good stuff (aside from an occasional *Hudson Hawk* or *Last Action Hero*), but with matinee prices edging towards $5 and refreshments **never** so reasonable, more people are waiting for the video. Besides, who wants to hear some old guy behind you narrate every scene to his wife?

Today, the video rental business is estimated to be an $11-12 billion industry. Over 25,000 mom-and-pop stores, and a few national chains, market **an inventory that keeps coming back**. As a result, unlike most retail operations, margins are quite high. It's not unusual for an outlet, after an initial investment in inventory, to operate with a 90-95% gross margin, and a 40-50% rate of profit after expenses. Try that, selling a product which doesn't have the boomerang trait. Although stores have come on line quickly, demand has outstripped supply. Seventy-five percent of American households now contain VCRs!

At first glance, one would think the industry had a bright future... unless your view was obstructed. Mine was blocked when trying to get a $1.2 million line of credit for the acquisition of three video stores and their respective inventories.

In March of 1992, Hercule Enright and Porter Stanwick had approached the bank with a request. They had learned, through personal contacts, that one of the national chains had decided to sell off its corporately owned outlets. So Messrs. Enright and Stanwick wasted no time. They negotiated an agreement for purchase before the plan was made public.

The following arrangement was agreed upon in principle, pending financing:

(1) Manatee Video Corp. (our proposed borrower), to acquire 3 strategically located stores. Each was operated from leased space, so the seller would assign all rights, and obtain the applicable landlord consents.

(2) The shops would continue to operate under the chain's name, as if franchises, allowing them to benefit from mass advertising campaigns. However, after the first fiscal year of transferred control, no portion of receipts would be due the seller.

(3) An agreement not to compete would be executed.

(4) Additionally, the chain would supply significant procedural support...

How to Obtain Business Loans

      (A) Staff at each location would be retained, including currently assigned store management.
      (B) An inventory control and budgeting computer from company headquarters would be included.
      (C) And, a senior person from within the chain would become the chief operating officer of MVC.

(5) The complete inventories of all 3 stores would go with the purchase. To include not only tapes, but video equipment, computer hardware and software, office furniture, antitheft devices, and leasehold improvements.

(6) Further, the agreement would make available another 12,000 tapes at vastly reduced cost. And thereafter would allow MVC to buy through the chain at similar volume discounts.

The financial terms called for purchase monies to flow to the seller on a staggered basis, according to operating results.

(7) At closing (anticipated to be sometime in May), MVC would pay an initial $1,080,000, plus another $60,000 towards the 12,000 tapes to be acquired.

(8) One month after the company's fiscal year end (8/31/92), MVC would remit $1.20 for every $1 above $1,500,000 in sales the three stores obtained in aggregate for the year just ended.

(9) Then, no later than the end of the first quarter following the next full year of operation, MVC would pay $0.60 for each $1 of combined revenues in excess of $1,200,000. Along with $48,000 for the balance of the 12,000 tapes.

    Fairly conservative projections were provided, indicating the stores should enjoy quite prosperous future operation. Assuming those in the approval process would largely disregard the information as too *optimistic*, I focused, instead, on historical data.
    From 8/31/89 - 8/31/90, only two of the outlets were in existence. On total revenues of $1,431,851 they achieved a net profit of $784,199. That's a margin of 55%! Even after including additional

Chapter Eleven

tape purchases of $387,459 the margin remains 28%. Not bad for ongoing cash on sales.

Last year (8/31/90 - 8/31/91), the three stores aggregated operations looked like this:

Revenues:		
Rentals	$1,728,518	
Sales	212,976	
Total Revenues	$1,941,494	
Cost of Sales	(102,382)	
Gross Income	$1,839,112	
Expenses:		
Advertising	(39,253)	
Salaries	(300,811)	
Benefits and Taxes	(29,596)	
Rent & CAM	(248,686)	
Utilities	(64,974)	
Other	(159,361)	
Total Expenses	(842,681)	
Operating Income	$ 996,431	51.3%
Tape Purchases	(339,664)	
Cash Flow	$ 656,767	33.8%

The figures clearly demonstrate that the new outlet came on line with profitability ratios in the same range as the existing shops. Using these numbers, the purchase figures would shake out as follows:

$ 1,080,000	Initial outlay.
60,000	Portion of the 12,000 tapes to be purchased.
529,793	$1.20 for every $1 above $1,500,000 in combined revenues attained for the fiscal year just ending.
444,896	$0.60 for every $1 of gross receipts in excess of $1,200,000 during the next fiscal year of independent operation. (using most recent year receipts for budgeting)
48,000	Balance of the 12,000 tapes.
$ 2,162,689	Total Acquisition Costs

However, these amounts are drawn from operating results from FYE 8/31/91. FYE 8/31/92's income statement is expected to show

How to Obtain Business Loans

an increase in both rental and sales revenues. Which would be in line with national averages showing:

- Due to a decrease in their prices, tape sales are increasing quickly as a percentage of total receipts. At a rate of 14% annually, to be specific.

- Rentals have also continued to escalate. About 2% per annum.

Given the fact year-to-date totals for FYE '92 approximate these trends very closely, in all likelihood, the final resolution of the purchase will approach:

$ 1,080,000	Initial outlay	
60,000	Portion of the 12,000 tapes to be purchased.	
529,793	$1.20 for every $1 above $1,500,000 in combined revenues attained for the fiscal year ending 8/31/92.	
483,529	$0.60 for every $1 of gross receipts in excess of $1,200,000 during the next fiscal year of independent operation.	
	$1,728,518 + 2% =	$ 1,763,088
	212,976 + 14% =	242,793
	Total Sales	$ 2,005,881
48,000	Balance of the 12,000 tapes.	
$ 2,201,322	Total Acquisition Costs	

Based upon even the newest of stores immediate operation at sales levels and profit margins identical to industry standards, estimates for ensuing years can be extrapolated easily... and with a high degree of validity.

In actuality, I provided senior management with memoranda detailing a month-by-month cash flow inclusive of tape purchases and line balances (whose seasonality required a maximum funding of $1.2 million). Attempting to be less tedious, I've here furnished only annualized cash flows and line balances. (Tape purchases are purposely budgeted on the high side.)

Chapter Eleven

	Year 1 FYE 8/93	Year 2 FYE 8/94	Year 3 FYE 8/95	Year 4 FYE 8/96
Revenues:				
Rentals	$1,763,088	$1,798,350	$1,834,317	$1,871,003
Sales	242,793	276,784	315,534	359,709
Total Revenues	$2,005,881	$2,075,134	$2,149,851	$2,230,712
Cost of Sales	(116,980)	(133,357)	(152,027)	(173,311)
Gross Income	$1,888,901	$1,941,777	$1,997,824	$2,057,401
Expenses:				
Advertising	(40,118)	(41,503)	(42,997)	(44,614)
Salaries	(310,912)	(321,646)	(333,227)	(345,760)
Benefits & Taxes	(30,088)	(31,127)	(32,248)	(33,461)
Rent & CAM	(256,753)	(265,617)	(275,181)	(285,531)
Utilities	(66,194)	(68,479)	(70,945)	(73,614)
Other	(164,482)	(170,161)	(176,288)	(182,918)
Total Expenses	(868,547)	(898,533)	(930,886)	(965,898)
Operating Income	$1,020,354	$1,043,244	$1,066,938	$1,091,503

YEAR ONE:

Acquisition Costs		Cash Flow	
$ 1,080,000	Initial outlay	$ 1,020,354	Operating Profit
60,000	Tapes @ discount	(435,000)	Tape purchases
529,793	% of Op. Revenues	$ 585,354	
$ 1,669,793	Total 1st yr.		
(585,354)	Funded via operations		
$ 1,084,439	Balance unfunded		

YEAR TWO:

$ 483,529	% of Op. Revenues	$ 1,043,244	Operating Profit
48,000	Bal. of tapes	(435,000)	Tape purchases
$ 531,529	Total 2nd yr.	$ 608,244	
1,084,439	Balance forward		
$ 1,615,968			
(608,244)	Funded via operations		
$ 1,007,724	Balance unfunded		

YEAR THREE:

$ 1,007,724	Balance forward	$ 1,066,938	Operating Profit
(631,938)	Funded via ops.	(435,000)	Tape purchases
$ 375,786	Balance forward	$ 631,938	

YEAR FOUR:

$ 375,786	Balance forward	$ 1,091,503	Operating Profit
(656,502)	Fundable via ops.	(435,000)	Tape purchases
— Acquisition cost retired —		$ 656,503	

How to Obtain Business Loans

Although the analysis (semi-concisely) illustrates MVC's routine retirement of the line from normal operations, blood befell the waters when "YEAR FOUR" was spotted on the summary.

"Addison, policy calls for loans of this type to be repaid within 3 years."

"I understand. Keep in mind that the applicant has requested 80/20s funding, which is acceptable according to policy, but I've presented the package based upon a 75/25 arrangement... in the interests of being conservative. So of the $1,140,000 up front, $285,000 will come straight from the guarantor's pockets.

"Whereas the cash flows *do not* fund any profit to the owners until the fourth year, they *do* allow for the $285,000 to be repaid prior to that, via operating profits after tape purchases. Only if this money were left in the company would a 3 year repayment be realistic.

"Messrs. Enright and Stanwick have requested 4 years, with an option for a 5th, as much for caution's sake as to allow the return of initial capital. If profitable operations permit, the latter seems more than reasonable given their complete willingness to have all other profits either reduce debt or be retained by the company. Especially over such an extended period."

"Addison... 3 years will be the maximum this institution considers. They'll just have to leave the money in." (No obstruction there.)

(Ding. Round 1 over.) I returned to the applicants to convey the shortened term decree. The tone of discussions with senior management, and Lightning, had me contemplating the probability of this request following the road of slow and arduous death. Many times, when bankers just don't like a credit, but have no specific reason for rejecting it, they'll nick away until the would-be borrower either bleeds to death or simply goes elsewhere. Then they exclaim, "Oh darn, I thought we were close to making this a do-able deal." When, in reality, they're tickled the matter has been removed from their dust-covered desks. MVC's proposal had the look of one destined to die in committee, a filibuster of questions, amendments, and caveats eventually draining the life from it. (Sigh.) I still have to play out the drama. It's my job. Besides... there's always an outside chance...

Going Through The Motions

I discussed chopping the repayment term with Mr. Enright.

Chapter Eleven

Surprisingly, though certainly not overjoyed, he took the news in stride. "You're really forcing the play here. Not only do I receive little to no return on investment for over 3 years, I don't even receive my capital back. Nevertheless, let's continue seeking an approval. My income down the line will justify the lack of monies received early on. This thing is going to be a cash-cow for **many** a year."

(The impediment cleared, I returned to the fight. Ding, Ding, Round 2.) "Addison, the problem as we see it, is that even under the optimistic analysis provided, there will be some shortfall at the end of year 3."

"Well, right... about $375,000, which is a result of reducing a 4 or 5 year deal into 3 to satisfy policy."

"Policy is set for the safety of this institution and its depositors. If requests don't meet our high standards, we move on. Now... you're admitting under the rosiest of assumptions the debt cannot be fully retired in 3 years. What happens if things don't go that well? "

"**I'm not sure the analysis uses the rosiest of assumptions. The figures are right in line with historical numbers and current industry trends, giving them a strong basis for reliability. Obviously, as with any business, unknowns could effect the course of operations. In this instance, given the percentage of revenue clauses, the effect would be a lower overall purchase price.**"

"You're assuming margins remain absolutely constant though. What if they erode as well?"

"**... That would seem highly improbable. Throughout the industry, outlets operate at fairly consistent ratios. I suppose salary expense might be the one item capable of varying somewhat significantly from store to store. But, in this situation, staff is already in place... and staying put. With the exception of the new COO.**"

"Right. Exactly. And your analysis does not account for the addition of his salary!"

(What glory there seems to be in finding a chink in the armor of one presenting a deal *the bank* is less than enthusiastic about.) "**True enough. I only recently learned of his coming onboard. But, we're only talking a $75,000 - $100,000 difference here. I'm not sure it's material... at least not to the extent of drastically changing the prospects of timely remittance.**

Remember, I've budgeted for annual tape purchases to be $435,000, when historically they've been between $340,000 and

How to Obtain Business Loans

$385,000. On average there's another $72,500 right there. Further, a good portion of the COO's compensation will be incentive based. Almost 25% of it. So if MVC's not prospering, those monies won't leave our vault... where they'll be on deposit along with the guarantor's funds and those of many employees. I thought I'd get their payroll set up on direct deposit!"

"I'd still like to see the numbers if sales fall off."

"**Are you speaking of *tape sales* or total revenues?**" (Okay, so line officers like to take pokes at senior management too. The whole process is truly combative.)

(Read this really loud.) "TOTAL REVENUES!!!!!"

(Ding. End of Round 2. Back to my corner... my tiny corner... office to prepare another analysis.) Consorting...

- Although revenues are expected to increase between 3.3 - 3.9% annually over the next five years, this analysis assumes a 4% drop from 8/31/92's anticipated FYE totals. Making budgeted receipts upwards of 8% less per annum than in the previously submitted analysis.

- A 3.5% increase is added to anticipated FYE expense categories... including salaries.

- Salaries are then further increased by $75,000 to reflect the COO's base compensation.

- And tape purchases, given the preceding changes in direct accounting, are assumed to run at their recent average of $362,500. This is appropriate since no additional cushion is necessary based upon the line item budgeting methods imposed, and with the realization that if sales are down, less tapes could be purchased.

Total Revenues		$ 1,863,834
Cost of Sales		(108,756)
Gross Income		$ 1,755,078
Expenses:		
	Salaries	(385,912)
	All Other	(576,887)
Total Expenses		(962,799)
Operating Income		$ 792,279

Chapter Eleven

YEAR ONE:

Acquisition Costs		Cash Flow		
$ 1,080,000	Initial outlay	$ 792,279		Operating Profit
60,000	Tapes @ discount	(362,500)		Tape purchases
529,793	% of Op. Revenues	$ 429,779		
$ 1,669,793	Total 1st yr.			
(429,779)	Funded via operations			
$ 1,240,014	Balance unfunded			

YEAR TWO:

$ 398,030	% of Op. Revenues	$ 792,279		Operating Profit
48,000	Bal. of tapes	(362,500)		Tape purchases
$ 446,030	Total 2nd yr.	$ 429,779		
1,240,014	Balance forward			
$ 1,686,044				
(429,779)	Funded via operations			
$ 1,256,265	Balance unfunded			

YEAR THREE:

$ 1,256,265	Balance forward	$ 792,279		Operating Profit
(429,779)	Funded via ops.	(362,500)		Tape purchases
$ 826,486	Balance forward	$ 429,779		

YEAR FOUR:

$ 826,486	Balance forward	$ 792,279		Operating Profit
(429,779)	Fundable via ops.	(362,500)		Tape purchases
$ 396,707	Balance forward	$ 429,779		

YEAR FIVE:

$ 396,707	Balance forward	$ 792,279		Operating Profit
(429,779)	Fundable via ops.	(362,500)		Tape purchases
— DEBT RETIRED —		$ 429,779		

Which brings us back to the customer's request. Four years with the option for five... if things turn really sour.

"Addison, I think what this scenario is telling us, is we better have deep pocket guarantors." (Ding. Round 3.)

"We do. I included personal financial statements and cash flow summaries in the initial memorandum. Here's another copy for everyone. Mr. Stanwick's information is included on page 15."

How to Obtain Business Loans

ASSETS:	
Cash	$ 31,292
Marketable Securities	13,800
Accounts Receivable	6,900
Partnership Investments	102,340
Residence	327,600
Income Producing Property	87,600
Personal Property	42,000
TOTAL ASSETS	$ 611,632
LIABILITIES:	
Miscellaneous Accounts Payable	1,020
Home Mortgage	203,760
Mortgage on Income Property	63,720
TOTAL LIABILITIES	$ 268,500
NET WORTH:	$ 343,132

"He's a real estate broker by trade, and has set that portion of his affairs up as a PA. Both PA and personal tax filings are included as addendums. His combining cash flow is accurately recounted on page 21."

	1990	1991
Commissions	$ 135,084	$ 163,800
Rental Income	0	11,520
Other	5,945	5,100
Total Income	$ 141,029	$ 180,420
Home Mortgage	(24,369)	(23,659)
Inc. Property Mtge.	(0)	(9,245)
Auto Lease	(6,422)	(6,422)
Taxes	(39,861)	(32,515)
Total Expenses	(70,652)	(71,841)
Net Cash Flow	$ 70,377	$ 108,579

"Which indicates his average net ratio for the past two years was 44%. That'd be 22% on a gross, or FANNIE MAE, basis... and his average cash flow after all expenses is almost $90,000 per year."

(Condescendingly) "Mr. Stanwick does fine for himself, but I

Chapter Eleven

wouldn't say he's capable of supporting the type of facility requested."

"No... but Mr. Enright, and his wife, who will also guarantee, *are* capable... Turn to page 24 of the same memorandum to review their joint financial statement. It runs through page 44, but the summary is on page 24."

ASSETS	
Cash	$ 399,098
Marketable Securities	203,640
Retirement Plan Monies	371,520
Trust Funds	360,000
Common Stock — Camelot Cable	46,600,424
Common Stock — GoGraphics, Inc.	1,288,560
Common Stock — AlaComm, Inc.	1,111,020
Common Stock — Vontel Ltd.	885,240
Common Stock — Fleet Development	377,520
Common Stock — Admin. Mgmt. Co.	48,000
Common Stock — Macy Enright, Inc.	360,000
Partnership Interests	793,080
Personal Real Estate	9,161,640
Aircraft, Yachts, Autos,	792,720
Art, Jewelry	1,092,000
Personal Property	179,880
TOTAL ASSETS	$ 64,024,342
LIABILITIES	
Mortgages Payable	$ 2,704,680
Note Payable — Camelot Cable	2,856,960
Line of Credit — Bank of The Hudson	986,880
Line of Credit — First National	3,360,000
Income Taxes Payable	180,000
Other Accrued Expenses	6,000
TOTAL LIABILITIES	$ 10,094,520
NET WORTH	$ 53,929,822

"Well now, this certainly is a large disclosure... fairly illiquid though... only $600,000 readily available. Hmmm... looks like most of their net worth is tied up in real estate and this Camelot Cable. Is that a publicly traded company?"

How to Obtain Business Loans

"No, and in point of fact, neither are the other stocks listed... the real estate is basically comprised of the Enright's three homes. Summer, winter, and vacation, if you will."

(Glibly.) "So what we've got ourselves is a giant statement with potentially very little behind it."

"I think it's... impractical... to whittle down a $54 million net worth so hastily. Particularly given the strength of Camelot. We're not talking about a corner merchant here. Camelot Cable has total assets in excess of our bank's. These are people of means.

Besides, if they didn't have their monies employed, we'd be suggesting they were unsophisticated... and decline the request based upon poor funds management. If you'll review their cash flow... on page 50... you'll see they are, indeed, enjoying a significant return on their investments... "

	ACTUAL 1990	ACTUAL 1991	ESTIMATED 1992
INCOME:			
Salary	$ 240,000	$ 248,022	$ 248,400
Consulting Fees	216,000	547,320	547,320
Interest	21,936	75,560	75,600
Corporate Dividends	1,427,468	2,061,427	2,060,400
Partnership Income	278,244	144,094	90,000
Trust Income	11,836	12,391	12,480
Tax Refunds	443,916	1,978	0
Total Income	$2,639,400	$3,090,792	$3,034,200
EXPENSES:			
Income Taxes	$ 407,594	$ 320,727	$ 559,440
Property Taxes	37,646	52,272	53,880
Mortgage Payments	192,098	234,992	236,880
Insurance Premiums	12,946	27,136	27,840
Other Personal Exp.	358,276	180,468	138,000
Total Expenses	$1,008,560	$ 815,595	$1,016,040
Cash Flow	$1,630,840	$2,275,197	$2,018,160

"*Specifically*... what does Camelot do, anyway?"

"They have very diverse holdings... it's a $350 million concern... but they are primarily engaged in the supply of cable TV

Chapter Eleven

systems, and cellular communications... telephones, pagers. They do exceptionally well. Mrs. Enright's father founded the company. She controls 20%, and her four siblings hold the balance of stock equally."

"How much of the Enright's income is derived from Camelot?"

"Again, let's review the cash flows on page 50. I've included accountant prepared recaps for the past two years, along with projections for this year. Of the corporate dividends listed, about 45-50% come from Camelot Cable."

"Addison, that being the case, I'd say *we've* really got to review the company thoroughly. And, I've gotta tell you, I don't feel comfortable going any farther until we do so." (Hear! Hear! Such a daring, proactive, stance.)

(Round 4. Looks like this one's headed for 15. I should be pacing myself better.) Mr. Enright reluctantly allowed me detailed information on what **was** a fairly private family company. Boy did he allow me information! He inundated me. Given the level of expertise within our credit department and the pace it moved at, I didn't think we'd be able to decipher the statements over the requested five-year term. Sure enough, we gave it a shot for a few weeks... and couldn't.

"Addison, I'm still not ready to move forward in our discussion of the credit without a better understanding of the cable company's operation. Our own analysis inconclusive, I'm not sure where we're left." (Fishing for a "no mas.")

"I've spoken with Mr. Enright in anticipation of this eventuality. (Jab.) **He has graciously offered to have MacKenzie Lawford, the company's Treasurer, fly down and respond to everyone's questions in a group forum."**

(Loud again.) "NO!" (Regaining composure.) "I'm not confident we'd benefit from that. Ummm... meet with him alone until you have a thorough understanding of the ins and outs. We'll then... reconvene for your report." (Hear, hear.)

"Wouldn't it be easier to allow Mr. Lawford the opportunity to answer your questions directly? I certainly can't anticipate all you would inquire about."

(Louder.) "WE'RE NOT GOING TO GET INTO ALL THAT..." (Regaining composure, again.) "That's your role as a line lender." (And also as a safety buffer.)

(End Round 4. Back to my corner. I think I'm cut.) Mr. Lawford flew in to meet with me one-on-one. "I'm a little disappointed the

How to Obtain Business Loans

bank's approval contingent couldn't find time to meet with me. You know, the Enright's are now spending most of their time here and are relocating both personal and business accounts to the area. I would think gaining their business would be a high priority for any bank with such an opportunity."

"Of course it is, and we truly appreciate your taking the time out of your busy schedule to help us make it happen. I apologize for senior management's absence. If possible, they'd be here (Fib.)... **we're just involved in preparing for a visit from the auditors** (1/2 fib, we always were.)... **and their time is very internally focused right now.**" (Not a fib.)

Over the next hour-and-a-half, MacKenzie Lawford cordially explained, in as much detail as possible, financial statements it took a Big 8^g months to compile and audit. It was a whirlwind delivery of a ton of information, but I took as copious notes as possible... and reported back the following day. (Ding. Round 5.)

"Highly summarized balance sheets are included before you."

	12/31/90	12/31/91
CURRENT ASSETS:		
Cash	$ 10,225,427	$ 1,628,136
Accounts Receivable	15,702,281	18,774,223
Inventory	3,021,744	3,806,066
Other	3,873,886	3,149,122
TOTAL CURRENT	$ 32,823,338	$ 27,357,547
PROPERTY, PLANT & EQUIPMENT:		
Raw Land	$ 4,960,360	$ 5,038,627
Buildings	15,369,415	23,642,022
Leases	7,438,985	1,440,000
Equipment	181,387,547	199,211,628
	$209,156,307	$229,332,277
Less: Accum. Depr.	(87,689,562)	(105,693,843)
NET PROPERTY, PLANT & EQUIPMENT	$121,466,745	$123,638,434
OTHER:		
Noncurrent Receivables	$ 14,584,183	$ 16,400,954
Broadcast Rights	56,733,856	40,339,074
Licenses, Network Affiliations	115,109,815	111,682,144
Goodwill, Other Intangible	16,817,846	20,014,427
TOTAL OTHER	$203,245,700	$188,436,599
TOTAL ASSETS	$357,535,783	$339,432,580

Chapter Eleven

CURRENT LIABILITIES:		
Accounts Payable	$ 20,550,198	$ 24,393,474
Current Portion Term Debt	3,008,826	4,192,292
Deferred Income	5,666,242	6,298,261
TOTAL CURRENT	$ 29,225,266	$ 34,884,027
NONCURRENT LIABILITIES:		
Leases Payable	$ 1,556,146	$ 1,561,860
Long Term Debt	357,326,124	394,788,143
Minority Interests	6,530,727	7,435,210
Pension Fundings	2,818,778	3,293,642
TOTAL NONCURRENT	$368,231,775	$407,078,855
TOTAL LIABILITIES	$397,457,041	$441,962,882
EQUITY:		
Class A Voting Stock	$ 325	$ 325
Class B Nonvoting	846	846
RETAINED EARNINGS	(39,920,087)	(102,529,131)

"My word, Addison... you've been talking about company strength, company strength... they've a huge deficit retained earnings position... and have had cash reserves fall about $9 million in the last year! I'm not at all sure this is something we want to get involved with."

"When presenting a credit whose borrower has a sizable cash position, we always say one can't put much stock in such because a balance sheet is just a snapshot. Let's remember that here.

"At year end 1990, Cash and Accounts Receivable totaled about $26 million; this past year $20.5 million. The difference, at first glance, seems enormous... but it's less than 2% of average total assets over the period. Hopefully, that adds some point of reference. We're just not used to looking at statements of this breadth."

"But look at that retained earnings position, and the difference from '90 to '91. They must've had a horrendous year!"

"I wouldn't say so, look at their income summaries."

	1990	1991
DIVISION:		
Cable Operations:		
Revenues	$ 60,220,378	$ 64,946,239
Expenses	(33,621,096)	(37,275,199)
Gross Profit	$ 26,599,282	$ 27,671,040

(summary continued on next page)

How to Obtain Business Loans

Broadcast Operations:		
Revenues	$ 39,205,282	$ 35,326,369
Expenses	(26,809,304)	(24,437,798)
Gross Profit	$ 12,395,978	$ 10,888,571
Cellular/Paging Operations:		
Revenues	$ 20,724,392	$ 25,252,864
Expenses	(16,294,524)	(17,922,674)
Gross Profit	$ 4,429,868	$ 7,330,190
TOTAL GROSS OPERATING PROFIT	$ 43,425,128	$ 45,889,801
Operational Expenses	(7,698,794)	(6,874,046)
Interest/Inv. Income	3,293,550	3,614,514
	(4,405,244)	(3,259,532)
OPERATIONAL CASH FLOW	$ 39,019,884	$ 42,630,269
Depr./Amortization	(48,107,045)	(51,610,722)
Interest Expense	(43,834,728)	(51,351,050)
NET	(52,921,889)	(60,331,503)

"The company posts strong operating profits..."

"Yes... but, Addison, they aren't sufficient enough to carry interest expense. It appears that was accomplished last year via the depletion of cash reserves and the increase of term debt. Which, in the absence of a future funding solution, means BK^g."

(In less than 3 minutes, we had a $350 million concern going bankrupt without the benefit of any knowledge of its *specific* operation.) **"They have the means to continue successfully. Spending time with Mr. Lawford allowed me to understand their methods."** (Jab.)

"How in the world did they pay dividends to the owners?"

"Well..."

"They appear insolvent."

"If I could just have a moment. These are complicated statements, which is why I hoped Mr. Lawford would be granted an audience. (Right lead.) **I'll try to accurately relay the information he bestowed upon me.**

Chapter Eleven

"Let's start with the cable division. About 1 1/2 years ago, the stockholders began trying to sell off this segment of the company. However, there was somewhat of a depressed market at the time, and a suitable price could not be procured. As I understand it, the early '80s had cable operations selling for around $3,000 per subscriber, versus $2,000 most recently. The expectation is for a seller's market to return, and liquidation to take place within the 12 to 18 months... FOR APPROXIMATELY $3.6 BILLION!! The reason the balance sheet looks so poor is the value of the division is stated at cost... about $95 million. (Strong left to the body, knocking the wind from 'em.)

"As for the broadcast group, there are two TV stations in Illinois and one in Texas, along with radio stations scattered across the South. A large portion of this segment's cash flow goes to retire debt to other family members. What's more, it is the area which has perennially provided dividends from the sale of stations. Which, I might add, take place well in excess of their reported costs shown on the balance sheet. Broadcast concerns trade at what's known as "stick value," a multiple of 8-10 times gross revenues... making this division worth more than $310 million! (A right to the head. Lightning Lou looks out on his feet. I wade in, fearing little retaliation.)

"Moving on to the cellular division. Here heavy start-up costs skew the overall cash flows, and explain the growth of long-term debt. Apparently, the Federal Communications Commission sells purchase rights on a lottery basis. Which gives you an idea of the demand for air slots. More suitors than ladies-in-waiting. Recently, Camelot won two drawings and had to shell out for purchases in Georgia and Arizona. About $84 million in debt is associated with these acquisitions. Rest assured, down the line they'll resell for much more." (What a flurry. One eye's beginning to swell shut.)

"But, Addison, you're saying the only real method of continuing to pay dividends is the sale of capital assets. How can you be confident this will continue?"

(What resiliency.) "One: There's a track record before you. Refer to the detailed financials on pages 34-41 of your newest memorandum. Dividends over the last two years were generated from the sale of assets. Last year it was a radio station, and a commercial office facility.

How to Obtain Business Loans

"Two: There are pending sales on the table. A paging company in Sante Fe for $4.5 million... with no associated debt, a cellular company in South Carolina for $3.5 million without encumbrances, and a paging firm in Alabama for about $1 million... also free-and-clear.

"Three: Due to the huge differences between asset and market values, there is ample latitude with which to sell off resources." (Ding. Big round for me. Huge. "Gonna fly now...")

An indeterminable period of silence followed. (Sensing the kill, I did not return to my corner. Ding, Ding. Round 6.) Finally, Lightning spit out his mouthpiece and said, "Perhaps if we had consolidating^g statements from all the divisions we could better understand the consolidated^g statements presented."

(Blow after blow shaken off with no effect. Unbelievable. An iron jaw.) **"Lou, those statements are not going to add anything meaningful. They're just divisions of the aggregated totals. The balance sheet will still be undervalued, and still be the source of future dividends."**

"Alright, well... get them anyway just so we have them."

Then Winthrop added, "Even if, giving them the benefit of the doubt, we assume capital sales going forward, I have further concerns related to the unknowns of how the Enright's value their ownership." (Short round, not much action, but I was dazed as I slumped onto my stool.)

(Ding. Round 7.) **"Here's a recap of ownership derivation..."**

CAMELOT STOCK VALUATION AS OF 12/31/91

LOCATION	PROPERTY	VALUES (at cost or contract price)
Sante Fe	Paging Plus	$ 4,536,000
Columbus	Azalea Cellular	3,528,000
Jacksonville	Gamecock Paging	902,200
Phoenix	Arizona Paging	173,433,600
Atlanta	Paging & Radios	1,944,000
Chicago	WXTO-TV	27,720,000
Springfield	WNOK-TV	12,810,000
Dallas	WGSV-TV	37,590,000
Pt. Charlotte	WBCU-FM	5,793,600
Knoxville	WPTU-AM	2,400,000
Little Rock	WKCW-FM	11,508,000

Chapter Eleven

Birmingham	Cellular Today	12,069,600
Miami	Camelot Cablevision	228,552,000
Pensacola	Camelot Cablevision	13,350,000
Charleston	Camelot Cablevision	26,952,000
Memphis	Camelot Cablevision	40,215,600
Orlando	Camelot Cablevision	71,660,400
Total		$ 674,965,000
Associated Debt		(441,962,882)
Value		$ 233,002,118
20%		$ 46,600,424

"Hmm... under whatever estimate of worth, I question what collateral value we add by accepting a share hypothecation."

"...Who said anything about a stock pledge? The Enright's have never offered... "

"Right, right. But we're driving the boat here. I think it's probably necessary under the circumstances."

"I don't think they'll agree. It's more likely Camelot would borrow the money and then loan it to them individually."

"Uh-huh, let's just suppose... for purposes of dialogue... the Enright's *will* agree. With it being a closely held company, how salable is the stock? I wonder how expeditiously the bank could liquidate its interest. If a market for the shares does exist, I doubt it is at the lofty level estimated."

"I would disagree. Again, most of the assets are worth some multiple of the cost basis they are reported at. I mean, some are of such great demand... lotteries are held for the right to purchase them."

"Um-hmm, but in the event a default occurs and we are unable to liquidate our collateral, the bank would *de facto* become a part owner of the corporation. To my knowledge, this would be a breach of federal banking laws."

(*De facto*? Who in the heck talks like that? Speaking of conjuring up problems... now we're concerned about liquidating collateral *not being offered*. Anything not to make a decision.) **"I think this line of discussion is irrelevant. We may as well discuss the enforceability of a second mortgage on their Colorado vacation home! We're not being offered that either... and it's equally unlikely they'd agree to."** (Overboard. Frustration starting to show. My opponent senses the kill now, will move in next round.)

How to Obtain Business Loans

(Ding. Round 8.) "Alright, if you wish to be so pointed, *we're* not altogether comfortable with the video industry either. (Nahhhh, so there.) The advent of new technology may render videotapes obsolete in the not too distant future."

Winthrop joined in: "I've heard local cable companies might soon put miniature satellite dishes on homes... in a move to charge for extended channel availability."

"I must admit, I'm not thoroughly versed on those details, but if they were true... Camelot would benefit many fold, offsetting any downturn in MVC's operation. I'd liken our position to an option straddle in the stock market. On the one hand, we'd be expecting the video operation to continue its blossoming course; but should it fail, we're hedged by a boon in the guarantor's primary holding. It would seem the best of circumstances for the bank."

"I'm not sure it's so cut and dried. *Let's* look into those satellite mounts." (Ding. I should've trained harder.)

(After some quick corner instruction. Round 9.) "In the municipalities where the outlets are located, zoning ordinances do not allow antennae — which the dishes qualify as — on top of residences, nor on pole mounts astride homes. The type of small, less costly, units we're speaking of... have to be mounted high above ground in order to function properly. So I'd say this is not an area of concern."

"Unless zoning changes to accommodate the technology."

"We live in communities which spend more to landscape their street medians than they do on school lunch programs, where ordinance limits the amount of time you can leave your garage door open. Local government is very concerned with aesthetics. Furthermore, many area developments are similarly as concerned. They restrict homeowners from placing anything on their roofs. I don't see the widespread use of satellite dishes being very probable."

Ever the technology buff, pen pack in tow, Lightning Lou chimed in, "Yes, but video-on-demand is on the horizon. I've heard some cable companies offer it now."

(Ding. Beleaguered, I trudged to my corner to research the long-term viability of an industry. Good thing I retained some library skills from English 101.)

(Ding. Round 10.) "I've included for your review, excerpts from a recent *New York Times* article by Peter Nichols. It's entitled,

Chapter Eleven

"Videotape's Growing Rival: Pay-Per-View TV" and I think it cuts right to the heart of the issue of obsolescence..."

Time Warner's start-up of its 150-channel cable television system within the New York borough of Queens sparked some debate about the future of the videocassette rental business.

"'By the mid-90s, the stores will have to confront more competition from pay-per-view for hit titles, but it's certainly not a killer for the video business,' said Craig Bibb, an entertainment industry analyst at Paine Webber." [1]

Within the next several years, technological advances in the area of digital compression will enable cable operators to readily offer hundreds of channels to subscribers. However, making this a reality for the end-user means replacing the cable equipment in every home. A costly, and time consuming, process not expected to be finished until sometime in the 21st century.

Time Warner's operation in Queens is, perhaps, a forerunner of what the future holds. Of the 150 channels offered, around 55 deliver a selection of 17 movies available at different time slots. The company bills service as video-on-demand.

Although the phrase suggest subscribers are able to order up any movie, at any time, it is not entirely accurate.

"'Video on demand is what the pay-per-view operator would like you to think he's offering, but he's not,' Mr. Bibb said. 'The time frame for that is 10 years away.'" [2]

Besides, the purveyors of video cassettes have a most powerful ally in their corner — movie studios. Statistics indicate that almost one-quarter of their total revenues come from home videos.

"'It's such an important source of income they'll always pay lip service to the video industry, and never do anything to hurt it,' Mr. Bibb said." [3]

And as to the effect of Time Warner's operation on video stores in the Queens area? Ron Castell, a senior VP with Blockbuster Video proclaimed that "we show no impact whatsoever." [4]

(Ding. Another big round for yours truly. In my mind, I'm leading at this point.) Days went by without any other questions, or requests for additional information. The applicant, now approaching contract deadlines, began calling constantly to see if an answer was forthcoming. I thought I had completely exhausted my stalling tactics, when Lightning Lou appeared at my doorstep. (Round 11.)

"Addison, I've been spending time thoroughly reviewing all the

How to Obtain Business Loans

memoranda you've supplied. And I've spoken, at length, to Winthrop about this request... (uh-oh)... we just can't get comfortable with this one. The way we see it, the industry has so many unknowns... who can really tell when technology breakthroughs will completely kill video rentals?

"And Camelot is a business we're totally unfamiliar with. I mean... assets supposedly trading at such multiples of book value, that's totally foreign to us. Given the unknowns, I don't think we can see our way clear to offer any financing... unless the Enright's wanted to post a letter-of-credit in the amount of the loan..." (Why not a CD?)

(Knockdown.) In retrospect, watching the fight *on video*, one thing was apparent. No amount of information, and no amount of mitigating answers to concerns, could ever have gotten this deal approved. Nothing could have overcome the bank's initial point of view. All the rest was simply *going through the motions*.

As a footnote: Subsequent to the denial, the Enright's maintained a small checking account with the bank. One day they requested a branch manager approve them for a $2,000-$3,000 overdraft[8] facility, to be backed by a credit card. To quote Mr. Enright, "Macy doesn't balance her checkbook very often, and it would be embarrassing to have anything returned."

The branch manager forwarded the request to the bankcard department and replied to Mr. Enright, "We'll get back to you as soon as your application and financial information has been reviewed." (Stop the fight.)

[1] Peter M. Nichols, "Videotape's Growing Rival: Pay-Per-View TV," *The New York Times*, page D-8.
[2] Peter M. Nichols, "Videotape's Growing Rival: Pay-Per-View TV," *The New York Times*, page D-8.
[3] Peter M. Nichols, "Videotape's Growing Rival: Pay-Per-View TV," *The New York Times*, page D-8.
[4] Peter M. Nichols, "Videotape's Growing Rival: Pay-Per-View TV," *The New York Times*, page D-8.

Chapter Twelve

CHAPTER 12:

THE Deal

Mortie had called an emergency meeting of all line lenders for 7:45 A.M. Times like this, I hated the fact he's an insomniac and a workaholic. As a boss, he set a tough standard. In the office by 5:00 A.M., there until around 6:00 P.M.; and then working at home until 2:00 A.M. nightly. "Banker's hours." What a laugh. Although Mortie **was** certainly an extremist... devoted to the company, despite its indifference to his efforts above and beyond the call of duty.

Leland Garvey had been much the same. Running the Business Development Department until just recently, his hours were only slightly different than Mortie's, 8:00 A.M. until 9:00 P.M. ... plus weekends. After years of plowing forward in this fashion, it would later pay off when our affiliate merged with another. He lost his department, along with his senior vice president title; and was

How to Obtain Business Loans

demoted back to trust representative. Rumor was they even docked his pay. In what amounted to a forced resignation, he left the bank.

The merger would not leave Mortie unscathed, either. He, too, lost his senior VP title, along with the senior lender position. (And banks continually wonder why turnover is so high... often in the area of 30% each year. With treatment like the preceding, and only the promise of a 3-4% annual raise as the upside, it doesn't seem hard to figure. Union? There's a word to terrify a bank president. During employee orientation, trainers lay out exactly how new hires are to react if ever approached by someone from, or seeking to form, a union. "Proceed directly to your supervisor and report the matter. If you received literature, immediately turn it over to your department head, making no copies for yourself, and speaking to no one else about the subject. A union could destroy our community institution. We must guard ourselves against the encroachment of organized labor." Yikes! To arms! Repel the Red Horde.)

But, the merger was to come later. On this early morning, Mortie was eager to forge ahead. He opened the meeting by sounding the alarm. "We've got to find some type of sizable commercial credit we can get approved. There's no way we'll meet our volume goals doing $5,000-$10,000 vehicle loans. We're gonna have to put our heads together and come up with something..."

"Winthrop wants officer calls[g] to be stepped up. He feels the lack of volume is the result of poor prospecting efforts."

"But, Mortie, we're not suffering from a lack of applicants. We just can't get anything approved."

"I know, and that's why we're here... to come up with a game plan."

"Did you ask Winthrop, or more importantly Lightning and the folks at the holding company, what type of business they're looking for?"

"Yes. Unfortunately, they won't be pinned down. Their comment is, 'the bank will review all types of *quality* credit.'"

"Exactly. It's the ambiguous nature of *quality* we're having trouble getting a handle on."

Camden Brainard, a long-time line lender, added, "All types except... what... (counting on his fingers) restaurants, hotels, motels, unanchored strip centers... "

Others jumped in, "Nonowner occupied office space... "

"Shopping plazas without permanent takeouts... "

Chapter Twelve

"Mobile home parks, congregate living facilities..."
"Mini-warehouses, lounges..."
"New ventures of any kind..."

Mortie put a halt to the free-for-all. "Alright you guys. We've got to try and be a little more positive."

"I think the pessimism from above is starting to trickle down."

"I think you're right... Maybe we should look to lend to retail and service firms. The holding company has intimated they'd like to see more applicants in those areas."

"Yeah, like Manatee Video Corp.?"

"Touché. I'll admit borrowers need to be in industries the bank is comfortable with... we could also look to finance more presold assets."

"Like dockominiums?"

"Now, Addison, the holding company definitely wasn't familiar with that product. But maybe condominiums. The focus is on residential real estate, and if we're lending on a presold basis, with a bonded construction contract in place... there's a minimal amount of risk. Especially lending in some of the established developments which experience very low sales fall-out."

THE p.u.d.

Planned Urban Development. More than your average neighborhood, or subdivision. Like a mini-city. PUDs are master planned communities which lay out exact property uses for huge plots of land. They must conform to locally dictated zoning, density, etc., and include blueprints for adequate supply of all infrastructure (roads and utilities), public education centers (libraries, schools), recreation areas (parks), and commerce districts (office parks).

The developer is usually a sizable conglomerate capable of funding the massive land purchase. The strategy is to sell parcels of property within the PUD to smaller developers and individual builders, at increased prices. The amounts are supported by an appreciation in value resulting from the area's harmonious improvement. Tight deed restrictions control the type and style of vertical improvements which may be added (right down to the mail receptacles) and mandate a high level of landscaping with indigenous plants.

The bank itself was part of, perhaps, one of the finest examples of

How to Obtain Business Loans

a successfully engineered PUD. Gull Harbor. Back in the very early 70s, a major multinational firm (Acme Development) teamed with a prominent family to bring about the world-renowned resort and retirement community. With over 2,100 acres, only 50% was designated for regular use. Care was taken to set aside vast beach, wetland and marsh areas. No expense was spared to preserve the natural flora and fauna associated with the pristine site.

Bordered on the west by the bay, and the east by a main highway artery, Gull Harbor was designed under a slow, controlled growth plan. Build-out was charted to take place over three decades. As defined in the PUD documentation, the maximum number of residential dwelling units was 9,600. At the period in question, they were accounted for as follows:

Type	Total	Complete	Remaining
High-rise	5,000	925	4,075
Low & Mid-rise	1,686	1,341	345
Cluster Villas	2,314	470	1,844
Single-family	600	458	142

An average Gull Harbor resident might be described as "older, quite affluent, and from the Midwest." However, an international contingent exists, with many buyers coming from Europe and Canada. About half to two-thirds of the residents are seasonal.

Refinements include championship golf around a 27-hole layout, multi-surface tennis facilities, miles of member-only beach access, nature and jogging trails, canoe areas, bike paths, parks, a yacht basin just to the north on a manmade island and the jewel, an 80,000-SF performing arts center showcasing the finest in cultural entertainment.

Commercial development also exists with four bank towers and another multistory office facility abutting the city's main thoroughfare, along with an upscale shopping center containing more than 250,000-SF of retail space offering the likes of Saks, Jacobson's, Victoria's Secret, and Ralph Lauren.

Gull Harbor is an established community with a lot to offer. Initial inhabitants were cultivated from the community's two world-class hotels. Together, the Ritz-Carlton (when not booked by

Chapter Twelve

OCC personnel), and The Registry provide over 200,000 visitors annually. Many purchase multifamily homes ranging from $150,000 - $1.5 million (for high-rise penthouses), and having an average cost of around $400,000. These residences often serve as incubators for seasonal folks ultimately purchasing permanent single family homes. Lot sales within the PUD go from $300,000 around the golf course to well into the seven-figure range beach side.

Historically, no project within Gull Harbor had failed.

THE Applicant and THE Request

Feeling something was accomplished by the line personnel's morning pow-wow, Mortie went across the hall for a face-to-face with the chief. Winthrop had just the reinforcement needed. "I think you're right on target, Mortie. Residential development is the way to go. We should be able to do great things in that area, so long as we stick to the major PUDs. And you know, I saw Jack Hudson the other night. I told him we wanted to finance his new condo project in Gull Harbor... Sunset Bay. You and Addison should make a call on him and his partners." Minutes later, I was on the phone making the appointment. Three moons thereafter, we gathered in their tepee to pass the friendship pipe.

The proposed borrower was Sunset Bay, Limited Partnership. The general partner, ASB Inc., a wholly owned subsidiary of Premier Locales, Inc., would act as construction manager and contractor. ASB was to have a 2.5% stake and Premier, the first limited partner, 8.5%. The second limited was Quixote Inc., a subchapter S-Corp. owned by the principals of Premier Locales — Jack Hudson, Rodger Norwood, and Grant Hobbs. Quixote was to have a 50% position. A newly formed corporation, called Sunset Bay, Inc., was another limited. Set up by a wealthy entrepreneur's family, the company controlled 14% of the venture. The balancing interest was retained by the fourth, and final limited partner, Frazier Prescott the IIIrd. An immoderate investor/developer/businessman from the other coast. In order to accomplish a 1031 Tax Free Exchange[g], Mr. Prescott purchased the land underlying the property's golf course sites, subject to Acme's mortgage. He then granted an option to the partnership to purchase the property from him for the same price. On an ongoing basis, the partnership could acquire any of the land owned by Mr. Prescott for

How to Obtain Business Loans

the payment of the master developer's corresponding mortgage. Mr. Prescott would then take back an unsecured note for his balance due... to be repaid by his priority distribution of the eventual cash flows from the undertaking. The semi-complicated nature of the applicant was never to be well received by the powers that be. They much preferred more "white-bread" borrowing formats. I had thought a family tree would adequately depict the relationship among the different parties, but the Sunset Bay partnership confused everyone from the outset.

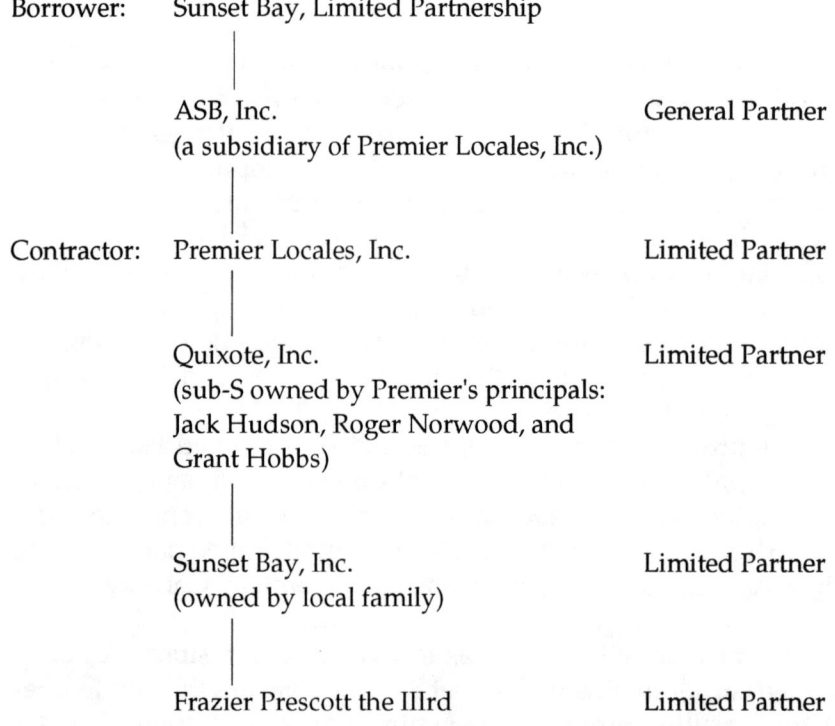

Borrower:	Sunset Bay, Limited Partnership	
	ASB, Inc. (a subsidiary of Premier Locales, Inc.)	General Partner
Contractor:	Premier Locales, Inc.	Limited Partner
	Quixote, Inc. (sub-S owned by Premier's principals: Jack Hudson, Roger Norwood, and Grant Hobbs)	Limited Partner
	Sunset Bay, Inc. (owned by local family)	Limited Partner
	Frazier Prescott the IIIrd	Limited Partner

Premier Locales, Inc. was a successful area developer. They had previously completed two outstanding projects within Gull Harbor. Royal Palms were stacked condominium homes which set absorption records for the PUD, averaging over 13 unit sales per month. And their latest endeavor, Seal Point Village, saw 35 units close immediately after the initial COs were provided, and another 15 contracts signed for future buildings. Additionally, the company owned one of the bank towers adjacent to our own financial center.

Chapter Twelve

Premier had enlisted David Hardaway, the leading local appraiser, to complete a study of Gull Harbor and its rival PUDs. His task was to identify the superior choice for multifamily development on the acquired property, and supply recommendations for construction based upon the optimum target market.

Mr. Hardaway's report concluded the site was best suited for lower-end luxury homes, priced less than $325,000. His analysis determined there would be very little competition in this market segment through the next year, and thereafter. The proposed project would stand alone, as little existing inventory would remain elsewhere, and additional sites for similar construction were unavailable within Gull Harbor. Further, he suggested stacked low- to mid-rise units, since his data clearly indicated this had been the fastest absorbing product line over the PUD's history.

Based upon the appraiser's findings, the architects and engineers joined forces to design truly distinctive condominiums (the individual unit floor plans won acclaim from the local builder's association while still in the planning stage), along with building layouts which afforded the best views possible. Fourteen four-story, low-rise buildings (3 habitable levels over a parking garage) and three six-story mid-rises (5 floors above parking) were taken through permitting. In all, 264 dwellings would be completed... the mid-rises (84 units) directly upon the golf course and most of the low-rises (180 units) surrounding a large lake whose island recreational facilities would be the focal point of the site's arrangement.

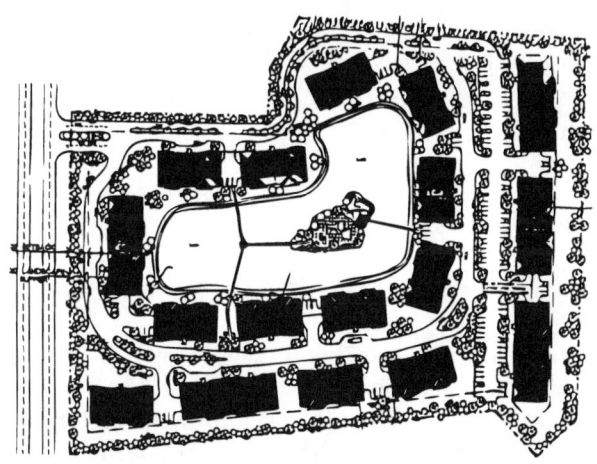

Golf Course

Now all that was needed was some financing.

How to Obtain Business Loans

THE Structure

Build-out of the overall project was such that the underwriting emphasis dealt with the relationship between golf course (mid-rise) units and non-golf course (low-rise) units. In working directly with Premier's numbers whiz, Grant Hobbs, the ensuing three-loan format was developed:

---

(1) A site loan in the amount of $5,590,000. These funds would provide monies necessary to take down the balance of the land off the golf course, and complete all project infrastructure and amenities. Below is an equity and loan fund allocation for the site's development.

	COST	DEBT	EQUITY
SOFT COSTS			
Architectural/Engin.	$ 313,178	$ 313,178	$ 0
Legal/Accting/Prof.	91,325	91,325	0
Permitting/Impact	300,612	300,612	0
Marketing	244,408	244,408	0
Real Estate Taxes	171,163	171,163	0
Closing Costs	571,587	230,050	341,537
Interest Reserve	520,662	520,662	0
TOTAL	$2,212,935	$ 1,871,398	$ 341,537
HARD COSTS			
Land	$5,153,200	$ 1,594,736	$3,558,464
Site Development	650,000	650,000	0
Entrance/Landscape	377,000	377,000	0
Amenities	650,000	650,000	0
General Conditions	234,000	234,000	0
Contractor's Fee	125,775	125,775	0
Contingency	83,850	83,850	0
TOTAL	$7,273,825	$ 3,715,361	$3,558,464
GRAND TOTALS	$9,486,760	$ 5,586,759	$3,900,001

Thus, the borrower's equity at this point would be 41%. The release provision, paid as units close, would be set at $32,500. Overall repayment would then be accelerated via additional cash flow provided by the latter three units in each building. (To be illustrated in a moment.)

Chapter Twelve

(2) The loan for vertical improvement of the low-rise pads would be for $4,056,000, whose fund allocation for the first three proposed buildings looked as follows:

	COST	DEBT	EQUITY
SOFT COSTS			
Architectural/Engin.	$ 47,436	$ 47,436	$ 0
Legal/Accting/Prof.	4,965	4,965	0
Permitting/Impact	386,751	386,751	0
Marketing	104,883	104,883	0
Real Estate Taxes	23,162	23,162	0
Closing Costs	135,997	135,997	0
Interest Reserve	110,265	110,265	0
TOTAL	$ 813,459	$ 813,459	$ 0
HARD COSTS			
Construction	$ 2,531,552	$ 2,531,552	$ 0
Landscaping	117,000	117,000	0
General Conditions	264,432	264,432	0
Contractor's Fee	198,643	198,643	0
Contingency	132,428	132,428	0
TOTAL	$ 3,244,055	$ 3,244,055	$ 0
GRAND TOTALS	$ 4,057,514	$ 4,057,514	$3,900,001

Site Costs	$ 9,486,760
Unit Costs	4,057,514
Total Costs	$13,544,274
Equity	$ 3,900,001

At this juncture, the borrower's equity is 29%. Repayment of the site loan and the low-rise construction revolver would take place as follows:

Average unit price	$ 197,903
Less closing costs/commissions	(19,790)
Net sales proceeds	$ 178,113
Site release	(32,500)
Available to reduce construction revolver	$ 145,613
10 units X $145,613	$1,456,130
Revolver apportioned to single building	(1,352,000)
Excess cash flow from 10th unit	$ 104,130

(continued on next page)

How to Obtain Business Loans

Remaining cash flow in each 12 unit building:
10th unit	$ 104,130
11th unit	145,613
12th unit	145,613
Total	$ 395,356

These profits would then be set aside as an equity reserve for the third loan. After the first three low-rise buildings are closed out, $1,186,068 would be made available. Enough to commence construction on a 28-unit mid-rise.

(3) Funding to be provided under another revolver, this time in the amount of $5,650,000. This broke down as follows:

	COST	DEBT	EQUITY
SOFT COSTS			
Architectural/Engin.	$ 36,895	$ 36,895	$ 0
Legal/Accting/Prof.	3,860	3,860	0
Permitting/Impact	307,394	307,394	0
Marketing	114,458	114,458	0
Real Estate Taxes	28,159	28,159	0
Closing Costs	406,133	166,494	239,639
Interest Reserve	195,303	195,303	0
TOTAL	$1,092,202	$ 852,563	$ 239,639
HARD COSTS			
Land	$1,996,558	$ 810,537	$1,186,021
Construction	3,129,100	3,129,100	0
Landscaping	72,800	72,800	0
General Conditions	323,896	323,896	0
Contractor's Fee	240,143	240,143	0
Contingency	160,095	160,095	0
TOTAL	$5,922,592	$ 4,736,571	$1,186,021
GRAND TOTALS	$7,014,794	$ 5,589,134	$1,425,660

At this stage of development, due to the anticipated timing of closings, construction would have begun on another two low-rise buildings. Assuming their total cost in an equity recap would mean:

Chapter Twelve

Site Costs	$ 9,486,760
Costs for 5 low-rises	6,762,523
Cost for 1 mid-rise	7,014,794
Total costs	$ 23,264,077
Initial equity	$ 3,900,001
Profits reinvested as equity	1,425,660
Total equity at this juncture	$ 5,325,661

Which indicates the borrower's equity would still be 23%. Repayment of the mid-rise construction revolver, and providing for the equity in the ensuing golf course building to be constructed, would take place as follows:

Average unit price	$ 304,720
Less closing costs/commissions	(30,472)
Net sales proceeds	$ 274,248
28 units X $ 274,248	$ 7,678,944
Revolver	(5,650,000)
Excess cash flow	$ 2,028,944

A portion of these profits would then be set aside as an equity reserve for the next mid-rise ($1,425,660) and the balance would flow through to the owners ($603,284).

In assessing the bank's position, two factors were predominant risk mitigators. One: In every 12-unit low-rise building to be constructed, 10 would be presold with 20% nonrefundable deposits. And in every 28-unit mid-rise, 24 units would be presold with similar money down. Certainly, few individuals would walk from deposits in the $30,000 to $60,000 range. What's more, *historically fall out among Gull Harbor projects has averaged less than 1%!*

Two: Due to the equity cushion provided, even under a worst case scenario, the loan-to-value position is still quite conservative.

How to Obtain Business Loans

Say the bank was forced to fund completion of the site and amenity work, five low-rise buildings, and one mid-rise:

Total costs	$ 23,264,077
Equity	(4,139,640)
Cost to complete	$ 19,124,437
Collateral created:	
60 low-rise units	$ 11,874,180
28 mid-rise units	8,532,160
Value of finished units	$ 20,406,340
Value of improved site	5,616,000
Total value created	$ 26,022,340
Loan-to-value	74%

Note: The value of the finished units alone would be well in excess of the maximum loan balance:

Site note	$ 5,590,000
5 low-rise buildings	6,760,000
1 mid-rise building	5,650,000
Maximum funded debt	$ 18,000,000
$20,406,074/$18,000,000	1.13:1 coverage

So I felt any land shortfall related to the underwriting structure should be considered a moot point.

Hardly. That's where deliberations began. As we've touched on previously, bankers absolutely loathe the possibility of being extended against raw land. Even the slightest possibility. So, although finished unit sales could retire the bank's maximum exposure... if sold at market prices... pessimism warrants the presumption of a fire sale, resulting in a residual loan balance against some dirt. When Little Louis was a tot at commercial lending school, this lesson must've really been the teacher's favorite (although Louis probably wasn't).

Lightning believed the release price set to reduce the site revolver was much too low. In his opinion, it caused the bank excessive risk by "having the site loan's repayment accelerated slower than policy's

Chapter Twelve

125%." This statement was myopic as it considered only the original rate of acceleration...

$5,590,000/$32,500 = 172   180 total low-rise units/172 = 105%

It ignored the monies which become available and which would be required to reduce the site balance after the first thirty-six low-rise unit sales had closed. I'm speaking of the funds created from the latter three units in each non-golf course building thereafter. Initially set aside as equity into the first mid-rise, monies would be available for site reduction at this point, as profits from the first mid-rise would generate more than enough funds to move into the next golf course building. Thus, the acceleration rate after the first six low-rises becomes:

72 X $32,500	= $2,340,000		made available from releases
	1,186,068		made available from units 10-12 in buildings 4-6
	$3,526,068/72	=	$48,973 reduced on an average unit basis
	$5,590,000/$48,973	=	114
	180/114	=	158%

Further, when you analyze the matter from the perspective of *marginal* acceleration; after the first 36 units, the rate is 212%.

	$5,590,000				
36 X $32,500 =	(1,170,000)				
	$4,420,000		against 144 improved sites		
12 X $32,500 =	$ 390,000		made available per building		
	395,356		made available via last 3 units/bldg.		
	$ 785,356/12	=	$65,446 reduced on an average unit basis		
	$5,590,000/$65,446	=	85	180/85	211%, or
	$4,420,000/$65,446	=	68	144/68	212%

How to Obtain Business Loans

"Uh-huh, but we still *would* be in this site loan thing for a long time, and..."

"Through the 114th low-rise closing. Which, according to the appraiser's best estimate, will take place 19 months from the commencement of construction... well within policy's two year maximum for development financing."

"Uh-huh, but we still could be in this site loan thing for quite awhile. How strong is the sponsorship portion of the credit?"

A W~~ord~~ Litany From THE Sponsors

Did I mention, at the point when this conversation was taking place, Sunset Bay had managed to presell all but 2 units in the first 3 buildings? No small feat, considering advertising had not been utilized and only land and plans were available to show those who came across the motor home parked on site as a sales center.

But no matter how hot a commodity any product line is, it must have *sponsorship*. (Remember, only the very rich might get richer, not those with an idea, plan, capability, and fortitude.) In this case, the guarantors did happen to be wealthy... just not downright (Enright?) wealthy. Sparing you the lengthy financial statements, because we're really going to get into some numbers shortly, I'll summarize the support portion of the credit very succinctly:

	Total Assets	Net Worth	Liquidity	Annual Income	Debt Ratio
Premier	$16,671	(709)	$676	NA	NA
ASB		New Concern			
Quixote		New Concern			
Jack Hudson	$ 3,796	$2,874	$ 7	$299	45%
R. Norwood	$ 2,581	$1,696	$ 92	$186	60%
Grant Hobbs	Due to non-millionaire status, guarantee adjudged non-meaningful.				
Sunset Bay, Inc.		New Concern	Not Offering Guarantee		
Frazier Prescott			Not Offering Guarantee		

Upon reviewing the unabridged information (at extreme length), Lightning questioned why we would take two new concerns as guarantors without requiring a similar pledge from the third, and Mr. Prescott. We spent days debating the difference between primary and secondary involvement.

"Lou, it's important we effectively tie up all means the developer might have of diverting cash flows. Obviously, only those

Chapter Twelve

with day-to-day involvement... Premier's principals... would possess a remote opportunity to do such a thing. Given our disbursement process, the potential for any diversion is next to nil, but we always nail down interrelated funds flow. Meaning all of Premier's peripheral concerns need to be on the hook — ASB, Quixote, and the individuals themselves. However, the Saville family's Sunset Bay, Inc. concern, and Mr. Prescott, have only tertiary involvement. They are simply equity contributors who will be returned their investment and pro-rata profits after the bank's debt is retired. They do not have the capacity to control the course of monies. What's more, requiring Mr. Prescott's guarantee would most assuredly cost Premier big bucks, as he would ask to be compensated for expanding his risk."

"We might have to require it though. Hudson and Norwood have very limited liquidity, and Premier has a deficit net worth, with basically no income stream in the last two years."

"Premier has almost $700,000 liquid and, although the company had to file tax returns, they basically sat out the last two-and-a-half years. As we prefer, they are prudent, conservative developers. They recognized a little softness in the market and stayed away. As for net worths, Messrs. Hudson and Norwood combine for one of four-and-a-half-million."

"Addison, I'm afraid we're totally reliant on a project here. Premier has no ongoing cash flow from other operations. What if their Seal Point project were to become a drain? Frankly, $700,000 is not enough to support them... and that deficit net worth really scares me." (I wonder if he sleeps with the light on?)

"Remember, it is not at all unusual for condominium developers to pay through all profits and retain as little as possible in their companies. This protects them from association suits. Which, as you know, our area has a lot of. Something about taking a bunch of retired CEOs and putting them together in a homeowners group. They've too much time on their hands, and a sense of purpose to fulfill. I've heard of litigation taking place over the color of pool tile, the number of trees planted, the type of window shades used, etc. And the courts typically favor the associations. It doesn't make sense to retain a lot of cash... it would just be judgment bait.

"As to their ongoing cash flow, the following should be helpful..."

How to Obtain Business Loans

VIA SEAL POINT VILLAGE

Costs — All operating expenses, including marketing, are funded via an existing construction line with Community Bank & Trust.

Developer & Contractor Fees — Premier currently receives $13,000 per month, funded via the aforementioned credit facility. And another $13,000, accruing monthly, will be payable at the back end of the development. At that time, deferred developer fees will total $234,000, and the deferred portion of contractor fees will be $481,000. With 52 of the project's 88 units having sold, these accrued monies should be realized within the next 4-5 months.

Equity Recapture & The Distribution of Profits — Over the next 30 closings, $5,900 per unit will flow back to Premier as a return of investment capital. Thereafter, the amount will be $4,600 per unit. Premier is entitled to 25% of the first $1,000,000 in net profit (up and above fees), and 50% of the earnings beyond that level. In total, approximately $650,000 in net profit will be received by the company.

FUNDS TO AUTOGRAPH WITHIN THE NEXT 120-180 DAYS

$13,000/month for 6 mo. via Community line	$ 78,000
Accrued developer fees	234,000
Accrued contractor fees	481,000
Equity recapture:	
$5,900/unit for the next 30 closings	$ 177,000
$4,600/unit for the following 6 closings	27,600
Total	$ 204,600
Distributed Profits	650,000
Grand Total	$1,647,600

"Also Lou, their building is fully leased and throwing off excess cash flow above expenses and mortgage service, plus... $30,000 per month and 7.5% of hard costs are included in our loan to fund operations during Sunset Bay."

Chapter Twelve

"I don't like that. They should support their own operations without debt... makes me especially nervous in light of that deficit net worth position."

"If they chose to put less equity into their deals initially, they could fund overhead without having dollars within their development loans allocated to operations. However, we banks like up-front equity in our collateral. Funding back operating money is an incremental wash, it just gives us more of a cushion."

"Still... that deficit net worth is unnerving. We need to better understand its origin."

"Some stockholder transactions are at the root of the matter. If you'd like, the principals would love to sit down with you and answer your questions one-on-one... "

"No." (Of course not.)

Later, I addressed the issue in more formal memoranda:

> Premier's deficit net worth is primarily the result of a buy-out of two-thirds of its previous ownership. A few years ago, about $2.9 million of Royal Palms' profits were distributed straight through to them as consideration for the purchase.
>
> Further, advancing equity positions on Seal Point and Sunset Bay, and incurring debt on Seal Point, does not enhance the balance sheet. Not until units are finished will the true "value" of those invested dollars heavily outweigh their corresponding debt.
>
> What's more, roughly $1,365,000 in balance sheet liabilities are comprised of two loans which will be converted to equity ownership in the company's office tower. The total debt on the building ($8,033,350), and the outstanding line balance associated with Seal Point ($4,033,712), make up 94% of their total indebtedness ($12,821,063). And lastly, remember all assets are carried at depreciated historical cost. For instance, Lake Liberty is raw land which was acquired for $1,955,200. However, its recent appraised value is $3,421,600. Adjusting for the debt/equity swap, and reflecting Lake Liberty's current value tells a different story altogether:

Change in Asset Value	Change in Stated Liabilities	Resulting Net Worth
As is		(709,000)
Building	Decrease $1,365,000	$ 656,000
Lake Liberty	Increase $1,466,400	$2,122,400

> And the office building has certainly appreciated since being constructed.

Although these factors seemed to explain the reported deficit, the impression of a weak ongoing concern was indelible.

"Addison, you're still looking at a lot of illiquid resources. In all cases, they've got to sell something in order to produce any cash. (Unlike most companies who don't have to peddle anything to create money.) Either Seal Point units or raw land has to be marketed. There's very little existing cash supporting this request."

"Isn't some of that mitigated by the fact that 34 of the first 36 units are presold?"

"Sure, that's good... but our site development loan isn't fully retired until 114 of the 180 low-rise units close. What happens if sales suddenly stop after this initial 30?"

"Seems unlikely... they've gotten 34 with zero marketing effort."

"But it *could* happen. You never know, we might have another Gulf War or something which could drastically effect sales." (No fooling, this was actually said.)

Resisting the urge to ask if I should more formally address Middle East tensions, I returned to the applicant. Who then offered to post a $650,000 liquidity reserve with the bank.

"Well, Addison, if we're in control of their existing cash, we'd have to be pretty confident they could cover ongoing expenses from Community Bank & Trust's line and the monies beginning to flow from Seal Point. In which case, the $650,000 would be a... relatively... decent backstop to the Sunset Bay project. Still though... what if their cost estimates are way off? $650,000 would only go so far." (Boy, isn't that always the truth?)

"They previously have successfully completed *several* other projects... Personally, I feel pretty comfortable with their ability to properly cost jobs, but to be safe, I'll have an unrelated project engineer review the legitimacy of the budget... line item by line item."

"Will bonding be available?"

"No. As I mentioned, Premier will be acting as the general contractor, as well as construction manager. Insurers won't underwrite completion in a situation where the builder could fail to perform, then benefit from the policy's funding provision."

"Hmm... in my mind that's a huge negative. It makes the $650,000 reserve appear wholly inadequate."

Back to the applicant. Who now offered to contract out all but a small portion of the construction to be completed, assigning work to other major GCs. A measure which cut deeply into Premier's overall profitability, but enabled 80% of the project to be bonded.

Chapter Twelve

"Addison, I'd feel so much better if the whole matter was covered."

Somewhat unbelievably, the applicant conceded to acting only as construction manager, thereby allowing for the bonding of another GC's total job contract. It was evident Premier was becoming desperate to get under way. Foolishly, they had committed all their eggs to one basket. Winthrop's statement to them ("We want to do your next project.") had been strength enough for the company to only apply with our institution.

Recognizing that things were a bit precarious, they had recently filed applications at other banks... but answers would take time. The *motor* home sales center had been upgraded to a *mobile* home, and momentum had really kicked in. Now having almost 60 low-rise and 15 mid-rise units presold, they needed to get started.

"Addison, the problem... really continues to be the amount of sales necessary to clear the site loan... and the lack of secondary support."

"They've presold over half of the units needed to retire the site note!"

"Right, but those sales could fall out. I'd feel infinitely better if we had a more substantial borrower... one with liquidity *outside* of the project. What's to happen if say... 50% of the sales fall out?"

"50 PERCENT! You've got to be kidding. Historically fallout within Gull Harbor has been about 1 percent! The average low-rise price is almost $200,000... people would be forgoing $40,000 deposits. Who would do that?"

"Crises prevent folks from going through with things."

"HALF of the buyers are going to have some personal calamity necessitating they walk from forty-grand?"

"Again, who can foresee the future of the overall economic environment? We could have another war, the stock market could crash... there are a lot of unknowns out there."

"I just think most people perform on contracts where they stand to lose $40,000... regardless of war or market vicissitudes."

"You don't know. It might, in some instances, make better sense to take a loss rather than further extend one's self. These are predominately second homes, remember."

"I still can't envision, under most circumstances, someone with the capacity to perform... not doing so. They could always turn right back around and resell the unit."

How to Obtain Business Loans

"You're assuming the property **would** hold its value..."

"**Mr. Hobbs has indicated people have already assigned their contracts to other parties for $10,000-$12,000 profits.**"

"That's now. We were talking about what **would** take place under dire conditions. (And in the world of make believe.) As to the capacity of these buyers... how can we be sure they can perform? Is there anyway for us to qualify them?"

"**As in pull their credit, get and analyze financials, etc?**"

"Uh-huh."

"**No. But if people are contracting to purchase $200,000 second homes, I'd say we** *can* **reasonably assume they have some substance to them.**"

"You know how I feel about assuming." (Yes. You keep extra candles about the house in case the sun doesn't rise one day.)

Chapter Thirteen

CHAPTER 13:

THE Deal Continues...

Panic began to set in. Word had gotten out Premier was, shall we say, *having difficulty* procuring construction funds... and buyers were becoming anxious. Sales associates had been guaranteeing commencement for months. As more and more time passed, their broken promises were harder and harder to explain away.

Acme became aware of the company's plight, and responded by offering to carry some of the site debt ($1,040,000) in a subordinate position to the bank's A&D loan, allowing the entire underwriting to be restructured around a few key points of emphasis:

(1) The bank **would** hold the $650,000 reserve offered, as an emergency backstop, with full right of offset in the event of nonperformance.

How to Obtain Business Loans

(2) An unrelated party **would** be retained as general contractor, enabling the entire construction contract to be bonded.

(3) In order to reduce the bank's exposure, the project **would** be undertaken in carefully choreographed steps:

Phase I   Horizontal development of 84 non-golf course unit sites.

Phase II   Vertical construction of 72 low-rise units, in 6 bldgs.

Phase III   Vertical construction of 28 mid-rise units, in 1 bldg.

(4) The master developer's debt would be apportioned against the latter 96 (of 180) non-golf course unit sites.

The numbers fell out as follows:

Loans		to	Cost	
Site loan	$4,550,000	Site development	$ 9,486,760	
Low-rise revolver	4,056,000	1st 3 low-rises	4,056,000	
Total bank funding	$8,606,000	Total	$13,542,760	
Loan from Acme	1,040,000			
Total debt	$9,646,000	Total LTC	71.2%	

A position well within policy, further enhanced by monies held by the bank, which under a default, **could** be used to reduce loan balances.

Up-front reserve		$ 650,000
30 20% deposits		1,187,418
Total		$ 1,837,418

Chapter Thirteen

Forget 50% fallout... if NONE of the presales closed:

Total bank debt	$ 8,606,000
Less: Offset monies	(1,837,418)
Leaving an unretired bal. of	$ 6,768,582

Against collateral as follows:

36 completed units (avg. price $197,903)	$ 7,124,508
48 improved sites (appraised @ $46,800 each)	2,246,400
96 unimproved sites (appraised @ $33,800 each)	3,244,800
Total value	$ 12,615,708
$6,768,582/$12,615,708	Exposure 53.7%

A pretty safe spot to be in at the outset of a development loan. **Should** it be assumed that all 36 units in the first 3 low-rise buildings close:

36 X $197,903	$ 7,124,508
Less: Closing costs & comm.	(712,451)
Available to reduce debt	$ 6,412,057
Construction revolver	(4,056,000)
Still remaining	$ 2,356,057
36 X $ 32,500 (site release)	(1,170,000)
	(Site bal. now $ 3,380,000)
Available for reserve	$ 1,186,057

At this point, the original $650,000 set aside by Premier **would** be released to the company, and these monies ($1,186,057) **would** be available for future offset. Note: No dollars are to be allocated to the

How to Obtain Business Loans

first mid-rise building to be constructed (as previously planned). The bank's exposure **would** be:

Total bank debt	$ 3,380,000
Less: Offset monies	(1,186,057)
Leaving an unretired bal. of	$ 2,193,943

Against collateral as follows:

48 improved sites	$ 2,246,400
96 unimproved sites	3,244,800
Total value	$ 5,491,200

$3,380,000 site balance/$5,491,200   LTV 61.6%
$2,193,943/$5,491,200   Actual exposure 40.0%

Being so bold as to surmise the next 36 units are successfully built, and closed, means the subsequent transpires:

36 X $197,903	$ 7,124,508
Less: Closing costs & comm.	(712,451)
Available to reduce debt	$ 6,412,057
Construction revolver	(4,056,000)
Still remaining	$ 2,356,057
36 X $ 32,500 (site release)	(1,170,000)
	(Site bal. now $ 2,210,000)
Available for reserve	$ 1,186,057

Now a total of $2,372,114 in reserve monies has been created from closings. Of which, half **would** now be released for equity into the first mid-rise... **should** the project remain on schedule with regard to

Chapter Thirteen

the appraiser's absorption targets. If not, the amount **could** be applied to the site loan's balance... *completely retiring it.*

As I promised when "THE Deal" began, we've really gotten into crunching some numbers. Let's not miss their importance. The financing package was restructured around an incremental funding format, in an attempt to lower the bank's exposure. The overwhelming concern all along had been the possibility of a land shortfall; anxiety centered around what balance **would** be extended against raw land at various stages of development... **should** the project fail. Here are those positions of advance:

Phase I Horizontal development of 84 non-golf course unit sites. Loan amount ($4,550,000) - offset monies ($650,000) = $3,900,000/value created ($7,176,000) = maximum site exposure of 54.3%.

Phase II Vertical construction of 72 low-rise units. At 36 units... Total loans now $8,606,000 - offset monies ($1,837,418) = $6,768,582/value created ($12,615,708) = maximum site exposure of 53.7%. At 72 units... 36 have closed, leaving a site balance of $3,380,000 - offset monies now available of ($2,135,991) = $1,244,009/value created ($3,806,400) = maximum site exposure of 32.7%.

Phase III Vertical construction of 28 mid-rise units. Just prior to this point, offset monies are in excess of the maximum site balance. No exposure.

At no time is true exposure in excess of 55% against land alone. This would appear to be a position without an actual chance of loss. And the rate of return seems to justify the risk related to a possible downtime of funds... if the project were to stall.

THE Opportunity Cost

"Addison, no matter what our actual exposure, I've seen these things become unglued and take months... even years... to piece back together once the attorneys get involved. And there the bank sits with outstanding balances not employed as earning assets."

"You *could* make the same statement with regard to any loan where we take a mortgage. *Should* the borrower contest foreclosure, you're at the mercy of the court's timetable... and eventual ruling. Unfortunately, signing a mortgage... no matter how all encompassing we endeavor to make default remedies... is not an act of forbearance. As you know, the property owner still has rights.

"Maybe the courts could be more expeditious in allowing banks clear title after a default... and they probably *would*, did they not have to ascertain the difference between the technical and monetary defaults we put before them. As the process is used now, the risk of downtime is associated with all mortgage credit.

"But, other than adversely effecting nonperforming ratios, the bank... in this instance... can sustain no harm. Yet it can benefit so greatly. I've completed proformas on the project's month-by-month cash flows. The printout allows us to look at what our outstanding balances *would* be at any given point of time, in relation to related funds on deposit, thus allowing for a rate of return to be calculated. It's quite a long analysis, with 'best' and 'worst-case' scenarios... but the 'most-likely' summary is on page 92.

"You'll note over the entire project period, the bank can anticipate the receipt of approximately $1,235,000 in interest. Additionally, $429,000 in fees *would* be collected... for a total income figure of $1,664,000. This against average loan balances of $4,628,662. That's a return of almost 12% annually over the three year period of development. And, on average, the bank will hold 58% of its outstanding monies in compensating deposits. 58%!"

"Certainly, **should** the project be a success, the bank stands to benefit. I don't think that was ever in question. We've just been seeking to limit our risk while obtaining an adequate rate of return. I wonder if, perhaps, there isn't a better way to structure the deal. I think we **should** have a larger affiliate look at our suggested format, and offer their input. You know... it might be even better if they led the underwriting and participated the outstandings. Our Metropolis bank has a lot more expertise in this type of lending."

THE Expert(s)

"Lou... to say the least... I've been working with the applicant for some time now. I don't think it's fair of us to ask they begin the entire process over with another line lender. They're already months behind their scheduled start date."

Chapter Thirteen

"That's not the bank's fault."

"Yes, it is. Winthrop told them we wanted to do the loan. I don't think they *could* have imagined we'd be embroiled in debate this long. Further, we always... always... say it is imprudent to lend outside our own areas due to an inherent lack of market knowledge. I strongly request this project, literally in our own backyard, not be handed over to someone a couple hundred miles away. I don't feel anyone stands to gain from doing so.

"Respectfully, there is ample information with which to make a decision and more than sufficient merit to justify an approval. I'm concerned, as is our applicant, that the matter is being drawn out without a direction. No conclusion appears to be on the horizon... after months and months of deliberating."

"Let me stop you right there, Addison." (Uh-oh, challenged his manhood.) "First of all, a second, third... even a fourth opinion... is always worth the time. Particularly when the ensuing feedback is to be received from those with advancing levels of expertise. This is the practical course of prudent lending. Second of all, starting from scratch won't be necessary, as all of your *preliminary* information can be used as a basis from which to move forward. And lastly, we **could** always just make a decision. However, it is only rational for us to come to a cautious conclusion under our own timetable... not that of the applicant."

"**Doesn't it make sense to be a bit more responsive when delay ultimately hurts the project we're contemplating? Procrastinating seems to ensure the undertaking ultimately doesn't make sense.**"

"We are not procrastinating! Besides, if the project is such a good deal now... why won't it be a few months down the road? You have vehemently defended the validity of Sunset Bay's presales, are you now saying they **would** fall out?"

"No. I'm saying you're ignoring the principal of momentum. If... "

"I don't wish to discuss this with you any further. I want you to get in touch with Crandell Worthington of our Metropolis office."

Crandell was his affiliate's Senior Lender. For days I tried to reach him by phone, only to be told he was "in meetings"... evidently booked to the point he couldn't return calls. Finally I asked for Mortie's help. "**Maybe he'll speak to another senior officer,**" I surmised aloud.

He did. And asked Mortie that I forward Sunset Bay's informa-

How to Obtain Business Loans

tion directly to him. I shipped all applicant-supplied materials, and my own memorandums. To aid in digesting the data, I sequentially ordered the information. If read start to finish, a full understanding of both where we were... and how we got there... **would** be obtained.

Days and days passed. Mortie was getting steamed, as Premier's principals began to apply a lot of pressure on us locally. We were reticent to explain how we'd been pulled from the game, and even more reluctant to tell them their deal was now being reviewed from afar.

Mortie blasted me. "When did you send that package to Crandell?"

"**About a week-and-a-half ago.**"

"Did he get it?"

"**He *should* have... I sent it by inter-office courier, but I can't be sure. He doesn't return my phone calls, remember?**"

"That's it. We've got to set up a system logging out information we send to the region, or other affiliates... and start tracking when they receive it. And most importantly, when they act upon it. This lack of teamwork needs to be addressed at the holding company level. We've got to document a file to present as evidence." (An inquisition becomes necessary in order to get someone to move on this project. The deal was being buried the old fashioned way... shuffled around, and basically ignored, until it went away. All the while, I was forced to fudge about how close the bank was to a decision.)

Mortie pushed and got a reaction from Crandell Worthington. Though not the one he wanted. "I don't have the time to sit and review all the information your guy sent. Have him do a summary for us."

I complied and included a plea for our wiser sibling to visit the site... and meet with the applicant. Mortie relayed an affirmative answer and I set an appointment. (Imagine, a senior lending officer gathering with a customer... now if I could only get a senior credit Administrator to do the same.)

My euphoria was short-lived. The day of the meeting, the esteemed Crandell Worthington was a no-show. In his place he sent two of his line lenders... Baldwin Dickerson and Aldrich McNaire.

I couldn't resist. On the ride to the project, I had to probe for experience levels. Aldrich quickly admitted he was straight from the commercial lending training program and was in attendance to learn. "I'm looking to start big," he said. "I've already contacted

Chapter Thirteen

Acme to see if we can do some financing for them. Wouldn't it be great to bank a company their size?"

"Aldrich, they share the same building with our affiliate. We already handle their deposit accounts. On the credit side of things, they're large enough to have access to the capital markets... at rates lower than we extend. We do, from time to time, issue letters of credit to the county on their behalf... back-stopping utility work within the PUD... but we have little direct credit with them."

"Too bad... what an ideal borrower."

"Actually, they hold a lot of land. Credit admin is not in love with that sort of thing."

Baldwin joined in. "Yes, but they have more than adequate reserves, and good ongoing cash flow. They're a high quality, bankable concern."

"I'm glad you think so. As you know, they have a subordinate position on Sunset Bay... a vested interest to protect in the unlikely event of any difficulty."

"How much debt are they carrying?" (Uh-oh... I smell a rat.)

"$1,040,000... "

"And you're confident they'd advance to cover their position?"

"Aside from the $1,040,000... being the PUD developer, they don't want Gull Harbor tainted by one bad project. They'd advance!"

"How much do the units go for?"

(I knew it.) "Baldwin, have you reviewed the package of information I sent up, or at least the summary I wrote?"

"Sure, sure... but I like to come into these things fairly fresh... without bias." (He hadn't read a word.)

"Done a lot of these projects, huh?"

"Well, er, no. Not really."

"When's the last one you guys did?"

"Well, ah... actually, we don't feel the market's been conducive for them. We haven't extended any condominium development loans for some time now."

"How long?"

"...about two or three years." (Ah... expertise!)

We arrived at the site, shook hands with Premier's principals, and walked around the property for awhile kicking dirt. After about 15 minutes, Baldwin proclaimed, "Well, we need to be going... we've another appointment to attend."

How to Obtain Business Loans

Mouths agape, the applicants stared at him as if he were a physician having delivered the message, "I'm sorry... we did all we could." Ten minutes after returning to my office, Jack Hudson called with a clear understanding of what had just taken place.

"Addison, you're not going to try and tell me that visit wasn't a polite kiss-off... are you?"

"Iyah, er... "

"An exhibition of feigned interest, if ever I've seen one. Your bank is playacting us until we go away. Who the *blank* were those two characters anyway?"

"Ubba... umm... "

"Look... if we're not already dead... our pulse is fading fast. What's it gonna take to coax you guys into some action on this thing?"

Momentarily regaining my composure. **"Everyone's still terrified of the site development loan."**

"YOUR MAXIMUM EXPOSURE IS LESS THAN 60%!! And the issue **should** be a moot point... given the velocity of sales. Besides, you know *blank* well Acme would protect. What the *blank* is there to worry about?"

"I understand your frustration. To be honest, I feel the same way. But... "

"I know, I know... we've got to offer some alternatives. Ain't a *blanking* thing gonna happen otherwise. What if we provided a bigger initial reserve, double what we've previously proposed... say $1,300,000? We've taken so long getting started, a lot of our money from Seal Point Village is now flowing in. We **could** get the balance needed from Mr. Prescott and the Saville family. Of course, you know it's going to cost us. But, I don't feel we're left with much of a choice. Can you get an approval if we front that kind of dough?"

"I'll sure try." (I had no confidence with which to offer anything more hopeful.)

Returning to my laptop computer (where I was fast developing a good case of carpal tunnel syndrome), I tapped out another lengthy memorandum for consorting about. An analysis of the bank's exposure at various stages of the project's development (again) highlighted the discourse.

Without a doubt, the numbers only improved from the previous scenarios; especially given that the first three buildings were now completely sold out. Sparing you the nought-by-nought calculations

Chapter Thirteen

this time, the following is a summation... which I hope you can appreciate:

Phase I   Horizontal development of 84 non-golf course unit sites. Loan amount ($4,550,000) - reserve ($1,300,000) = $3,250,000/value created of $7,176,000 = maximum site exposure of 45.3%.

Phase II   Vertical construction of 72 low-rise units. At 36 units... Total loans now equal $8,606,000 - offset monies ($2,724,902) = $5,881,098/value created ($12,615,708) = maximum exposure of 46.6%. At 72 units... 36 have closed, leaving a site balance of $3,380,000 - offset monies now available ($3,435,991). No exposure.

Phase III   Vertical construction of first mid-rise. No exposure.

Lightning spoke with the Metropolis *experts* on the latest information I had put together. After a week or so, he phoned Winthrop to explain what the bank's new stance **would** be. I was allowed to sit in on the conference call, *in the event anyone had questions relative to the project we were contemplating*. It quickly became apparent only Mortie had a grasp of the numbers. Winthrop didn't, as he exclaimed, "Man, you gotta sleep with this deal to understand it!"

How ironic. The request began fairly straightforward. The bank's own paranoia had been the driving force behind the ever amending structure. Each ensuing analysis only illustrated our ever diminished position as to dollars, cents, and percentage exposures. Now some **couldn't** understand what we created. (Maybe I **should** have tried some pie charts, or snappy graphs.)

Lightning summed up the determination he and Crandell (our absentee authority) had made with regard to the latest rider to the Sunset Bay debate. "I'm afraid there's still no liquidity *outside* of the project to support the credit."

(Time to be insubordinate in a crowd.) **"WHAT?!! YOU'VE GOT A $1.3 MILLION RESERVE FROM DAY ONE. None of it is project specific... those aren't deposit monies... are you out of... "**

"Let me stop you right there." Lou rumbled firmly.

"I've got to go," a previously quiet Crandell Worthington cut in. "You fellas can take it from here." (Thanks) "If something reasonable is worked out with *your* borrower, call us back and *we'll* lead this thing. Have a good one..." (Click.)

How to Obtain Business Loans

Lou continued, "Those funds, or a portion of them, are equity contributions from other partners. They're not *all* company profits available to use as ongoing reserves... as you **would** have with a more stable concern. Yes, Premier has a little cash coming in from their other project, but let's remember... they still have a deficit net worth."

"WE ADDRESSED THAT! And besides... now you're also saying equity contributions can't be used to reduce our loan balances in the event of default? We'd be in control of the money. We'd just offset, and let partners, buyers, etc. litigate it out with Premier."

"I'd still like to see some entity with viable liquidity on its statement... not associated with the development itself... come on board as a backer." (I guess the color of the reserve money wasn't quite green enough.)

How in the world would I convey this one to the applicants? Walking back to my office I picked up messages. One was from a Carleton Lawrence, the note explained he was an officer with our Metropolis affiliate. Hoping to gain some expertise via osmosis, I returned his call immediately.

"Yeah, Addison, we've got a real good customer who's apparently having some trouble with you guys. We're concerned because he's not only a good borrower of ours, but a major depositor. He says... although he's not dealing with anyone at your bank directly... he and his partners are getting jerked around... and have been for months.

"I'm only calling because his is such a valued relationship at the holding company level. We're talking long-time, big money customer... with major contacts all the way up our corporate ladder. And I mean all the way up. (No one likes to say a customer knows the holding company CEO. That information must always be whispered, or veiled in some manner... like a spicy rumor... or threat.)

"Anyhow, he had your name as the responsible account officer. The project's called... Sunset Bay... and our customer is Henry Saville. Do you know anything about what's going on?... Hello?... Addison?"

(Incredible. Absurd. Ludicrous. Ridiculous. Preposterous. Bizarre. Disgraceful. Appalling. Offensive. Reprehensible. Asinine. Intolerable. Shocking. Disgusting. Sickening. Nauseating. Astonishing. Amazing. Unbelievable. Inconceivable. Overwhelming.) I think

Chapter Thirteen

I blacked out after managing to suggest he check with his boss... Crandell Worthington.

After some smelling salts, and a saline IV, I had recovered enough to face Premier's principals who had just happened to be hanging out in the lobby.

THE Newest Guarantor

You can't imagine how good it is to have a paramedic right there when you need one. IVs for everybody... on me. They lamented aloud for over an hour. Pouring out onto my terrace to smoke a pack of cigarettes each... as well as contemplate a jump to the parking lot below.

"How close are you with the other banks where you've applied?" I asked.

"Not very. We're going through similar hoops all across town. *Blank* it all. We never **should** have put in so much money up front. Everybody used to like that. Now it's cash on the balance sheet," Jack said.

"And don't just use historical cost for asset values, either. You better do a separate disclosure raising your statement to market... recognizing explanations after the fact are useless," added Grant.

"No... you guys are both missing the point!" Roger interjected. "It's an all-of-the-above sort of thing. Big bucks up front, cash balances *outside* of the venture, good net worth, ongoing income from other sources, *and* deep pocket guarantors. Our only choice is to pay Prescott for his signature."

Soon I was back in the typing pool whipping out another lengthy document. (Ouch. Hopefully it's just tendonitis.) This memo would deal with the financial statement summary provided by Mr. Frazier Prescott the IIIrd. A highly condensed version looked like this:

Assets		Liabilities	
Cash & Equivalents	$ 6,651,823	Notes Payable	$ 3,092,291
Marketable Securities	445,563	Mort. Payable	1,739,764
Notes Receivable	130,000	% Part. Debt	37,152,775
Real Estate	2,405,000	Total Liabilities	$ 41,984,830
Partnership Inv.	79,044,573		
Personal Property	5,526,777		
Total Assets	$94,203,736	Net Worth	$ 52,218,906

How to Obtain Business Loans

(Downright Enright-like numbers... eh?) Lou wasn't so impressed. The most he **would** say was, "*Maybe* we **could** do something here." (Spoken to the tune of: "You *may* be eligible for a cash award...")

"Addison, what kind of ongoing cash flow does he have?"

"Mr. Prescott does not wish to supply his tax information. He feels the project's cash flow and offset monies, along with his own cash position... *outside* **of the venture... adequately address the concerns we have presented."**

"But if his ongoing projects happen to be draining his indicated cash position, of what substance **would** his guarantee be? We'll have to require full disclosure."

After chastising all parties involved for their ineptitude, Mr. Prescott forwarded his last two tax filings. This was an expensive proposition, as the volume of his returns filled a DC-10... chartered to fly in the information. And guess what? Our subsequent analysis of them proved inconclusive.

The wisdom of Lightning rolled forward. "We just aren't in a position to accept the risk of the site loan as it stands now." (Let's recap for those of you at home: That's a maximum exposure of around 30% with a personal guarantee showing almost $7 million in liquidity supporting it.) "I think we might have been able to do something... were the loan amounts not so large."

I went to the applicant's office in person to deliver this bit of news. Normally full of smoke, the air was as clean as can be. **"What's going on Grant? It smells different in here."**

"We're all trying to quit smoking. We've each had some health problems over the past few months... and the cigarettes we've been sucking down haven't helped. What's the latest?"

I told him. I've never seen anyone swallow a pack of Lifesavers whole. The paramedics applied the Heimlich maneuver before I even left my chair. I suppose it was a good idea they'd been added to staff.

THE Last Gasp

A few days later, Premier's principals requested I submit one last ditch effort on their behalf. Community Bank & Trust, who had funded the Seal Point project, was ready to come on board at Sunset Bay. Outstandings at Seal Point had kept them from being involved previously, as they were up to their legal lending limit with Premier.

Chapter Thirteen

However, due to reductions in their loan, they had room to participate some of the debt associated with Sunset Bay. The numbers would now shake out altogether differently, as even Acme agreed to up their subordinated stake.

The main points of the new structure were:

(1) The three mid-rise buildings along the golf course **would** not be developed with the other portion of the project. Instead they were to remain a separate undertaking entirely, to be contemplated only after the close-out of all low-rise units.

(2) The bank would not have to fund for any horizontal improvements whatsoever. No site loan... no chance of a land shortfall. (No rash on Lou.)

This was to be accomplished from the debt being apportioned across the following parties... in subordinate positions, or on adjacent plots of land:

Acme	$2,190,500
Community B&T	1,105,000
Total	$3,295,500

The balance of funds ($1,254,500) which had been requested under the originally proposed site revolver, **could** then be included in our construction loan for vertical improvements... as the monies actually dealt with direct prep of the building pads themselves.

(3) The bank's extension, providing for the completion of the first 3 low-rise facilities, **should** be in the amount of $5,200,000. Given a borrower-supplied average net unit proceeds of 97% (other closing costs now included in loan amounts), the debt is then retired within 27 closings. Which is 75% of the phase... dead on (poor choice of words) policy.

Addressing concerns relative to the fallout of the presales necessary to retire our proposed loan, almost 100 contracts existed at this juncture. The majority written for "the first available unit in the same bedroom/bath configuration." Out of these, the bank only need close 27 sales. Or about 1 in every 4 presales. And remember, historical fall out in Gull Harbor was about 1%.

How to Obtain Business Loans

Lou asked, "Have they recently surveyed the buyers to see who's willing to move around? I mean, some might want only an end unit, or only an interior one, or only second floor. Have they checked that out?"

"No." (Nor did they ascertain what buyers are willing to turn to their left when entering the compound versus those willing to turn only counterclockwise. And no study was done to discover who'd be willing to drive in full circles... as I've done with this deal.)

"I think without that type of data, we have to look at a good percentage of the presales falling out. Say 50%."

Voilà:
Counting only deposits of the units within the first three buildings, and not including any reserve or other offset monies previously discussed:

Average unit price	$ 197,903	
20% deposit	39,581	
36 20% deposits	1,424,902	
Max funding	$ 5,200,000	
Reductions from 18 closings		
(90% avg. price)	(3,206,029)	
	$ 1,993,971	
Forfeited deposits	(712,451)	
Unretired balance	$ 1,281,520	
Against 18 units valued at	3,562,254	LTV 35.9%

"That's against finished units now, Lou. Not land."

"Sure, sure. But now how are Acme and Community paid?"

(Who gives a *blank*? A better question might be, "How do you get paid?") **"In each 3-building set completed, after our debt is retired, there's an additional $1.3 million in cash flow available. Community *would* be paid out after the seventh building. As would $1.3 million of Acme's debt, and under their agreement with Premier... they would carry the balance until the last building of the low-rise phase."**

Even The Great Detractor was left at a loss. His best negative conclusion was, "I'm afraid the deal's just too convoluted now. Too many cooks in the kitchen." (And not a thing to eat.)

Chapter Thirteen

THE End

Hooked to his respirator, Jack Hudson could only mutter over what might have been. "Your bank had so much to gain from doing this deal. I just don't understand why such a brick wall was put up." (That's the only thing we've constructed in ages). "You'd have made a big chunk of money off this one transaction... and we'd have certainly then done others with you."

"Well, as Lou says, 'The bank doesn't want to be project or just transaction lenders... we want to be *relationship* bankers.'"

"How do you develop a *relationship* without doing the first loan?"

"I haven't figured that part out yet. Maybe I'm supposed to do several CD loans with someone first... you know, build up a track record."

"This ended up amounting to the same thing didn't it? With $1.3 million in a reserve account, and average compensating balances of 58%... you'd basically have been lending us our own money. Just as banks like."

"As I said, I haven't quite figured things out, yet. What are you guys going to do?"

"I don't know. We're sitting with an almost sold-out project, and no way to bring it to market... although... you're gonna love this, the subcontractors we've been using have agreed to carry the construction debt through unit closings."

"How *would* that work, Jack?"

"They're going to be the bank. We won't pay them for the work they'll have done... until units close. Acme and Community still carry the land debt. The approach costs us big, but we don't have a lot of alternatives.

"We're going to give it a few more weeks in hopes of getting a positive response from one of the other institutions where we've applied. Do you mind forwarding the information we've supplied you to other folks? Like Reece Melbourne at First Township."

"I'll have to check to see that I'm allowed to." (Such authority.) I asked Mortie, who said ask Winthrop, who said ask Lou, who said... "Hey, we still might be able to work something out."

Which I told Winthrop, who said tell Mortie, who said... "Heck, we're not going to do anything. You think we **should** send the stuff out, Addison?"

So we asked Winthrop, who in a command decision said, "Go ahead."

How to Obtain Business Loans

For the next couple of weeks we tried to sell the deal at other institutions on behalf of Premier. Mortie felt doing so would keep us in good graces with them and Winthrop thought it might enable us to retain the project's escrowed deposits. (Dream on.)

It was a tough sell (the deal that is). Think about it... **"Really, Mr. Competing Banker, it's a great deal. You guys *should* do the loan for them."**

"Why don't you do it?" **"We don't want to... you do it."** "No, you do it." **"No, you do it."** "No, you do it first." Needless to say, we found no takers for a project now perceived, within the community, to have leprosy. ("Why else would they be passing it on?")

Mortie suggested trying any and all capital sources. We worked very hard *attempting to do the deal... while not doing the deal*, of course. I contacted an extremely wealthy individual I had previously dealt with on another loan request. He had $65 million in marketable securities and sometimes borrowed against them to fund deals banks wouldn't without holding a CD... or marketable securities.

I put him in touch with the Premier's principals. Shortly thereafter I received a call from Grant Hobbs, whose EKG alarm was going off in the background. "Your Mr. LIQUID wants to charge us 5-6% above Prime, and 3 points! He's a *blanking* loan shark!" (No wonder he's got $65 million in marketable securities.)

What a racket. Take $5,750,000 in stocks, and pledge them as collateral for a bank loan. Enjoy, say a 7% dividend yield — $402,500, and pay around the same rate to the bank on a loan of $4,000,000 — $280,000. For a subtotal of $122,500. Then require a three point fee on the $4,000,000 passed through to a third party — $120,000. And charge 5% higher than you borrow at — $480,000. Net — $722,500. Bringing the yield on $5,750,000 to 12.6%. And that's a conservative estimate. Nice business for a pension or mutual fund... eh?

Grant's parting comment was, "Addison, he's talking about an APR of around 15%. Does this look like a three point deal to you?" (Nowadays... apparently.)

As Premier's principals and partners pondered the attributes of simple hemlock versus formal hara-kiri, the mailman delivered. North Dakota National Trust & Credit Bank offered a commitment more palatable than Mr. LIQUID's. (And the heavens opened, and music flowed forth, the choir sang, and children rejoiced.)

The day before, a newly hired Credit Administrator at the local level, Fabian Faulkner, had asked me to set down what had tran-

Chapter Thirteen

spired with the Sunset Bay request... start to finish. After which he wanted to discuss the matter and head through the region himself seeking an approval. When I was less than enthusiastic, I was told, "You can't be so negative."

Hearing the news from Premier, I penned one last memo.

> TO: Approval Group Distribution
> FROM: Addison Parker
> RE: Sunset Bay of Gull Harbor
>
> I received word today that Premier Locales has obtained a commitment to finance their above referenced project. The lender is NDNTCB, an institution located outside our marketplace. This renders any additional internal polemics immaterial, as they will be accepting the terms offered by NDNTCB.

Mortie asked, "What's polemics?"

"Let's just say it's the nicest way I can describe debating without purpose, but for drama alone," I explained.

Fabian scoffed, "I think it must be a nice way of saying *blank* off."

In this case, I guess so. I was exhausted. I'd been working on the deal for 11 months.

There are probably several conclusions one can draw from **THE** deal, and almost as many morals to the story. However, if there's one overriding notion, it's this: Don't put all your eggs in one basket. Not as in: Don't rely only on one bank. Although that's certainly true as well. But rather: Don't put all your money into a project on the front end.

Doing so might make LTVs look great, but if one thing **should** be pounded home by this point... banks aren't collateral lenders. Even when the collateral might be supplemented by reserves. A balance sheet showing cash and an income statement showing decent funds flow will carry you much further.

Witness a project known as Magnolia Woods. The owner, Edward Dunstin, poured well over $7 million into its horizontal improvements. Roads, water, sewer, etc., and even a golf course were all completed out-of-pocket. Confident that banks would be excited

How to Obtain Business Loans

over the absence of any land debt, he applied for a $1.5 million construction revolver to build four-unit condominium buildings. And he applied, and applied, and applied. With no additional cash resources and limited ongoing income, he never stood a chance. When last heard from, he was faced with bankruptcy... or loans with APR's in the mid-teens.

The most inventive businesspeople come up with ways to use other folk's money, keep some of their own on the balance sheet, and show a little continuing cash flow. Barry Rhodes was an attorney turned developer, who when I first met with him declared, "I'm not worth a billion dollars, but I have a method of supporting your underwriting."

His project, Robin's Nest, raised capital in a unique way. Buildings F & G, numbers 6 and 7 in a cluster to be constructed, were marketed first. Buyers were given the opportunity to purchase condos at $65,000... although the exact unit in the other buildings would be priced at $97,500. Thus, giving one the chance to make over $32,000 simply by closing on a purchase. That is, closing prior to construction. The risk being the cash paid up front.

The developer in turn, used the monies as equity into the earlier phases of the development. (Local laws allowing escrowed monies to be used anywhere within the same project, not necessarily to construct the unit purchased.)

Certainly this gives up some profit. But it gets a loan in place... in fact, two. One from the buyers in buildings F & G and one from a bank which is happy to see equity and cash on the balance sheet.

And ongoing income? How about an *investment consulting fee* charged to the buyers in the first two buildings marketed?

Perhaps the boys from Premier **should've** done something of this fashion. They **could've**. And they probably **would've**. As Mortie said, "Oh well, maybe they'll let us look at their next deal... " (After all... we do a great job of looking at stuff!)

Chapter Fourteen

CHAPTER 14:

HOW THE BANK LOOKS AT YOU

I'm sure you now have a much better feel for this than when you started the book. However, some subtleties need expanding upon; and a bit of repetition is in order with regard to a few key premises.

It has been contended prospective borrowers have a selective sense of hearing, discerning only what they wish to and ignoring the rest. For instance, a request for complete tax filings... inclusive of all schedules, supplements, and K-1s... is sometimes heard as "Supply the first page of your tax return." And the statement, "We're interested in your next deal," is occasionally interpreted as "You're pre-approved."

It's possible (just possible, mind you) that a portion of the information narrated in previous chapters was *discounted* a bit. You

How to Obtain Business Loans

might have said to yourself, "Maybe that happens at some institutions... but not mine." In today's environment, I might categorize that as blind faith. So permit me to re-emphasize some things. As your mother used to say... "For your own good."

What light will your deal be seen in? Perhaps, it is self-evident that *where* your request comes from can make all the difference. It, of course, emanates from you, but can arrive at the bank courtesy any number of different envoys. Suppose the ambassador is a mortgage broker. When undertaking large, complicated ventures, it may be best to allow a broker to "shop" a deal on your behalf. Through established networks and outright hustle, they cast a larger net when attempting to boat a lender and alleviate the need for you to fish from bank to bank.

But you should recognize a lender's first response to a brokered request. "What's wrong with the deal? There has to be a problem if a broker's involved." The presumption exists; all good deals are presented directly by the prospective borrower.

Accepting a brokered application means acknowledging the undertaking is being reviewed all over town. And no institution wants to be the "bigger fool." That is, the one who extends a loan... has it go bad... then has to listen to competing bankers say, "Yeah, we looked at the deal, and took a pass. We recognized the risk." (This said in a superior tone, with thumb to nose, and fingers wiggling about.) Thus, many banks avoid such requests like the plague. My own institution had an unwritten policy to contemplate no brokered deals. Any application for credit had to come straight from a viable potential borrower.

When time is of the essence (or even reasonably important), it may still be appropriate to enlist the aid of a broker... or brokers. However, it is important you overcome the initial perception your agented request will carry. This can be accomplished by adding a personal touch. To do so, you'll need to obtain a list of where your proxy will be submitting packages.

You should then preface any contact with an institution by phoning the senior lender, or even the bank president. It will be incumbent upon you to explain why you have retained a broker. Answer honestly, but tactfully. "In today's regulatory environment... with the burden the government has placed upon y'all (the southern gentleman approach is a personal favorite) and the resulting time it takes you to comply with their force-fed policies... it seems

Chapter Fourteen

only prudent in my mind to, shall we say, have more than one oar in the water." Or something of the like.

It's even more beneficial if you can (truthfully) state you have a working relationship with said broker. Or better yet, employ him on a "consulting" basis. (Consultant = good word. Broker = bad word.) I recall one incident where a "consultant" accrued wages in fee form... payable if the deal in question closed. Otherwise, a highly reduced amount was due at the discretion of the applicant. But you needed to read the fine print of their "employment agreement" to figure that out. In conversation, the bank was only apprised of a consultant's involvement. And that was fine, just keep those brokers away.

Conversely, should your request be championed by an influential benefactor, the formal approval process (previously spoken of as regulatory burden), can be... circumvented... to a large degree.

(Read this section in hushed tones.) One Monday morning, my phone rang around 8:15 A.M. "Hello, Mr. Parker. This is Olivia Gordon, I'm Talbot Wetherby's secretary. (The holding company's CEO... shhh!) Mr. Wetherby asked me to call. You see, he sits on the board of a company called CompuTel. And one of the other directors is a gentleman named Carvell Benton. Well, Mr. Benton's son is moving to your area. He'll be some sort of assistant manager at a local hotel. And Mr. Wetherby would like you to see he receives... *employee treatment*... on his residential mortgage application. He'll be building a home right away."

Hmmmm. *Employee treatment*... what exactly does that mean? Is she saying approve the loan no matter what? Or is she just talking about extending beneficial terms? Or both? Maybe I should ask. Then again, I don't want to come across as being difficult.

"Mr. Parker, did you understand?"

"Well... you mean Mr. Wetherby wants me to waive any financing fees, as we do with employees?"

"He wants to ensure Mr. Benton's son *gets the best deal possible, with minimum cost.*" (Comprenda?)

"...oohhhh Kay. Would Mr. Wetherby like me to call him after I meet with Mr. Benton's son? Just to let him know what transpires?"

"No! Please contact **me** by Friday so that I may apprise him of what you've done. He'll need to know by then, as CompuTel's next board meeting is the following Monday."

How to Obtain Business Loans

I'm sure Mr. Big would disavow any knowledge of the directive I received. However, although delivered by a secretary; the "applicant's request" commanded... most favorable treatment.

Know anybody in high places? Should your deal arrive from the top down, you, too, could be standing in the best possible light.

All That Glitters Is Not Gold

A methodical comparison of business balance sheets would be a diverse and daunting proposition. An entire set of encyclopedias could be filled with examples of how statements from assorted industries should look, and how their line item composition might vary according to a company's breadth.

Actually, there are just such reference books. They're produced by Robert Morris Associates (RMA), which is a trade group of bank credit officers. (Hey, LOOK OUT when they get together... Tailhook '91 looks like a Sunday church service in comparison. These guys really know how to let their hair down.)

When working, however, they compile untold volumes of data to be separated by industry type, and specific area of operation. Basically, they list averages to be used in comparing a loan applicant's concern to the "norms" of its particular commerce segment. This can be done with not only balance sheet and income statement items, but also key financial ratios. For example, say your bank is contemplating a request from a company who manufactures something as obscure as coated and laminated paper. You'd contrast the firm's historical operation to RMA data on that "industry."

In this instance, say the averages are determined as a percentage of asset size. Your applicant has total assets of $5.5 million. The RMA survey was done on 19 concerns. Almost half, of which, presented unqualified audited statements... the highest quality financial disclosures available. Unfortunately, your prospective borrower supplied compiled statements prepared by an in-house controller. (Not so good.)

For the record, companies should attempt to provide statements of a quality typical for their size and line of business. Banks will often add loan covenants requiring particular statement quality subsequent to a loan commitment... if not prior to. A quick accounting lesson will help you develop an appreciation for the levels of financial reporting.

Chapter Fourteen

Compiled: A preparer formats totals for a firm, but does not verify any of the numbers presented, or express an opinion as to their validity.

Reviewed: An accountant procures general information about the company's operating methods, and perhaps, does some physical confirmation of inventories and receivables. This adds a measure of reliability to the statements.

Audited: These differ from the preceding forms, and among themselves, according to the degree of certification undertaken in affirming presented totals. There are four types of accountant opinion letters which accompany audited statements. In ascending caliber:

Adverse: Declares the numbers do not accurately reflect a company's position.
Disclaimer: Pronounces that limitations in the analysis make commentary impossible.
Qualified: Notes the information is a fair representation, but includes certain qualifications as to the scope of verification undertaken in testing the legitimacy of reported totals.
Unqualified: Announces the statements accurately reflect the firm's state of affairs, and indicates the information is set forth in accordance with Generally Accepted Accounting Principals.

The more detailed statements prepared and provided to the bank... the higher the cost, and coincidentally, the higher the probability of approval... as the bank will feel more comfortable with the information they are being asked to rely upon. This is not an area to skimp. Consider the money well spent.

Returning to RMA statistical analysis, you can compare your applicant's balance sheet make-up directly to industry averages. (Or, at least, to 19 industry respondents.) Meaningful items of asset comparison are: cash holdings, and both receivable and inventory concentration. The percentage of fixed assets is also important in some industries where property, plant, and equipment are an integral part of bringing the company's product to market.

Further, the composition of a company's debt is always vital. Do

How to Obtain Business Loans

they appear to properly match sources and uses of capital? Are they disproportionately reliant upon trade debt? Does the current portion of long-term debt appear to weigh them down? It's all right there for comparison in the RMA figures.

As is income data, and the aforementioned key financial ratios... which I promise we will not go into. (That's on the itinerary for Credit Hook '95.) However, one item might be of interest... owner/officer compensation. This is a favorite of credit administrators. The range within the coated and laminated "industry" (or, at least that of 19 respondents) is between 1.7% and 4.3% of asset size. With an average of 2.6%. And what if the owner of an applicant company takes out money at a higher rate, for instance, 9.5%. Listen for it... "Omigosh, he's raping the company. We've got to include covenants to limit his annual compensation." (Not surprisingly, this isn't a favorite among owners.)

Obviously, no one can attempt to force-manage a business to industry averages. Doing so would be dangerous, at best. Suffice it to say, however, some effort should be made to remain cognizant of what others in the field are doing. This would make beneficial manipulation possible and prepare an owner to justify differences from the established "norms."

In this chapter, though, I wish to focus on how banks view the balance sheets of individuals. First off, one should be aware any information listed on a personal financial statement is looked at with a jaundiced eye. It helps to have an accountant draft the statement, as this adds a degree of credibility which can prove invaluable time-wise.

If an institution questions presented figures, it will ask for proof and conduct independent tests to ascertain the validity of the information supplied. It will require savings and brokerage account summaries, life insurance policies, appraisals, and a host of other time consuming documentation, when they are uneasy with the numbers.

I remember one gentleman who halted the process before it got started. He had supplied his financial statement for consideration on a Monday. On Thursday, just as a list of tests were being decided upon, he called the bank.

"Addison, I'm afraid I've made a mistake on the information I presented to you. I feel terrible and I want to set things straight immediately. I'm sorry, but I incorrectly disclosed my notes receiv-

Chapter Fourteen

able... by $90. I apologize for the misrepresentation, it was an honest mistake."

This COLOSSAL error took place on a statement with total assets in excess of $2.1 million. The $90 difference was inconsequential. The bank adjusts out any value given to notes receivable anyway. However, the gesture did one thing... it put the prospect's integrity beyond reproach. Character was no longer an issue... so, no checks were conducted on the totals he set forth.

In the case of the proposed loan to our local laminator, it's to be guaranteed by a Mr. Ambrose McGee who supplied this statement:

Ambrose & Georgia McGee	
Cash	$ 1,981,200
Cash Value of Life Insurance	57,810
Coin Collection	101,000
Retirement Accounts	401,500
Securities Traded on the New York Stock Exchange	126,100
Securities Traded Over-The-Counter	8,163,290
Club Memberships	85,000
Bequest Receivable	5,000,000
Stock in Closely-Held Firms	1,379,300
Partnership Concerns	81,581,680
Trust Involvement	7,697,500
Vacation Home, South of France	812,000
Primary Residence, Miami	1,520,500
Commercial Real Estate	12,710,420
Personal Property (Cars, Boats, Art, Jewelry, Furs, & Furniture)	1,325,000
Total Assets	$ 122,942,300
Total Liabilities	(8,840,000)
Reported Net Worth	$ 114,102,300

Immediately, there's a problem. Only Mr. McGee has offered to guarantee. Yet he has provided a joint statement. When asked to forward a breakdown of solely held assets, he replies, "Shoot, Georgia has ownership in almost everything I do. I don't think I **can** do a separate statement... not and have anything on it. I suppose you could just take our joint total and divide it by two, and that would give you some idea of what I'm worth alone."

No can do. Either the bank needs a separate accounting, or Mrs.

How to Obtain Business Loans

McGee needs to sign a guarantee as well. And here's the tricky part. By law, you can't ask her to. She has to offer.

Assuming some *sponsorship* was necessary to justify an approval of C&L's request and Mr. McGee isn't able to show anything on his own, you're left with only one choice. Turn the loan down.

Well... in practice, it works a little differently. To illustrate: Once, Mortie scheduled a big luncheon with some prospective borrowers. Both had presented joint financial statements with their wives, but offered only individual guarantees. Mortie handled the matter most deftly...

"We have an issue with the *sponsorship* portion of your credit request."

"What's that... I mean the sponsorship portion?"

"I'm referring to the personal guarantees... they're not sufficient to backstop the extension requested."

"**What? Have you seen our statements? We've plenty of assets to support the facility, and good liquidity, too!**"

"Well, yes, the statements you provided do indicate the ability to support... but those are joint statements. We've only been offered your individual guarantees... and they wouldn't justify the proposed extension."

"**So you're telling us our wives have to guarantee.**"

"Not at all. I'm precluded from doing so. I'm only telling you additional support is necessary because you don't qualify on solely owned assets."

"**So our wives have to guarantee.**"

"Not at all. You could bring in outside parties to guarantee."

"**And pay them to do so? No thanks. We get the message. Our wives will sign.**"

We'll presume Mr. McGee catches on too... and comes to a similar conclusion. Even then, the statement provided is going to require some work before the bank will embrace any of the information presented... and rely on same for support. Adjustments to asset totals, and the (sometimes deranged) reasoning behind them are as follows:

Personal Property ($ 1,325,000)
Always inflated. Salable only at a small fraction of perceived value.

Chapter Fourteen

Commercial Real Estate (12,710,420)
>Occasionally left in when substantiated by independent appraisals. Then at 70-75% of reported value. Otherwise, just zeroed out. The S&Ls lost too much money in this area. Take no chances.

Primary Residence (1,520,500)
>Remember the axiom: Always the last thing to be relinquished by a debtor.

Vacation Home, South of France (812,000)
>Bank has no practical recourse against foreign assets. Which explains why non-U.S. citizens have such a tough time borrowing in the states.

Trust & Partnership Involvement (89,279,180)
>Minority, and noncontrolling interests, cannot be relied upon as a source of capital. To the contrary, the bank must ensure they are not cash drains.

Stock in Closely-Held Firms (1,379,300)
>Without an established market to trade shares, how can any value be factually attributed? Besides, most owners inflate their company's worth by assigning too much value to goodwill^g.

Bequest Receivable (5,000,000)
>If you happen to be a trust baby anticipating a windfall gain upon a wealthy relative's demise, don't ask the bank for a bridge loan while you wait. How could the term be set... actuary tables?

Club Memberships (85,000)
>Probably a sore spot with your local banker. Who, even if time permitted, can no longer play at the local county club. Corporate memberships have been widely discontinued. The members will say because they allowed too many folks the run of their club without paying the same proportionate fees as individuals. I wonder, instead, if it's because fewer loans are being made at the 19th hole.

Over-the-Counter Securities (8,163,290)
>Market lacks breadth. Sometimes penny issues fall off the board. Nasty business.

Retirement Accounts (401,500)
>The McGees aren't that age yet. They'd pay a tax penalty to withdraw these monies. So the bank assumes they won't. Regardless.

Coin Collection (101,000)
>Buyer demand is fickle. Assigning a value is anyone's guess.

These... adjustments... have a profound effect on the statement presented:

How to Obtain Business Loans

Reported Net Worth	$114,102,300
Total Adjustments	(120,777,190)
Adjusted (Deficit) Net Worth	(6,674,890)

Which is then further altered by the treatment of contingent liabilities:

Adjusted (Deficit) Net Worth	(6,674,890)
Total Comm'l Debt	
— Carrying Personal Guarantees	(21,427,003)
Reconciled & Adjusted	
— (Deficit) Net Worth	(28,101,893)

(Can it be this easy? With the new Adjuster® by Ronco, you can slice, dice, and julienne net worths to the bone.) From $114,102,300 to a negative ($28,101,893) in just a few quick chops. In theory, <u>this method of analysis is supposed to provide the bank with a solid understanding of an individual's capacity to immediately support all current and proposed obligations.</u> (Question: How many Americans can instantaneously pay off all their obligations at one time?) In reality the process could be shortened to the following:

Liquid Assets	
Cash	$ 1,981,200
CVLI	57,810
NYSE Securities	126,100
Total Liquid Assets	$ 2,165,110
Less: Direct Liabilities	(8,840,000)
Adjusted (Deficit) Net Worth	(6,674,890)
Commercial Guarantees	(21,427,003)
Reconciled Net Worth	(28,101,893)

No credit is given for anything being semi-liquid. I remember lampooning this process when one of my customers indicated a sizable holding in collectible coins. Silver dollars to be exact. An over zealous credit analyst had zeroed out his value attributed to the collection, and I argued, **"Can't we give him some credit for his coins?"**

Chapter Fourteen

"No. It's too hard to assign a value with any degree of certainty."
"How about one dollar per silver dollar. They're still a medium of exchange you know?"
Sure, they may be shiny... but they're not gold from the vault of Ft. Knox.

Mind Your Own Business

We already know, when the bank is unfamiliar with a particular industry, it will hide in the closet rather than come out and play. All the RMA comparisons in the world have little effect on changing that tendency. But, for the record, RMA does publish the identical information we went over earlier... spread as a percentage of sales.

Although the percentages themselves differ, they should convey a message similar to when the figures were apportioned by asset size... or for that matter if they were calculated as a percentage of another base footing... total liabilities, net worth (or water cooler volume). Assets and sales are just used because returns are often calculated against them... and equity... and leverage... Anyway, the important thing is, RMA data helps lenders compare a prospective borrower's operation to other concerns within the same field. This is only helpful, though, after identifying the applicant's area of business. Which, from the banker's perspective, is often not as straightforward as one would think.

Remember the huge adjustment made to Mr. McGee's statement? $21,427,003 for commercial debts he personally guaranteed. This type of reduction will have a significant effect on most everyone's net worth position. Such alterations are a precautionary measure taken to ward off The Contingent Liability Plague, a killer of previously reliable borrowers.

To illustrate, take the case of Mr. Cogs who owns an upscale widget manufacturing business, which is the bank's primary obligor on a loan. Although, obviously, Mr. Cogs' personal guarantee on the debt was required. All analyses indicate the business is doing quite well, albeit cash flow is a bit up and down due to the seasonal nature of the widget industry. Restitution to the bank, however, has always been made on a timely basis.

Mr. Cogs' sons are in real estate. Competing institutions have supplied them monies to build and make speculative purchases based upon the strength of their father's guarantee. (Somehow

How to Obtain Business Loans

always... offered.) In the eyes of many bankers, it is the extension of such guarantees that poses great risk to the widget company itself, for they indirectly place the manufacturing concern in the real estate business.

Now Mr. Cogs' primary bank will see fit to analyze things like the construction risk of his sons' business, including, but not limited to, issues surrounding possible worker injury and public liability. Not to mention the financial risk associated with possible capital calls arising from cost overruns, subcontractor claims, and losses on sale.

Proponents of thoroughly analyzing contingent liability risk will argue that even though all signs relative to Mr. Cogs and his manufacturing business may be positive, he might struggle with difficulties in his sons' real estate affairs at any time. *And he may not want the bank to know.* Walter Bradshaw, President of 9th City Bank recommends the use of third party financial investigation firms. Such companies are engaged to make all-encompassing reviews of a borrower's business... and personal... affairs. Mr. Paranoid advocates this type of investigation become a regular part of a bank's due diligence process.

(Headed to your depository to request a loan? Watch your rear view mirror... you may be being tailed.)

Are the Rumors About You True?

I'm always amazed when it comes to the general public's lack of knowledge in the area of credit reporting and their complete miscalculation of its importance. In an information-based society such as ours, access to previously *personal* material has become widespread. Where your credit used to be checked only when purchasing a home, or maybe a vehicle, now you needn't be surprised to have someone pull a credit bureau when you procure a service... like cellular air time, cable TV, or electricity for goodness sake. Or even when you move into a community controlled by an association. Or, how about this... when you apply for a job.

The use, and misuse, of readily accessible private credit information has opened the door to a whole new area of litigation for attorneys... and lifted the lid on a Pandora's box of evils for the public to deal with.

Other than race, perhaps no one thing can predetermine your treatment, and the opportunities you receive in life, more than your

Chapter Fourteen

credit rating. You should guard it religiously. And don't be naive enough to make either of the following statements:

- "I've always paid back exactly what I've owed. I have a perfect credit rating."

    Restitution isn't the only issue. Did you pay the debt exactly to term? If you were ever 30 days behind on a payment, you have a blemished credit rating.

- "I've always paid everything on time. I have a perfect credit rating."

    You might have written the checks on schedule, but that in no way ensures the creditor posted them in a timely manner. One giant retailer is absolutely notorious for misapplied customer payments, to the extent that many finance institutions disregard late payments noted by the company on an individual's report. (Ask any banker to find out who the guilty party is.) However, this is the only exception. In all other instances, it is assumed reported information is factual.

You have to periodically check to see that your bureau is clean. At routine intervals, have your credit file pulled by a local agency and make sure no one has incorrectly posted derogatory information. (Your financial institution cannot give you a copy of the bureau data they used in assessing your request. It's against the law. Makes sense... banks have to comply with umpteen disclosure issues if they rejected a request, but they can't show an individual their own credit file.)

Reporting mistakes happen altogether too often. Individuals with common names, John Smith, Mike Jones, etc., need to be especially diligent in monitoring their credit file. Negative information from one John Smith is often misplaced into the database of another John Smith. In theory, this is supposed to be controllable by the cross referencing of social security numbers to name and address information. Unfortunately, practice in the field is far from infallible. And once a mistake is made... it is often difficult to set right.

That in mind, be sure to watch where and how you offer your social security number. Today, it seems like anyone and everyone requests it. From creditors, to retailers, to colleges, to employers... all

How to Obtain Business Loans

have a need to know those nine private digits. In and of itself, they often have singular good reason. The problem is they are a bit loose with the recirculation of the numbers. Doesn't it seem odd how when you obtain a credit card from one institution, you are suddenly "pre-approved" by a host of others? And, isn't it strange how after making regular purchases at Store A, you receive volumes of advertisements and perhaps more "pre-approved" credit from other retailers? And how after college, the alumni association has the ability to track your whereabouts better than the CIA? And employers, of course they need the information for tax purposes. Everyone (except for those who work within the homes of public officials) need to supply the numbers for withholding. And, guess what? Your own firm may be the loosest of all with your social.

For instance: Due to a lack of new loan volume (gasp) my bank had been on a big push to ascertain where business was coming from (or, rather, where it wasn't). They wanted a method to track each and every loan, as well as deposit and service accounts, which entered the bank. The idea was to have a way for senior management to assess true performance.

Myron enlisted the help of a local computer programmer and, after a few months of work, announced that a software package and system were implementation-ready. All officers were sent to training and there the computer technician explained, "This program will allow you to follow your referrals to other departments in a state-of-the-art manner. Suppose, Addison, you have a commercial customer who also needs a residential loan. You wish to refer him to Ira Haskel in that department. You just enter Ira's database by using his social security number, and type in the information for the referral. You don't need to send him any hard copy. It will all be on his computer screen; and the data will roll up into a management report without any additional work on your part."

"How am I going to know Ira's social security number?"

"Myron's provided me with a list of all officer's socials to use as their call numbers. Each branch will get the list, and be able to access a person's file remotely with the use of the numbers."

Now considering all bank personnel also had easy access to my address information, I had a problem with them having my social security number. Because with those two items, they had the ability to apply for all sorts of credit... in my name!!! And seeing as how bank personnel are a bit transient (one in three faces changing annually),

Chapter Fourteen

I was more than a bit hesitant about everyone having access to my credit bureau.

Thankfully, my protests ultimately got the system changed to use other password codes. But to finish the story, as we continued our education in how to use the program, I found an interesting shortcoming. Initially expected to allow referral tracking between all branches and departments, its eventual application would fall far short. Cost was the major reason.

"So if I want to refer a deposit customer to one of the city's southern branches, I just access their database and type in the information... and that's it."

"No... you'll need to send them a hard copy, and one to Myron as well for reports."

"I thought you said that wasn't necessary?"

"I said if you referred to the residential department it wouldn't be... they're in your same building."

"So anything down the hall from me... where I could just walk the information... I can send by computer without hard copy backup. But anything at a more remote location... where the ability to contact via the terminal would be helpful... I must type into the computer, print, then send a hard copy to both the individual and management... sort of like what I could do with a typewriter."

"Look, we tried to set it up the other way. Myron just didn't want to pay the additional $5,000."

"So the bank spent, what, $15,000-$20,000 for software which doesn't enable us to do anything more than we already can by hand... and we don't want to spend another $5,000 to have it work as intended?"

After taking the time to train all officers in the use of the system, it was basically junked. Management thought it better to just type referral slips and keep a handwritten log accounting for what went where.

But I've drifted, it's your credit file we should be discussing. I'll presume you understand the importance of maintaining and routinely monitoring your record. Now you'll need to know how to decipher the material a credit agency composes. There are articles and pamphlets on how to become proficient at *credit-ese*, but I'll summarize the essential elements.

Suppose you applied for a $100,000 loan to purchase a second home, and your credit file looked like this:

273

How to Obtain Business Loans

12/25/93
PROVIDER
Inside Scoop, a credit information service. 123 Public Ave. Los Angeles, CA

(A)   **FOR THE CREDIT FILE OF**
Dwight Edgerton 22854 Palm CT Hollywood (owns) (213) 555-0345 Age 40, social security number 999-99-9999

(B)   **EMPLOYMENT INFORMATION**
Entertainment Management, Inc. D/B/A Agents to the Cartoons Hollywood (213) 555-0356 President 12 years
Self-employed Income not verifiable

CREDIT HISTORY

(C) Grantor	Highest Opened	Credit	Owed	Past Due	Rating	Terms	Times Late 30	60	90	Last
Walkonya 46904739444	5/85	186,600	149,535	0	I-1	1,257 **(D)**	1	0	0	R2 8/88
Kingdoms 42002053338	9/90	20,000	18,188 **(E)**	237	R-2	237 **(E)**	3	0	0	R2 12/93 **(E)**
CMAG **(F)** 3201857463	8/92	25,000	24,704	0	I-1	380	0	0	0	
Pursue 915884736	6/90	12,500	5,461	0	I-1	265	0	0	0	
Jacket 9843564386	9/92	10,500	9,682	0	I-2	234	2 **(G)**	0	0	R2 8/93 **(G)**
Civic-Cache 312483058	9/81	9,000	826	0	R-1	41	0	0	0	
VaultAmerica 84305392	2/78	5,000	1,126	0	R-1	68	0	0	0	
EMXA 87674	6/70		741	0	R-1		0	0	0	
Bags 52047373	2/68	500	0	0	R-1		0	0	0	
Burns 25039847987	1/67	250	0	0	R-1		1 **(H)**	1	1 **(H)**	R8 5/71

PUBLIC RECORDS
Clear/No judgments Subject has been previously married.
(I)

INQUIRIES   **(J)**
8/20/92...CMAG 9/4/92...Assistance Wares 10/12/92...Baldwins, NY
12/2/93...Kingdoms 12/4/93...Civic-Cache 12/5/93...Pursue

Chapter Fourteen

(A) Your address, phone number, social, and even age are given. Often, it will indicate how long you've been living at a certain location and, when applicable, will disclose rental history.

(B) Place of work and position held are noted, as well as income for many salaried individuals.

(C) Columns separate information provided by creditors. Data is included, by account number, from highest to lowest credit balance.

(D) Walkonya holds your primary mortgage. They show you were once 30 days behind... back in 1988.

(E) Kingdoms holds a second position on your home, whose loan proceeds were used to buy a boat. They indicate you have been 30 days delinquent 3 times... and are past due currently.

(F) This is a lease payment Entertainment Management makes on a company vehicle.

(G) With you as a cosigner, Jacket financed your son's car purchase. Looks like he's been late a few times.

(H) And Burns shows you, like many of their customers, to have once been 90 days late.

(I) The bureau is even kind enough to show you were previously married. (At least they don't disclose details of the fiasco.)

(J) Inquiries are from a company called Baldwins, and three local banks, all within the last month.

As a credit applicant with this file, you had some legwork to do. You contacted Walkonya for an explanation as to why they showed you thirty days past due back in 1988. They had no record of the incident, other than the "fact" the loan was delinquent. Finally, you remembered this was when your interest rate initially adjusted, and *the bank was late* getting a new payment book out. Walkonya graciously agreed to remove the erroneous item from your bureau.

You are not, nor have you ever been, delinquent on the boat loan. After fighting through Kingdom's automated response line, you were ultimately informed the whole matter had to do with a computer foul-up... arising from Kingdom's simultaneous acquisition of three mid-size institutions, of which your old bank was one of the casualties. They, too, agreed to amend your record.

How to Obtain Business Loans

After a firm discussion with Junior about taking his responsibilities seriously, you contact Jacket to remind them of theirs. They neglected to notify you when Junior's loan fell in arrears, but nevertheless posted the delinquency to your credit file. As a result, the branch manager decided to have the blemishes removed from your report.

You weren't even aware you had an account with Burns. Perhaps your ex-wife had opened it, but even she wouldn't have let it lapse 90 days. You started the appeal process, well aware nothing would happen overnight.

All those inquiries. Your second home application was met with a high degree of skepticism because of them. The bank had asked you to explain the origin of each one... in writing. Your reply stated you had no idea why CMAG had checked your credit... you hadn't requested anything. (Creditors often retain the right to update their loan files with periodic customer bureaus. Such being one of their "early warning" methods to detect future repayment problems.) Assistance Wares had sent you a flier promising 10% off your next jewelry purchase in return for opening an account... and your wedding anniversary **was** coming up. You had no idea what Baldwins was and the remainder were simultaneous applications for commercial credit in Entertainment Management's name.

The officer reviewing your second home request accepted your explanation and moved into repayment analysis. You had reported your average annual income taken from the company was approximately $95,000. However, you informed the officer you didn't take a salary, but rather drew money down as needed, then took a lump-sum bonus each December.

This received a frown, and a big sigh. You were told you'd have to supply complete company tax filings for the past two years... to verify your income. "But for now, let's see if you'd qualify off the income you've asserted," he continued. "Your total monthly obligations are $2,482, not including EMXA... which is another $741. So, on average, we'll say you've got $3,200 per month in servicing requirements. And your total annual income divided by twelve is... $8,000. That makes your debt ratio... 40%. We use Fannie Mae qualifying guidelines... 36% is the maximum acceptable... you're 4% higher before we count the proposed obligation. Including that payment... $665 per month..."

"Excuse me, I calculated my payment would be $492 per month

Chapter Fourteen

on the one year ARM... it is at 4.25%, right? That's what I saw advertised."

"That's the primary mortgage rate. The rate for investor purchases is actually 5.5%, but the bank uses 7% as a minimum qualifying rate."

"Even though your 5-year ARM is at 6.25% and most people refinance more often than that?"

"Uh-huh. So your ratio would actually be... 48%. Way too high."

"Do you mind? Let me see how you're doing the calculations. Let's see... you've included the CMAG lease payment my company makes. Plus the Jacket loan my son pays. And monthly interest on the Civic-Cache, VaultAmerica, and EMXA balances which can all be paid to zero from my cash holdings. Look..."

Total Obligations	$ 3,865/month
Less: CMAG	(380)
Jacket	(234)
Civic-Cache	(41)
Vault America	(68)
EMXA	(741)
Revised Monthly Obligations	$ 2,401/month, or 30%
Including this Obligation at @ 7%	665
Total	$ 3,066/month, or 38%

"And that's on my *average* income from the past two years, my earnings have actually been going up as my company's business has expanded. I made $82,000 two years ago, $98,000 last year, and I should bring home around $110,000 this year. Can't you give some consideration for that?"

"Well... it's difficult to... when you don't draw a salary. We'll really have to look hard at Entertainment Management's statements, but even then... we're really compelled to take an average from the last two years. It's policy." (Self-employed individuals: Save a lot of grief. Pay yourself a salary. Put it on all credit applications, making sure it covers your existing and proposed obligations at a rate better than 2.78:1. Then name a financial officer within your company, and disclose them as a contact person to verify income. The bank will then

How to Obtain Business Loans

confirm your last year's and current salary from them... and qualify you off of the latter.)

"You see, I'm even supposed to look at your credit card lines as if they were fully drawn... and figure your ratios accordingly. We, generally, don't turn people down if that throws them over an acceptable ratio, but we like to factor it into the decision making process. Just like we do your son's car payment and your company's lease obligation. Because if either of those parties weren't able to pay... you'd have to."

"I've got news for you. If the company can't make that lease payment, I can't pay anything... 'cause the company's not able to pay me."

"Which is why we'll analyze the company statements very closely." (What else is new.)

"Man... did you see that guy? He never comes to the bank wearing anything more formal than a Polo golf shirt. I don't think he's ever heard of a coat-and-tie."

"You're just jealous."

"Yeah, right. You know, it wouldn't hurt him to dress a little more appropriately when he comes in to ask for a half million here and a half million there."

"Doesn't he already have a ton of debt now?"

"Yeah... come here. I'll show you what all he's got going on."

"No thanks. When the subpoenas are being handed out, I want to be able to say I have limited knowledge of his affairs."

"Funny guy. You really think he'll eventually go under?"

"Matter of time. He's got so many irons in the fire... big irons, mind you. All it will take is one problem, and the whole thing will go like a house of cards."

"Makes you wonder how I can keep getting stuff approved for him, huh?"

"Not really. He's a sacred cow. Buddy-buddy with all the directors. Wouldn't matter what he'd ask for... he'd get it. You can bet your bottom dollar he's talking to the board about his latest deals before you ever get wind of them."

"You'd think at some point he'd pull back. You know, let some

Chapter Fourteen

cash accumulate, put something in a savings or pension account... Say, are you in the bank's 401K program?"

"**Absolutely. It's never too early to start saving for retirement.** (Spoken by a 25-year-old.) **I put in the max, 6% of my pretax income.**"

"Whatcha doing for lunch? Did you hear Wal-Mart's got a sale on knit golf shirts? Let's head over there. I'll drive... I need to gas up the ol' Buick for the drive home tonight anyway. Hey, did you here Addison is talking about buying a Mazda MX-6? A sports car! I don't know about that guy. Seems a little loosy-goosy for a banker."

"**Yeah, I heard he wasn't in the 401K plan either.**"

Chapter Fifteen

CHAPTER 15:

HOW TO GET YOUR DEAL APPROVED

In a way, it could be said the whole book fits well within the confines of this chapter's title. In essence, the inside information and the illustrating anecdotes hopefully have afforded an understanding of...

- What you should do.
- What you shouldn't do.
- What you mustn't do. And...
- What you MUST do to get your deal approved.

The blueprints have been provided. Though, as with any lesson learned, a lack of finesse can hamper the use of the newly acquired

How to Obtain Business Loans

knowledge. More often than not, difficulties may arise from not knowing your opponent... that is, the bank. If honest, I doubt many participants would say the lender-borrower relationship is a true team effort. Each party hopes to impose their will in various ways. *Understanding your enemy is half that battle.* (As a kid I learned this from one of David Carradine's <u>Kung Fu</u> episodes.) You, too, must master this premise.

One man did just that. He had called a bank seeking information and got the run-around from the institution's automated response system. As retaliation for wasting his time, he designed his own computer program, which he used to contact several different departments at the bank. Regardless of what the answerer did, they were patched through to additional recorded messages... each carrying a complaint. He recognized who he was dealing with and responded in kind.

Who are the people who scoff at your polo shirt, then rush to buy discount knock-offs? Who are these folks who feel any vehicle more elegant than a Buick Skylark is affected, conspicuous, and pretentious? They are **The Bankers**. And they are different from the general public. Born missing a particular chromosome, or perhaps without certain genes, they are unable to comprehend the concept of *utility*. In economics it's defined as:

> The want or desire fulfilling capacity of a good or service; the sensation of enjoyment or gratification felt from their consumption.

Much like a toddler can't quite grasp quantum physics, bankers can't quite get a handle on paying a little more for a higher quality product, or spending money to collect an experience. *A polyester suit does just as nicely as wool, a hand ironed dress shirt looks almost as good as one sent to the cleaners, a meal at home is just as enjoyable as one out, and for goodness sake... don't go to the theater, wait for the video.* This is **The Banker's Pledge**, an industry credo which parallels the Hippocratic oath taken by physicians.

Most institutions have opened brokerage departments and suggest customers take advantage of the service, while their own employees put money into regular savings, 401K plans, or government savings bonds. The "do as I say, not as I do" method of guidance stems from those pre-described genetic irregularities. The banker

Chapter Fifteen

allows himself to live vicariously through his customers, but must be true to an inherent conservative nature. The lifestyle differences seem obvious:

Topic	Banker	Businessman
Favorite Film	Wall Street (High rollers get taken down)	Barbarians at The Gate (A classic in "ruthless and rapacious finance.")
Favorite Book	Not this one.	The Art of the Deal
Weekend Activity	Mowing the yard.	Skydiving
Vacation Plans	Grandma's house.	Vegas
Number of Children	More than the avg. Catholic family	1 or 2 at boarding school
Ultimate Vehicles	'86 Olds Delta 88 Royale Any station wagon	S Class Mercedes BMW 850i
Most Overworked Saying	"A penny saved is..."	"When do we close?"

Okay, okay, so maybe Vegas was a bit over the top, but the innate contrasts are undeniable. Those in private business loathe bureaucracies, while bankers deify form above function.

"Who Do You Think You're Dealing With?"

What's in a name? The title's the thing. I once offered the introduction: "This is Fabian Faulkner, the bank's Credit Administrator." Only to have Fabian pull me aside later and scold, "Don't tell people I'm a credit administrator... I'm a senior credit officer. Credit administrator sounds like I just push paper all day long." Which is exactly what he did, but that wasn't the point.

All sizable corporations are big on titles. Everyone knows it's easier to bestow a glossy new designation to someone's business card, rather than offer them additional compensation.

It's the intrinsic way of giving raises. Cash rewards are always promised for sometime down the road. ("You'll receive no money now, but on your death bed... ") In the meantime, a snappy new title every so often can keep natives from becoming restless.

I have to laugh when I hear someone say, "We've always dealt

How to Obtain Business Loans

with so-and-so. He's a vice president at such-and-such institution." In banking, who isn't a vice president of some sort? Only the degree of an individual's vice presidency is worth discerning. To help you understand the personnel you're dealing with, I've broken out the following list. Generally speaking, ascending from left to right are the promotional titles by department, and the power structure runs sequentially from phone recorder to CEO.

> Phone recorder... ..courtesy phone operator... ..customer service line specialist... ..hotline representative... ..SUPERservice technician... ..marketing aide... ..marketing assistant... ..marketing specialist... ..marketing officer... ..director of marketing
>
> Teller... ..drive-in teller... ..peak time teller... ..safe deposit box attendant... ..vault attendant... ..vault teller... ..peak time vault teller... ..lead vault teller... ..vault manager... ..central vault manager... ..teller supervisor... ..head teller
>
> Secretary... ..administrative assistant... ..administrative assistant II... ..executive staff assistant... ..executive secretary
>
> Proof operator... ..operations clerk... ..reconcilement clerk... ..internal control specialist... ..compliance officer... ..CRA compliance officer... ..head of compliance
>
> Loan clerk... ..loan processor... ..loan processor II... ..loan doc preparation specialist... ..loan closing technician... ..operations officer... ..manager of loan operations... ..accounting clerk... ..accounting assistant... ..assistant controller... ..controller... ..chief financial officer
>
> Collector... ..loan adjuster... ..mobile home repossessor... ..asset recovery specialist... ..collection manager... ..head of special assets
>
> New accounts clerk... ..customer service representative... ..consumer lender... ..relationship banker... ..business development officer... ..manager trainee... ..platform manager... ..assistant branch manager... ..branch manager... ..district manager... ..city manager
>
> Credit trainee... ..junior analyst... ..analyst... ..senior analyst... ..credit officer... ..credit manager... ..senior credit officer... ..THE POPE

Chapter Fifteen

Portfolio banker... ..private banker... ..trust representative... ..personal trust sdministrator... ..trust officer

Commercial lender... ..maintenance engineer... ..CEO

The rankings by position then go like this:

Basic title
Title followed by specialist, technician, etc.
Title followed by manager, administrator, etc.
Title followed by officer
    THEN:
        Those awaiting VPship
        Junior or double-secret vice president
        Assistant vice president
        Vice president 3rd level (degree?)
            2nd level
            1st level (3rd chair from the door, last
                to go for coffee during board
                meeting)
        Senior vice president
        Executive vice president
        President
        Olivia Gordon, or any holding company level
            executive secretary
        CEO

As part of the corporate banking division, responsible for getting money to businesses in our area of the country, my position fell just below building maintenance. However, my department head always reminded me... "Future CEOs begin a path to the top in commercial lending, take pride in that fact." (So don't call me a commercial *administrator*. I'm a commercial *lender*... whether I extend any credit or not.)

"Who Do You Think You'll Be Dealing With Tomorrow?"

Now you know who you're dealing with... **today**. Unfortunately, although the industry likes to give the impression of great stability...

How to Obtain Business Loans

as I said before, a turnover rate between 20-30% is not unusual. Recently, I was riding in the elevator with two Acme project managers. One said to the other, "Over the last couple of years, I've dealt with so-and-so... a vice president... at such-and-such bank." And the other fella answered, **"Wow, a banker in the same place for two years... unheard of."**

The point is, don't be surprised when you call to speak with your account officer, Thaddeus J. Billingham, 1st Vice President of Commercial Lending... only to find he's "no longer with the bank." And that your *relationship* has been turned over to Thad G. Young, Junior, a Commercial Lending Specialist. Which may cause problems, as you start from ground zero with an inexperienced person.

Why is there a here today, gone tomorrow *modus operandi* in banking? Because the prevailing belief is that almost all personnel are simply interchangeable, or easily replaced. The system is considered much bigger than the parts. And the way policy constricts individualism, star players are virtually nonexistent. The cadence thumped out by procedural standards tends to bring everyone to the same level.

Obviously, this causes frustration, and when income no longer compensates for the pains and indignation of bureaucracy... people bail out. However, from the time one begins working for a bank, management attempts to instill (more like brainwash) the notion skills are not transferable... that workers are only qualified to toil in banks. Then they offer the secondary argument that industry problems are universal, and things would be no better on the next corner... so why break continuity of employment. Nevertheless, people do. It's the trade's way of conferring true promotions. Witness a line lender's review:

POSITION:	(A) Commercial Lender II, Assistant Vice President
CURRENT SALARY:	$40,000
SALARY RANGE OF POSITION:	$32,400-$54,400 (B)
MIDPOINT:	$43,400
COMPA RATIO (SALARY/MIDPOINT):	92%
RATING SCHEDULE:	(1) Always drastically exceeds job requirements (C)
	(2) Always exceeds job requirements

Chapter Fifteen

    (3) Attains and sometimes exceeds job requirements **(D)**
    (4) Periodically does not attain job requirements (probable probation)
    (5) Regularly does not attain job requirements (automatic probation, possible dismissal)

(E)

(1) Max Raise	(2) Max Raise	(3) Max Raise
Salary < midpoint 6%	Salary < midpoint 5%	Salary < midpoint 4%
Salary > 75% of midpoint 5%	Salary > 75% of midpoint 4%	Salary > 75% midpoint 3%

A few items are especially meaningful:

(A) Position grades are usually subdivided I, II, III; although little justifies the differentiation. However, a Roman numeral can feel like major advancement to some.
(B) Fact: No one reaches their maximum. It is banking's equivalent to the quest for the holy grail. But it looks great on the form... it's the carrot at the end of a stick.
(C) Remember our discussion of star players?
(D) Probably 90-odd percent of an institution's employees fall within this category.
(E) Coincidently, the low point of the position's salary range is... 75% of the midpoint. So if your making the minimum your position pays, your maximum raise is curtailed.

How could you make less than the minimum? Say you're a commercial lender I, assistant vice president, who has just been promoted to Roman numeral II. Just because your subtitle changed, and possibly your responsibilities, doesn't mean your pay scale will. Generally it does not. Instead, the institution agrees to review you biannually rather than annually... "in an effort to get you to the minimum." This is not a big thing when skipping along I, II, III, etc., but say you go from being a relationship banker III to a commercial lender I (salary range $29,160 - $48,960). Your existing pay is $16,500. Assuming you get a 4% raise every six months after the move, it will take a mere 7 $1/2$ years to climb into the compensation range for a job you'll be doing day in and day out.

This happened to me personally. After a couple of years had passed (and I finally figured out what was taking place)... I went to

How to Obtain Business Loans

another institution to do the exact same job. And received a 51% pay increase for doing so. My old boss had known this would eventually occur, stating as much and adding, "I'm fighting the hardest I can for you. Policy doesn't allow me to do any more than I already am. Making a change is your prerogative."

Similar incidents transpire throughout banking. The institution I moved to had an annual award presented to the company's outstanding employee. (In reality only non-officers were eligible, as senior management thought the motivational effect would be lost if the tribute were imparted to "a higher level individual within the organization.")

Tess Casey, a Loan Processor II, accepted the coveted Exalted Falconer trophy for 1992. A few weeks later she received her performance review, and was given a 3.45% pay increase.

Less than excited about her monetary reward, she wrote a formal rejoinder to her supervisor and copied the human resource department. Her boss countered by explaining she would be going into an incentive pool in the near future and would receive a proportionate share (with other processors) of a new $50 charge to be imposed on customers... under the auspices of a doc prep fee.

Tess still wasn't a happy camper, since she felt the bank wasn't directly repaying her for her efforts. They were merely adding another fee to the consumer. Human resources finally got involved, and it was explained to Tess that she wasn't looking at the matter correctly. She needed to "take into consideration the no point home mortgage loan the bank had extended she and her husband earlier in the year."

Perhaps you're beginning to understand. Here's a joke which made the rounds at my bank during the most recent year-end review period:

PERFORMANCE REVIEW — CHARLIE HUSTLE

Category	Rating
I. Task awareness and proficiency	2
II. Level of efficiency	2
III. Client Service	3
IV. Individual Improvement	3
V. Daily Strategy	3
VI. Analysis/interpretation/discretion	4
VII. Adherence to policy	4
OVERALL	3

Chapter Fifteen

Supervisor's comments: Last year was a tremendous one for you, Charlie. The 80-hour work weeks paid off big, as you closed over $20 million in new loans. In the process, however, policy was far from completely adhered to... and preferential terms were often extended to entice borrowers. What's more, approval packages contained a writing style that was regularly too black and white. In the future, an effort should be made to include more "what if" scenarios and discussion should focus more directly on statement analysis and accrual commentary rather than simply whether or not the bank has a chance to lose money.

Nonetheless, your hard work benefitted the bank tremendously, as did your community involvement as a director on four civic groups and as a volunteer with two others. And, hey, that computer program you wrote allowing management to more thoroughly track the composition of a line lender's day was fantastic. It should save the bank big bucks in terms of efficiency. Coincidentally, your lunch hour has been getting a bit long lately. All in all though, congratulations on a job well done.

RAISE: 3% Your colleagues will not be rewarded quite so handsomely. You'll note Joe Slacker won't be smiling after review time. As you know, Joe only closed about $10 million in new credit... while cruising through 40-hour work weeks. And he neglected the bank's community image by failing to participate in any charity work.

> (Joe's raise: 2% The difference after taxes, insurance, compulsory PAC contributions, and semi-mandatory donations to charity are automatically deducted... is about $12.75 per month.)

Keep up the good work. Remember, I'll be retiring in another 15 years, and my slot could be yours if you keep at it.

How to Obtain Business Loans

With the dollars and cents so tough to come by, some workers find great solace in a title. A customer's recognition of this adds a sense of self-esteem... which can only return good things to the imparting individual. Failure to appreciate this can only be bad news for the desecrating party... whether internal or external.

One day, I overheard a trust officer's conversation with a customer. The discussion took place as they were walking by the commercial lending division. The visitor asked, "What's this department?"

"I dunno, some sort of lending or operations. Listen... " To the speaker's detriment, the majority of the division's personnel were. His arrogance cost him, and his department, heavily. No request for assistance with, or information on, mutual customers was met by the commercial group with any more enthusiasm than a Sunday afternoon nap.

Know Your Audience

The amount of cooperation received from the bank will correspond directly to your treatment of the personnel encountered. Ego gets the better of too many applicants and they attempt to bludgeon their way through the loan process.

Before adopting this approach, I suggest you objectively weigh your relative significance to the institution. Ask yourself: "How do I stack up with other customers?" You may find you're not altogether as important as you thought. And this is a critical thing to acknowledge. No one deal makes or breaks matters for an institution.

Say you follow the advice presented in the last chapter and direct your application from the top down. After politely discussing your request, the bank president will refer you to a line lender. Who can... "help."

Here's how one such handoff took place: Duff Warford had contacted Winthrop about a small business loan. His computer service company had done work for the bank before, which allowed him to use the *acquaintance factor* to gain an appointment. The request was, truly, small. So after a brief amenity period, Winthrop referred him to Serena Osbourne, a relationship banker located in the same building.

As he left, rather than taking a moment to meet Serena, Mr.

Chapter Fifteen

Warford chose to phone her from his car once he reached the parking lot. "Listen, Serena, I just met with Winthrop about a little loan I need. He said I'm all set, but that I should check with you to see when the paperwork will be ready. How 'bout tomorrow?"

"I'm sorry, I haven't spoken to Winthrop today. I'm sure he just hasn't gotten a chance to... "

"Honey, just go talk to him, and get the papers underway. I'll buzz you later. Bye now." Click.

In Serena's eyes, Mr. Rude just became public enemy #1. She marched right to Winthrop's office to try and find out what was going on. He explained, "Yes, I met with Duff just a few minutes ago. He's looking for a small business loan, and I referred him to you."

"So you're okay with his request... it's basically approved?"

"No. Treat him like anyone else... tax filings, credit bureau, the whole thing. Take care of him, though. Unless there's some major problem. He did computer work for the bank you know."

Shortly, Serena's phone rang once more. "Hey, Duff here. How we doin' on those papers, hon? You speak to Winthrop yet?

"Yes I did. Now... I'll need your tax filings from the past two years... personal and business... plus I need you to fill out an application form."

"No way!!! I don't have time for all that nonsense. Hon, I used to get money from my bank back home on just a phone call. Talk to Winthrop, would you."

"As I said, I did. He indicated I should go through our regular credit approval process. The bank has to comply with government regs you know."

After some heavy-duty grumbling, Mr. Impatient hung up and dialed for Winthrop. Who didn't take his call. (Presidents are public relations, good news folks. Rarely will they involve themselves with the sordid details, and certainly not the conveyance of any negative information.) After trying desperately to make contact for the next several hours, Mr. Anxious decided to play by the rules.

Later, when Serena pulled his credit report, she was delighted to find several slow pays. Three 30, and one 60 day delinquency... all within the last eighteen months. With blinding speed, she filled out and sent an adverse action[g] form; and with a smile on her face, called to turn down Mr. Tardy.

After communicating the rejection to him, she was berated with a storm of profanity. Culminating with the statement, "*Blank* it... if

How to Obtain Business Loans

you don't turn this thing around pronto, honey, you'll be working at Burger King next week! Do you hear me!??"

She, along with everyone else in the office, did. Serena responded courteously, **"Have a nice day."** Click.

Winthrop dodged Mr. Temper Tantrum's calls for the next several days, as Serena had not informed him of the adverse action. Winthrop evidently thought he was phoning simply to complain about the process. Finally, Winthrop did take his call... and moments later, he called me. "Addison, are you familiar with this Warford deal?"

"Serena's mentioned it."

"Yes... well, he's not such a bad guy. I suppose he's a little abrasive, but I'd like to see us work this out... "

"I understand he has bad credit."

"Yes, but he explained that to me. Would you see that Serena goes ahead and does the loan for him. (Not delivered as a question.) Just approve it yourself... there's no problem."

Serena was not excited about this turn of events. She angrily threw a credit package together, had me sign, and forwarded it to Daphne Hampsted, one of the bank's Loan Closing Technicians; for documents to be prepared. In the next two days, Mr. Sunshine called five or six times, each time restating the profound question, "What's taking so long?" He pestered Daphne, whose name Serena had gladly given up, incessantly. "C'mon, honey, what's it gonna take to get this done already? Move it along, alright babe?!!"

This put Daphne in low gear. In fact, darn near park. Another week went by as now Daphne artfully ducked Mr. Wonderful's calls. Soon he was back to phoning Winthrop, who also refused to talk to him and instead contacted me. "Addison, will you intercede and get this matter concluded?"

After letting off some steam at me, Daphne agreed to close the loan. When she reached The Borrower From Hell, he responded, "It's about time! You know, you guys have got to take better care of your important customers. People like me are the lifeblood of your institution. Listen, I'm a ways north of town right now, but I can zip down in a flash. My new BMW will have me there within 45 minutes at the outside. We'll close at noon. Hey... ever ride in a Beemer?"

Ignoring the last comment, Daphne replied, **"Fine, I had a lunch appointment, but I'll cancel it. Let's get you closed."**

A couple of hours passed without any sign of Mr. Motorhaus of

Chapter Fifteen

Bavaria. Finally, he arrived in the lobby and bellowed, "Somebody get Daphne for me, I need to button up some business."

Daphne entered the waiting area to hear, "I'm running a little late sugar. Got tied up ya' know. Hey, hon, when are you due?"

Daphne was a little overweight, but most definitely not pregnant. And she furiously informed Mr. Faux Pas of this. He never even blinked. "Well, I just figured someone as pretty as you would've had somebody get ya' pregnant."

It's a wonder she didn't deck him. She chose rather to prolong his punishment. As Daphne handled the signing of documents, she intentionally left out nonessential compliance forms. Realizing, of course, internal controls would require her to have Mr. No-Time-For-That back in to endorse them. Then each time he returned, Daphne managed to *forget* to have something else properly executed. And had to have him stop by again, and again, and again. All in all, Mr. I'm-In-Too-Big-A-Hurry-To-Fool-With-Details was forced to go through four or five closings before she decided he had had enough.

It should go without mention, treat others with respect. If not out of a sense of common decency, then because it's to your detriment if you don't. No matter how much of a big shot you think you are, or even if you ARE a big shot, bank personnel can make your life miserable if your actions do the same to them. You may ultimately get your loan, but what price will you pay along the way?

One gentleman understood this better than any other I've met. John Q. Public was a hotel developer on the Forbes 400 list of wealthy Americans. He was the richest, most influential, borrowing prospect our institution ever had. He began his application with a call to the bank's president, then set up an appointment with the senior lender, and yours truly.

The day of the meeting, he entered, shaking everybody's hand on the way in... including all secretaries, specialists, and technicians. He formally referred to each one as sir or ma'am... even if they were 40 years his junior. These actions left an indelible impression. Although his request came with several policy exceptions, the bank eagerly rolled out the red carpet. And I'm 100% convinced it was not due solely to his financial prowess. (Hey, I've written a book about rejecting wealthy applicants.)

Basically, he was given free reign... *carte blanche*. He met the one restriction we tried to impose with such aplomb, it was waived without a word being said... literally. I was instructed to obtain an

How to Obtain Business Loans

environmental audit on one of the *vacant land* parcels he was pledging as collateral. (That's right, we were doing the impossible, loaning against — gasp — *vacant land*.) When I requested the report, the conversation went something like this: **"Mr. Public, it's our policy to obtain environmental audits on all loans of this type. I'll need to ask that one be provided for the Main Street property."**

"Mr. Parker, I've given you a copy of the one I had done when acquiring the Heron Avenue parcel. It's worth more than 5 times the other site, and about 3 1/2 times your loan amount. I hope your bank will be comfortable with that fact, and not require me to expend several thousand dollars for another audit... which, perhaps, isn't totally necessary."

Remembering my training, I jumped in and gave all the reasons why another audit was absolutely essential. And then waited for a response... and waited... and waited... and waited. Finally, it became very awkward, so I restated the rational I had just given. This time with a lot more ahs, ers, and buts. Still no response. I knew he was there, I could hear him breathing. Suddenly my office was 110 degrees (again). The awkwardness turned into an insufferable pressure not to give in and be the first one to speak.

I cracked. **"On the other hand, Mr. Public, I see your point. Let me see if we can get by without that report."**

"Mr. Parker, I would really appreciate that. Are you a basketball fan? Who do you like in the final four this weekend?" I had just attended a clinic on business negotiations.

When I relayed the fact that no environmental report would be forthcoming on the Main Street property, the policy exception was ignored. Not approved mind you... **ignored**. The loan closed, and that was that.

Make Every Sales Pitch Count

My father always used to say, "If you're not going to do your best... why bother?" Vince Lombardi went a step farther, and applied the sentiment to obtaining financial services, "Getting your loan approved isn't everything... it's the only thing." Certainly, missed opportunities are hard to live with, so it's important to do all you can... when you can.

You're now well-versed on how institutions **choose** to operate under government security, you're aware of the personnel you'll be

Chapter Fifteen

dealing with (at least initially), and you've politely suffered through a refresher course in applicant etiquette. What else could further optimize your chances of success? Understanding and knowing how to combat *The Silent Killer*.

In selling your deal to an institution, you need to find out who is the ultimate approval authority and you must flush out the aforementioned assassin. Either actually or effectually, credit administrators are often one in the same individual. They play Caesar with most requests... and without having met with those they give the thumbs-down to. As illustrations have shown, <u>at most lending institutions, the lending decision has been removed from the lender</u>.

In reality, the person with whom you'll meet to begin with is better referred to as a "loan advocate." (Or, perhaps, a *credit lobbyist*.) If your deal is a good one, no one will work more diligently to get it approved than your "advocate." Make sure to help as much as possible by providing your hired gun all the ammunition in your favor. As you sell the deal to your "advocate," so shall it be sold to Caesar. Don't rely upon an individual's total retention of verbally supplied information. Although fewer loans than ever are getting approved, there is still no shortage of applicants. The officer you meet with is probably talking to six to twelve *would-be* borrowers a week. Make sure details of your conversations don't get lost in the shuffle. Forward comprehensive summaries after any discussions.

Also early in the process, perhaps even during the initial meeting, it's important to determine the capacity of your "advocate" to work on your behalf. Ask probing questions:

- Are you from this area?

- How long have you been with the bank?

- Were you previously with a different institution?

- So is this the type of loan **your** bank is interested in?

- What are some similar ventures your institution has done recently? (Confidentially, to the wind... bankers will tell you!)

- And how were you involved in those?

The responses can prove invaluable. Don't make the mistake of

How to Obtain Business Loans

relying upon one's title... or age... as an indication of their corporate prowess. Remember, the executive and senior VPs have been at things for awhile. True, that can mean they are effective users of the system, but it can also mean they are dinosaurs in the process of fossilization.

Brigham Stoddlemier was an Executive Vice President in charge of commercial lending at an institution where I previously *lobbied* credits. Brigham was in late 40s, a career banker, and had been with the institution for a decade or so. He was one of only two EVPs with the affiliate, sported a penthouse office adjacent to the president's and chaired loan committee.

On the surface of things, how could you ask for a better "advocate?" Unfortunately, for many who sat down before his desk to discuss deals, the best part of the meeting would be the opportunity to view "babes" at the park across the street through the telescope Brigham kept on his credenza. For he had next to no experience in commercial real estate lending and hadn't been actively involved in the analysis and preparation of many other types of commercial credit in years.

His most meaningful input to loan committee was overseeing the preparation of an agenda and occasional prompt: "Is there a motion on the floor?" Brigham had attained his position through longevity, and by comfortably aligning himself with bank policy to the point he contemplated little other than cookie-cutter (liquid-secured) loans on his own. It was apparent he had evolved by not rocking the boat. (Question: How dynamic would this sort of "advocate" be on your behalf?)

In practice, the local credit administrator carried the big stick in committee. This became abundantly clear when Brigham stepped out of his comfort zone to personally present a deal on one occasion. Packages had been out to committee members long enough for everyone to review what was truly a borderline request. It had been referred by another affiliate and our bank was being given the opportunity to participate the debt.

Brigham began his presentation at the top of the agenda. Immediately, lowly line lenders of the AVP fashion began asking questions... which Brigham could not answer. After awhile, it became evident that he grasped very little of the proposed undertaking and was unable to either defend the credit's weaknesses or bring out its attributes.

Chapter Fifteen

Eventually, the credit administrator said, "I'm not hearing anything which merits the continuation of this discussion. I think we should pass on this deal in its entirety. Let's move on." (And the applicant never heard the shot.)

Brigham rolled over. "Sure, sure. This credit has a lot of problems. Hey, I never said I was in favor of it... I was just presenting the deal." (Who works harder for an applicant... an insulated member of senior management coasting along, or a line lender with heavy volume goals to reach?)

At any rate, it's the unidentified gunman from the depository that does you in more often than not. Rarely is there a second shooter. It's incumbent upon you to bring the *would-be* assassin out into the open... out from behind the mounds of memoranda on his desk... out from behind those horn-rimmed glasses.. and out from an introverted personality.

Credit administrators have no loan growth goals whatsoever. They are responsible for **credit quality**. That is, not just making sure the bank will be repaid, but protecting the institution from outside criticism of its portfolio. With this kind of occupational direction, you can see why there is little pressure to *extend* credit, more emphasis being placed on *talking about it*.

To ensure the success of your request, you must gain the concurrence of the controlling credit Guru. And make no mistake, they are in charge. No matter how many VPs (of any degree) are in love with your deal, it can be trumped by one diffident detractor from the back room.

So bring them out of anonymity. There is an adage in banking that says, "It's always harder to turn down someone you know." Which is why credit folks prefer to remain the unknowns in the process. Don't let them. **Insist upon meeting with the head of the credit department no later than your second meeting with a bank**.

You should expect to have your request for an audience with Caesar denied. This can be overridden by contacting the bank's president and explaining your desire to have the "decision maker" involved from the beginning. This does two things:

(1) It more than insinuates the president has less control over new loans than the credit administrator. While, in some cases, this may in fact be true... it rankles any president to be reminded. By making the statement, you throw down the gauntlet. Implying

How to Obtain Business Loans

that if the credit Guru turns down your request, the President couldn't do anything about it even if he wanted to. This may be an ace in the hole for later, one you can play against the President's ego if your loan is rejected.

(2) It puts the bank on notice you will shop the deal elsewhere unless the credit administrator is personally involved from the outset.

You'll get your meeting. For as much as banks reject loans, they shudder at not getting a chance to review requests. They don't want you going to the next corner before they've had a look-see.

The goal for the first face-to-face with Little Caesar is simple: Get him to talk as much as possible. If it's true in negotiations, and in the court room, that the more one speaks the more they are likely to hang themselves... it is especially true here. Talk about anything and everything to begin with, just to thaw some ice around what will be a rather cold personality. Then probe for experience level, etc., as you did with your "advocate."

Finally, and most importantly, after developing as much rapport as you can, have the credit administrator tell you about your business. Ask such leading questions as:

- How do you see this or that market or industry right now?

- What's your outlook on the local economy?

- You're probably not very familiar with my type of business... I don't know... you probably are. What do you know about _____?

What's going to happen? (Remember, this fella is not used to dealing with the public. I've seen several who have a tough time handling waitresses in restaurants.) He'll be as affable as his social skills will let him and the way in which he answers questions will have him painting himself into a corner.

He will not sit before you and spill out negativism about your industry, the market, or the economy. Instead, he will try and appear optimistic... and knowledgeable about your specific area of business. Your conversational feedback should encourage him to be verbose. Have him lay a solid foundation for you. After saying lots of wonderful things in relation to your request, it certainly limits the reasons he can later put forth to reject it.

Chapter Fifteen

Subsequent to the meeting, you should continue phone discussions in the same manner. Little Caesar will be fairly easy to lead, as your typical credit administrator is actually quite nonconfrontational. Only on their own turf, so-to-speak, do they readily offer dissenting opinions. And they do so then with an audience who has limited latitude in questioning their decisions. **They are not used to having to justify their conclusions.** Your staying in direct contact with them forces them to do so at each step towards an approval. This is the most valuable lesson in the entire book. Use it well.

By the way, credit administrators never get to play much golf, but they really like to be included in the fun. (Remember the kid on your block always chosen last for pickup games?) It's interesting... I have never seen a loan rejected when the head of credit teed it up with the applicant. No matter what he shot. Maybe that's just a coincidence.

How to get your deal re-approved. No, I'm not necessarily talking about getting a renewal upon a loan's balloon maturity. Although, practically speaking, the bank has already made that decision well before the loan comes due. Sometimes years in advance. They do so in Annual Key Credit Quality Committee meetings, or AKCQCs. (The sound made when one sticks their finger down their throat.)

As reviews are done, their analyses are presented to a committee which addresses the continued credit worthiness of the borrower. The reality is that the meetings are held for appearance sake. For the benefit of internal loan review and to show external auditors the bank "stays on top of its current portfolio." Little productive result can come from a forum discussing existing loans not in arrears.

With no constructive purpose, the gathering becomes an opportunity for analysts and lenders to take pot-shots at one another. The real loser is the existing customer, whose credit worthiness is infringed as battles rage over trivial matters of financial disclosure. The result is that the ongoing, and future, banakability of the entity is eroded.

Eventually, the decision is made on many credits that their... *imperfect nature*... would have them best regulated to a lower loan classification, then moved out of the bank at the earliest opportunity. Regardless of their payment history.

How to Obtain Business Loans

This was the case with Art and Vivienne Sullivan's credit, The Harbor House Restaurant, which we discussed in Chapter 8. After denegrating a perfectly paid loan over many AKCQC sessions, the credit was downgraded to a 'D' classification. After a few more meetings, it was dropped to an 'E' rating.

Months later, frustrated with the bank's requests to go on line with the restaurant's registers, the Sullivans refinanced the loan elsewhere. Upon finding this out, the leader of the AKCQC get-togethers, *Credit Officer* Fabian Faulkner exclaimed, "That's a shame. We should've been able to keep that deal on the books."

Whether purposely pushed, or *accidently* nudged, many good paying loans leave the bank unnecessarily as a result of being needlessly worked over. After calculating total run-off, senior management then cries for new volume... to be comprised of certain types of extensions, not just those that remit interest like clockwork and are collaterilized to the point they have no chance of loss, but those so perfect in nature that no auditor could possibly find something to criticize.

Chapter Sixteen

CHAPTER 16:

THE CLOSE OF (ALL) BUSINESS

Another seminar. It must be twenty degrees in this barn. I've found that to be a rule of thumb. The more tedious the subject matter, the colder they keep the room. By the looks of the icicles forming along the ceiling vents, this sales pow-wow is going to be a real yawner. One full week of dullsville.

I'm dumbfounded the company has spent this much money to foster the illusion of a dynamic sales culture. Talk about putting on airs. On the way in, conversation among "lenders" centered around the glut of deals rejected by senior management. Now we're to be tutored on where to *locate* new business opportunities? (Get real.)

I remember discussing the matter with another line officer from my institution. We estimated, between the two of us, *our turn-downs* outstripped the bank's *total commercial volume* by more than 3 to 1! Given the number of other "lenders" involved, and their respective rejections and contributions, we calculated that senior management was at least six times as likely to dismiss a commercial credit application as they were to approve it.

This illustrates the banking community's avidity for deals perfect in every way, as the number of turn-downs I spoke of refers only to loans rejected by higher approval authorities. It does not include applications denied directly by line lenders due to poor credit quality. Rather, the 6:1 ratio represents the inclination to refuse loans based upon a fear of audit reprisal.

As we have discussed throughout the book, the primary focus is no longer repayment risk, but risk of reclassification. After-the-fact scrutiny by both internal and external review bodies serves to narrow the field of acceptable (or should I say, "bankable") deals. And even when pristine applicants are uncovered, they many times don't accept the financing packages offered by banks in light of particularly onerous terms.

A growing trend has institutions outsmarting themselves by imposing increasingly restrictive loan covenants. Target coverage ratios, compensation caps, debt/worth requirements, etc., can all work in ways contrary to their intent.

(1) They increase the bank's liability by evoking questions of *managemental control*; which carries not only lender liability exposure, but the risk of being held culpable in the event a *controlled* borrower inflicts environmental damage to a collateralized property and surrounding area.

(2) Given their technical default nature and their accompanying lack of practical application in the courtroom, the provisions are rarely acted upon. Which, according to one bank's corporate counsel at the holding company level, "Only serves to water down the non-technical default provisions provided for elsewhere in the loan docs." If an institution stipulates technical default provisions (which allow few real world remedies), and doesn't attempt to enforce them, judges can invalidate other conditions based upon the institution's lenient adherence to the established loan agreement. Selective enforcement sets a precedent that defaults may not be acted upon. In which case, the question becomes whether or not such is an act of forbearance with regard to other stipulated covenants. (I don't know. Throw two lawyers in the ring and let them argue it out.) The point is, banks are generally fooling themselves by putting in a lot of loan provisions that look great when reviewed, but may erode the actual

Chapter Sixteen

collectibility of principal and interest in the event of a true default by the borrower.

And to what end do these means justify themselves? Ultimately, they show regulators how tightly loans are sewn up and what little chance of loss there is given all the colorful bells and whistles added to the loan agreement. Although the sense of well-being provided is somewhat of an illusion, you'll find many bankers who will tell you these measures are needed "to ensure the safety and soundness of financial institutions, and to protect depositor's money... nay, to protect the deposit insurance system itself." They'll argue, "In terms of safeguarding the system's funds, no amount of overzealous providence can be considered excessive."

My own institution certainly followed this rallying cry... well, actually only on the lending side of the bank. Lengthy procedures were followed so that virtually anything to do with a presented deal was handled away from the submitting officer. Credit analysis, the review of appraisal and environmental reports, the composition of commitment letters and loan docs, title policy examination, closing itself, and, of course, disbursement. (Good. Fine.)

Meanwhile, branch managers had the authority to wire an unlimited amount of money in $25,000 increments... anywhere in the world... without so much as a second person's initials corroborating the transactions. The big joke at staff meetings was whether banks in Switzerland or the Cayman Islands gave their numbered account holders better service.

Don't feed me the "tighter underwriting policies are justifiable because it's the only area of great risk" argument. First-hand knowledge notes possible loss isn't the issue which drives policy and procedure... government regulation is. Yet, public perception has been slow to embrace this fact.

Witness an article written by a Mr. M. Arthur Gillis, president of Computer Based Solutions, Inc. In it, he states that "too many bankers are squawking about regulatory burdens and unfair competition while they overlook their own shortcomings." [1] He goes on to say what really bothers him is "that bankers are losing their grip on what legitimately belonged to them until a number of outsiders decided to share the wealth." [2]

Mr. Gillis then recounts how Merrill Lynch made him "fill out tons of forms," but that his request to refinance his home mortgage was ultimately approved, lowering his monthly payments by 40%. [3]

How to Obtain Business Loans

Which led him to ask: "Should I have stuck with my bank for dumb loyalty or a 'relationship?'" [4]

Moreover, he shared an experience in which a computer store granted him an instantaneous credit line the moment he made a purchase and shared his DUNS number[g] with them... Making him wonder why banks can't do the same thing. "I suppose that all happened because the regulators would not allow my bank to offer a legitimate loan to a solid customer." [5]

He concluded with a comparison of credit card rates. First Chicago at 19.8% vs. AT&T at 11.9%. "Which one would any smart consumer choose? Did the regulatory agencies establish these rates?"[6]

Mr. Gillis shares some interesting opinions. In fairness, his views are probably similar to that of 90% of Americans in business. Actually, he makes an excellent point about banks beginning to overlook the market for which they've long held a monopoly of sorts. And he's right on target about the choices of informed consumers. Naive "purists" (or should it be "puritans"?) will tell an assembly of bank officers they must *sell themselves* in order to obtain new business.

This theory grounds itself in the belief that if someone likes you, they will gladly pay a premium for the goods and services you offer. Despite the fact they are the same ones available at rival banks on every street corner, and now mid-block by competing non-banks. So blindly do many long-time bankers steadfastly hold to this tenant, it propels them past the point of rational thought. Witness the recent instruction I received to include the following (narcissistic) sentence in credit packages submitted to higher approval authorities; "Although the applicant has been issued a commitment by another institution, it is expected he will accept any approval we might put in place... because of our superior products and services." I suppose if you recite this type of thing enough, something of a David Koresh effect takes hold.

So here I sit awaiting further indoctrination. I understand the group is to be led through a personal advancement series by some motivational Guru. Apparently the holding company paid BIG bucks for his tapes and literature. Word has it they felt it was necessary to improve the *esprit de corps*.

It's ironic that management often fails to focus on the cause(s) of morale problems, choosing instead to try and reshape perceptions. I recall how somber people were a few months ago when the latest round of spending cuts were announced. MUZAC was to be discon-

Chapter Sixteen

tinued, saving $6,000 annually. Plant service was to cease, which according to estimates, would conserve in excess of $2,000 (inclusive of the cost to haul away dead vegetation). And, well... you get the gist.

I remember Winthrop's address to the officer's third quarter meeting. "It's important each of you instill in your respective staffs the need for these cuts. Without them we simply won't make budget," he said with an anguished expression. "As it stands now, we are on pace to net only $4.5 million this year... and plans call for a $4.8 million profit. So as you can see, without trimming costs, we're just not going to make it. And you've got to make your staff understand this, because we don't want them thinking the company is being chintzy or something." (Tough sell.)

I hear you. "W..a..i..t.. a minute, Addison. $4.5 million profit! What panhandling, what lack of income? Why the necessity for all the nickel and dime service charges? Looks to me like somebody's crying poormouth while raking it in. If things are so bad for bankers, where are these profit levels coming from? And, while we're at it, how come stock prices keep escalating?"

Healthy Banks, Anemic Economic Future

1992 was a record year for bank profits. 1993 was even better. So much so that FDIC[g] Acting Chairman Andrew C. "Skip" Howe was quoted by *Bankers News* as saying that the industry didn't "even have to wait for the fourth-quarter numbers to be able to claim another record year for bank profits."[7] The trade article went on to say that earnings through the first nine months of the year totaled $32.6 billion, outstripping the previous *annual* record of $32.1 billion" (achieved the prior year). I understand the figures for the first three-quarters of 1994 are similarly impressive. Stock prices have reflected the strength of earnings, with investments in bank shares outstripping what might be characterized as a nervously bullish market.

So how has this been done? A lay person might assume such earnings growth would be impossible without strong loan volume. On the contrary. Banks were able to set record marks in profitability by simply sitting back and taking a glorious ride down the yield curve.

Rather than investing heavily in their respective communties, bank controllers allocated available funds to various government

How to Obtain Business Loans

backed securities. As predictions were for a prolonged decline in interest rates, senior management took care to invest for the mid- to long-term when possible.

The effect? Net interest margins, or the difference between the bank's cost of funds and the yield on their earning assets, widened appreciably. With earners locked in, and costs dropping, the gap increased over time. For every 1% increase in net interest margin, the typical regional sized bank "earned" $1 million on each $100 million in employed assets. (Did we say it before? ... fish in a barrel.)

Now, as rates have bottomed out and are beginning to climb, sandbagging... in the form of over-funded reserve positions... has created a healthy cushion for future profitability. Consider: *The Game Within The Game*. Banks assign loan loss reserves for various credit types and categories of risk. (As discussed in Chapter 1.) The consolidation of which can best be illustrated in table form:

RESERVE FOR LOAN LOSSES ($000's)

	Grade	Outstanding	% Reserved	$ Res.
UNFUNDED ITEMS (Letters of Credit)				
Not Criticized	('A' - 'C')	$ 0	0.00%	$ 0
Risky	('D')	349	5.00%	17
Substandard	('E' < $250M)	0	10.00%	0
Substandard	('E' > $250M)	714	10.00%	71
Doubtful	('F')	0	50.00%	0
		$ 1,063	8.32%	$ 88
CONSUMER AND CREDIT CARD (All Grades)				
Consumer Direct		$ 3,977	0.75%	$ 30
Consumer Indirect		0	1.50%	0
Credit Card		1,711	4.50%	77
Executive Lines		574	3.00%	17
		$ 6,262	1.98%	$ 124
RESIDENTIAL REAL ESTATE (1-4 FAMILY)				
Not Criticized	('A' - 'C')	$ 170,495	0.25%	$ 426
Risky	('D')	0	3.50%	0
Substandard	('E' < $250M)	479	7.00%	34
Substandard	('E' > $250M)	553	7.00%	39
Doubtful	('F')	0	50.00%	0
Equity Lines	All Grades	6,193	0.50%	31
		$177,720	0.30%	$ 530

Chapter Sixteen

COMMERCIAL					
Not Criticized	('A' - 'C')	$ 15,262		1.00%	$ 153
Risky	('D')	592		5.00%	30
Substandard	('E')	0		10.00%	0
Doubtful	('F')	0		50.00%	0
		$ 15,854		1.15%	$ 183
COMMERCIAL REAL ESTATE					
Not Criticized	('A' - 'C')	$ 39,101		1.00%	$ 391
Risky	('D')	1,840		5.00%	92
Substandard	('E' < $250M)	1,236		10.00%	124
Substandard	('E' > $250M)	7,702		10.00%	770
Doubtful	('F')	0		50.00%	0
		$ 49,879		2.76%	$1,377
GRAND TOTALS		$ 250,778		0.92%	$2,302

ACTUAL RESERVES FOR LOAN LOSSES:	$5,869
REQUIRED RESERVES:	2,302
EXCESS RESERVES:	$3,567

The table provides for *required* reserves. *Actual* reserves are set by senior management during the company budgeting process. With banks "investing" in security instruments rather than lending money... and net interest spreads widening, many institutions chose to build up excess reserves... rather than recognize available cash as profit in the current accounting period.

Why? What characteristic is most commonly associated with banking? (Okay, other than the "Just Say 'No' Campaign") Consistency. Think about the advertising you see... "rock solid," "reliable," "steadfast," "dependable," "safe"... these are all self-proclaimed adjectives used to describe institutions. They are what the masses, and Congress, are comfortable with. Banks are supposed to grind out a certain return annually, without a lot of variation. Which is why management tinkers with loss provisions in order to smooth out profits from one year to the next.

Also, recent years have seen deposit insurance premiums exceed costs by $1 Billion! These monies are paid to the FDIC[g] in order to establish a pool that backstops the operation of banks. The fund insures individual account holders against the loss of their deposits (up to $100,000) in the event a member institution becomes insolvent. Ask yourself: between bloated deposit insurance coffers and loan loss reserves, should this much money... investible in American business... be underutilized to such an extent?

How to Obtain Business Loans

Is the industry now over-insured? Perhaps from a businessperson's viewpoint, but not from the vantage of the general public. Think about the clamor which arose over Whitewater. At the heart of the uproar... a failed financial institution. Joe Citizen seems to say, "Okay Tom Brokaw, touch on the genocide in Bosnia, give me a blip about drug use among American teens, and you can mention the federal government is going bankrupt... but don't tell me about another failure within the financial community or I'll take up arms. Besides, shouldn't we be talking about Tonya, Lorraina, OJ, or the Buttafucos?" The public will numb itself to a lot, but bank failures appear to be an intolerable issue.

Washington has aligned itself accordingly by imposing stiff regulations on the industry, and banks have adapted by altering their *modus operandi*. Rather than recirculating community savings back into local business (creating more products, services, and jobs), institutions "invest" more in government-backed securities (in effect loaning money to the government). **Meanwhile, the very same debtor government insures the lending institution's depositors against the possibility of loss stemming from loan defaults.**

Anybody read what happened on an overcast Monday back in 1929? That's right, the stock market dropped like a stone, and The Great Depression followed. Many have attributed the calamity to pyramiding. Until banking Regulation U came about, you could purchase stock and borrow heavily against its value to buy more stock.

$100,000 of Company X	$80,000 of Company Y Purch.	$64,000 of Company Z Purch.
80% Advance	80% Advance	80% Advance
$ 80,000 Loan Proceeds	$64,000 Loan Proceeds	$51,200 Loan Proceeds

...and so on. Once the market drop began, the momentum from the pyramid's collapse created a landslide. With banks lending more and more to the government and the government insuring those loans, isn't a similar debt being built by pharaoh? Not only do your taxes subsidize a mismanaged government, so do your savings.

Where's the investment in America? Who handles the process of intermediation (As spoken of in Chapter 6.), so vital to our capitalist economy? The answers to these questions have led many to proclaim banks obsolete.

Chapter Sixteen

Daniel R. Smith, CEO at First of American Bank Corp., and current President of The American Bankers Association, has theorized on things to come. A recent article quoted him as saying, "I see the future of banks more as managing financial assets than intermediation..." The article continued: "There will always be lending and there will always be deposits, he explains, but, again, they may not be on the balance sheet as now." Furthermore, Smith foresees "the development of mutual funds that invest in commercial loans, which would address the funding concerns that some bankers have raised. He also believes that total assets will cease to be an important measure of a bank's size, and will be replaced by earnings."[8]

In other words, banks, as members of the private sector, have stockholders to answer to. Stockholders who are most interested in earnings. If, over time, government regulation makes traditional intermediation an unprofitable line of business, institutions will move away from that area of operation. Smith's answer? Mutual funds which "invest" in commercial loans. The purchasers of fund shares would themselves be "investors," their money not privy to FDIC protection. What will be the consequence of this process clearly designed to circumvent the current regulatory requirements of lending? An inflationary bias for the future.

What would entice funds out of government-backed interest bearing bank deposits and into mutual funds? Answer: Obviously, higher rates of return. Meaning, when coupled with increased packaging and administration costs, the ultimate borrower... American business... can expect to *pay* higher rates. Meaning companies must then generate higher internal rates of return to justify the costs of borrowing. Meaning the pricing of goods and services has to rise.

Entrepreneurs take heed. There is a boom industry for the latter '90s and beyond. It will be comprised of firms who, in effect, specialize in intermediation. The economies of scale necessary to profitably package mutual funds "investing" in commercial loans will squeeze out many small- to mid-sized borrowers. Banks will continue to meet the needs of a portion of the smaller concerns via a more traditional basis, but mid-sized borrowers may find themselves locked out and forced to work exceptionally hard to obtain funding at palatable rates.

The financial machinery constructed by change will be much less efficient than that previously used to obtain commercial credit. You reap what you sow, and America may harvest...

How to Obtain Business Loans

The Grapes of Wrath

Back in the mid-1980s, when the good times seemed to be rolling, then Federal Reserve Chairman Paul Volker proclaimed the U.S. to be "in a real sense living on borrowed money and borrowed time."[9] What he meant was that the country was in the midst of spending and enjoying what it would have to pay off in the future. Now, almost a decade later, as our collective stupor has worn off, the question is whether or not we can pick up the tab.

The national debt is approaching $5 trillion. (That's trillion with a 'T'.) Is anybody paying attention? Not long ago, a study indicated that 75% of the population followed the Nancy Kerrigan story closely. About 67% knew the details surrounding Michael Jackson's difficulties and a similar percentage know just why Lorraina Bobbitt did it. But only 30 odd percent of us are conversant when it comes to the state of the union. That's less than watch the Super Bowl (37%).

Come on folks... wake up... we've got a serious problem. $5 trillion is about 7 times what the government collects in corporate and personal income taxes each year! This is the very same government which backstops the safety and soundness of the banking system by guaranteeing FDIC deposits. Ironically, under criteria it was instrumental in setting, our government wouldn't appear to qualify for a loan from the institutions it stands behind.

Think of it this way. Take that $40,000 salary held down by your average commercial banker. Say the individual applies for a loan to purchase a single family home, but already has a $400,000 mortgage on another piece of property. The existing debt is amortized over 30 years at 7.75%, so the annual remittance of principal and interest is $34,167... or about 85% of the person's total income. Obviously, they don't qualify for additional credit. In fact, it's highly questionable they'll be able to retire their existing obligation without some extraordinary event(s). This is the position our government finds itself in... except that Uncle Sam's 85% ratio is based upon making interest payments alone — forget *reducing* any debt.

How in the heck did this happen? And on who's watch? Actually, our national credit card has been run up while in the hands of every President since Lyndon Baines Johnson. (Although some were more compulsive spenders than others.) LBJ got things started by trying to finance a war on poverty and one against Vietnam, at the same time. The battle to stamp out poverty required the creation of

Chapter Sixteen

entitlement programs such as Medicare, Medicaid, etc. And similar legislation has been readily penned ever since. Spending programs which make good social policy are easy to approve, they're just difficult to handle fiscally. Elected officials are hard pressed to properly address the funding issues of programs providing benefit to significant organized segments of the public. This helps explain why entitlements have expanded substantially since President Kennedy's administration. A man whose candidacy, it's worthwhile to note, was bankrolled by his father... and not special interest groups. During his time in office, entitlement spending made up about 30% of the budget after interest expense... versus a figure of roughly 65% today.

Furthermore, there are matters that severely compound the initial difficulties in finding funding solutions for social legislation.

(1) Somewhere along the line, I believe while President Carter was at the helm, it was determined that inflation was eroding the value of social security and other benefits paid to recipients. To combat this, it was decided that future benefits be indexed[g] in a manner to ensure that real dollar[g] payments remain constant for those entitled. This was great from the perspective of those receiving checks, it just happened to be poor long-term fiscal policy because...

(2) Entitlements don't come up for some type of review — ever. In other words, once they find their way into the budget... they are there perpetually. And given that they are now indexed, what our government has done is ensure this part of the federal budget will grow hand over fist... even if no new programs are approved. And that, as we know, is a whole other matter. Promising special interest groups various consideration is a tried-and-true method of being elected to both the executive and legislative branches of government. (I liken it to buying something with money that's not yours. Like using a stolen credit card.)

(3) Assuming, at some point, we come to the conclusion we truly can't pay for everything... where will cuts be made and who will suggest them? Certainly not someone who wishes to be re-elected.

Remember when George Bush dared to go back on his campaign

How to Obtain Business Loans

promise of "no new taxes?" We, the public, promptly bounced him out of office. Which illustrates fairly clearly how ready we are to pay the piper. (Not very.) Instead, we tend to ignore a problem that just gets bigger and bigger...

The National Debt
(In Billions and Billions Spent)*

Year	Annual Deficit	Administration Total	Adjusted Total Deficit
1964	$ 5.9	$	$ 316.8
1965	1.6		323.2
1966	3.8		329.5
1967	8.7		341.3
1968	25.2	45.2	369.8
1969	(3.2)		367.1
1970	2.8		382.6
1971	23.0		409.5
1972	23.4		437.3
1973	14.8		468.4
1974	4.7	65.5	486.2
1975	45.1		544.1
1976	66.5	111.6	631.9
1977	45.0		709.1
1978	48.8		780.4
1979	27.7		833.8
1980	59.6	181.1	914.3
1981	57.9		1,003.9
1982	127.9		1,147.0
1983	207.8		1,381.9
1984	185.3		1,576.7
1985	212.3		1,827.2
1986	220.7		2,132.9
1987	149.7		2,345.6
1988	155.1	1,316.7	2,600.8
1989	153.5		2,881.1
1990	220.5		3,266.1
1991	268.7		3,688.1
1992	399.7	1,042.4	4,082.9
1993	267.3		4,350.2

*These figures are from the annual editions of the U.S. Bureau of the Census, Statistical Abstract of the United States: Successive years 1964-1993. Washington, DC. The differences between both annual and administration total(s), and the adjusted total deficit(s) are unexplained.

Chapter Sixteen

As you can see, in the years since LBJ, only Richard Nixon **ever** had a budget surplus during a single year. However, over 6 years, he that was "not a crook" charged our bill up some $65.5 million. His appointee, Gerald Ford, continued the trend... seeing deficit spending as a way to jump start an economy in recession. His two-year bill... $111.6 million.

Jimmy Carter was dealt a tough hand. Inflation was already a problem by the time he took office. What's more, he had the misfortune of manning his post during a period of great change in the American workforce. The largest portion of baby boomers had entered the workplace looking for jobs, plus more and more women were choosing to seek full-time careers outside the home. Although the economy was, indeed, growing, it wasn't doing so at a rate fast enough to accommodate all those who wished to be working. The unemployment rate was a serious problem. Carter decided to exorcise that demon prior to addressing inflation, which he decided was the lesser of the two evils. More deficit spending added fire to the economy, thereby providing an increased number of jobs for applicants. However, the flames of inflation began to burn out of control as interest rates topped 20%. People received gainful employment, unfortunately they were paid in dollars that were worth less each day at the grocery store.

Next The Gipper strode onto the field with a platform which included a balanced federal budget. He exited the game with the U.S. $1.32 trillion further behind. He had basically tripled the country's debt in only 8 years, managing to do so by engaging in an arms race that he hoped would end The Cold War by bankrupting the Soviet Union. (Which is a little like setting out to drink someone under the table. Even if you succeed, and the other person passes out first, you both wake with one heck of a hangover the next day.) Reagan's plan worked. And as a result, rather than continuing to spend money for military build-up, we now use those dollars to help stabilize the region of the world that was the U.S.S.R.

George Bush stepped into the oval office next. Four years later he had amassed almost as much debt as Reagan did in 8 years... $1.04 trillion. Let's be fair though... he didn't start this fire. In fact, by the time he eased into the big chair at 1600 Pennsylvania Avenue, much of the ability to even control the blaze was gone. When taking into consideration all the mandatory expenditures that had to be made...

How to Obtain Business Loans

interest payments, entitlement benefits, etc... only about 1/3 of the budget remained for him to play with.

People voted for a change in 1992, and Bill Clinton took center stage. The cost for a one-part ticket to his four-part show... $267 billion. Flames, rather than hope, burn eternal.

I've always been struck by our country's fascination with John F. Kennedy. Today, three decades after his assassination, his life and times still command an immense amount of programming on our airways... as well as space in the publications we read. Why? It's certainly arguable, but could his era be the last time we truly believed our tomorrows would be brighter than our yesterdays?

Putting On Our Best Face

Most, Americans truly tend to believe "the buck stops" at the President's desk. I'm guilty of it. Look how I just chronicled the way a $4.3 trillion debt was amassed... holding seven people responsible in the process. Of course, that's hardly realistic. To build up that kind of a deficit took a monumental effort on the part of a lot of people. Let's give credit where credit is due. It required an immeasurable amount of waste, inefficiency, and (my favorite) pork barrel politics. None of which would have been possible without the help of Congress.

Now our tab grows exponentially on its own. Indexed entitlements and rising interest rates on the debt make sure of that. Which leaves everyone time to focus their attention on putting circumstances in the best possible light. I believe this requires even greater effort than creating the debt.

Consider how budget increases and decreases are portrayed to the public. We often hear of tens of millions being sliced from the deficit. Which makes us all rest a little easier (at least momentarily). However, these cuts aren't made in *real dollars*... they are in *budget dollars*. Bear with me, this is confusing because our government doesn't want us to fully understand. Let's take an imaginary line item from the budget, Grift & Swindling (G&S). During 1992, G&S cost the government $200 billion. For 1993, policy makers budgeted growth in G&S, anticipating expenditures in the area to total $300 million. Later, they revised the budget to $250 million and announced the budget was cut by some $50 million, giving the appearance of significant "savings." When in reality, spending went up by $50 million. Any decrease was as compared to budget... not actual.

Chapter Sixteen

What's more, looking at the budget as a whole and projecting into the future, becomes even more fanciful. First, congressional budget writers take the most optimistic approach imaginable in forecasting revenues. They'll budget for economic growth to be exceedingly strong (at close to, if not, unsustainable levels). This makes anticipated tax receipts as high as possible. Next, on the other side of the equation, these "experts" predict interest expense will trend lower based upon falling interest rates. Now we have revenues as high as possible and expenses as low as possible. Bingo... an annual surplus has been created with which to trim the aggregate deficit. While this helps everyone feel better in dream-land, back in the real world the scenario can never transpire. You don't get booming economic growth coupled with continually falling interest rates. Basic economics insists that rates rise during periods of expansion because more and more dollars chase fewer goods and services. Prices get bid up.

Now comes the best part. All these gyrations, taken together, still would not be enough to put an acceptable face on our situation. Thus, many things (which are real costs to taxpayers) are considered off-budget items. You'll love this... the following are not even counted:

Direct Financing
A myriad of public agencies offer loans directly to the private sector. For example, the Small Business Administration.

Indirect Financing
There are a whole host of programs under which non-government entities offer direct loans... where Uncle Sam just covers any defaults. Some examples are: the Federal Agricultural Mortgage Corporation, the Federal Home Loan Mortgage Corporation, the Student Loan Mortgage Association, the Federal National Mortgage Association, the Veterans Administration, the Federal Housing Administration, and... the Federal Deposit Insurance Corporation. (The cynic in me wonders... if only the budgetary deficit is at issue, not the real one, and FDIC costs are excluded from the budget... why is the government regulating banks at all? Any reasoning which calls for tight scrutiny due to a need to safeguard depositor's money would also demand the Pension Benefit Guarantee Corporation be under as strict a level of control. That government insurance program

How to Obtain Business Loans

backstops private company pension plans, guaranteeing benefits to those entitled in the event the employer can't pay. The system calls for participating firms to pay a premium in order to have their workers covered. Thus, companies with well-funded programs don't usually come into the system... but you can bet those with under-funded plans do.)

Can you take some more? Even after a complete facial is done to all the facts and figures, there is still the matter of...

Paying For the Make-Over

With things as they are, you might ask, "How have we been able to keep our head above water this long?" How else... by finding ways to borrow *more* money. In the early 1980s, Congress made an excellent move to bolster the Social Security System. At the time, with all the baby boomers paying in, over 20 worker's contributions went to support each individual receiving benefits. However, recognizing a significant drop in the birth rate after the mid-sixties would cause a drastic change in this relationship by the time boomers came to retirement age, Congress raised the rate of Social Security deductions. This meant, after a few years, the system began running a very sizable surplus.

So what did Congress do next? They borrowed almost $1 trillion (again with a 'T') from the Social Security Fund. They then went on to borrow additional monies from the trust funds of many civil servant programs. In each case, they replaced the *real money* borrowed with government paper... treasury securities. Ask yourself: What will be the value of those securities once it is widely recognized our government is insolvent? Even if the debts are actually repaid, the funds remitted will have far less buying power than those borrowed. Why? Because all indicators point to a highly inflationary environment down the road.

Certainly, at some juncture, our nation's creditors are going to begin assessing investment in U.S. government securities as an increasingly riskier proposition. In which case, and this is especially so in terms of our foreign creditors, they are going to demand advancing rates of return in order to compensate them for the commensurate repayment (and currency) risk being taken. As the

Chapter Sixteen

rates on government securities go, so follow borrowing rates in the private sector.

The government has to feed the deficit. Which means it pretty much *has* to pay what the market demands. Not only will perceived risk drive rates up, but the borrowing necessity does the same. In a situation where government and the private sector are competing for a limited pool of available capital... the government *has* to be the higher bidder. This hasn't happened yet because many of the world's largest economies have been in the doldrums for some time now, but as economic expansion(s) begin to take place... and the demand for capital increases... interest rates will rise appreciably. They have to.

So where does this leave American business? With the highest premium ever imposed on the ability to efficiently compete for capital. Because of the foregoing reasons, many small- to mid-sized concerns will have to fight hard in order to keep from being crowded out of the credit markets. Since 1980, the government's consumption of available domestic credit has risen from 20% to better than 55%. And, when you consider federally sponsored borrowing, the government's consumption over the same time period has gone from slightly less than 40% to well above 80%!

This means the level of challenge facing the business sector is going to be greater than ever before. Both in the competition for a limited amount of funds, and in the realization that higher internal rates of return must be generated in order to cover borrowing at advancing rates of interest. That's why I feel this book is important. Hopefully it gives the American businessperson one more tool that can be used to their advantage. Which is critical because our future... and the futures of our children depend upon the success of private business.

Consider for a moment the only plausible ways our national debt can be addressed. (1) The government could just repudiate, or turn its back on the obligations it owes. For obvious reasons, the consequences of this action prohibit its consideration. (2) The debt could be monetized. In other words, the treasury could just print dollar bills to repay the debt. This choice would also have disastrous results. As stated before, putting more and more dollars in circulation chasing the *same amount* of goods and services only bids up prices. Which leaves only one alternative. (3) **<u>Real</u> government spending has to be curtailed, and gross domestic product [8] must grow.** The conclusion isn't new. Nor is it especially profound in its derivation.

How to Obtain Business Loans

Most anyone with a fairly basic knowledge of economics seems to arrive at the same end.

Some things we know will work. Reagan's tax cuts served their intended purpose. Through growth in gross domestic product, the government collected about 75% more in tax receipts during his term as President.

Some things we know won't work. Unfortunately, Reagan and the seated Congress outspent those revenues several times over. We've got to quit fooling ourselves with this weathly super-power image we like to project. We are the globe's largest debtor nation. We can't afford to ship money all over the world.

Some things aren't even worth debating anymore. Time and again, raising tax rates has proven itself to be a disincentive for Americans everywhere. It seems like common sense to me... if working more, harder, and taking on additional risk brings increasingly less to the table, why would anyone do so?

I think the only reason this issue still comes up is as a result of projections similar to those we spoke of earlier. Proponents take a period of economic expansion and apply increased tax rates to the revenue streams. And just like that you get an analysis which shows you will collect more money if taxes are raised. Of course, this methodology ignores the fact that the expansion itself was (at the very least) significantly enhanced by lower tax rates. With government poised to crowd private borrowing out of more and more of the domestic credit market, the last thing needed is one more item conspiring to bring about stagflation[g].

And some things are just down-right funny, if you can get by the frustration. Hopefully this book has fallen into that category, and so should something else. If you recall, a recurring theme during the last presidential campaign was that... "wealthy Americans needed to pay their fair share."

Let me give you some interesting information a friend of mine obtained from the Internal Revenue Service. Of the total amount collected in personal taxes, over 46% is paid by those *filing units* earning in excess of $75,000 annually. A group which made up only 5.6% of the population at the time these statistics were drawn (1990). To put that in perspective, look at it this way... out of every 100 Americans, the tax receipts of 5 amount to almost as much as the total remitted by the other 95. Relatively speaking, of course, I'd say folks towards the top end of the pyramid are paying their fair share.

Chapter Sixteen

Taking a step up, those *filing units* indicating incomes in excess of $200,000 represent only 1% of the population... however, they remit one-quarter of the total taxes paid. Seem fair?

If not, other interpretations of "fair share" must have the imposition of taxes serving as something of an equalizer in terms of standard of living. Maybe that was the meaning behind the rallying cry that swelled during the last election. Perhaps that kind of thought process is the same type which leads to the development of more and more entitlement programs... instead of systems that offer greater opportunity and support for Americans through private business. Remember, government can only pay for entitlements... and reduce deficits... as tax receipts allow (that is, without creating greater deficits). And growth in tax receipts can only — truly — come from increases in gross domestic product (a/k/a economic growth). All the rest seems like smoke and mirrors to me.

Some things are simple. You can't provide opportunity for the few, heavily tax them (creating a disincentive to use the very opportunities made available), and then take care of the many through ever expanding entitlements (abrasively a/k/a "handouts"). It just *has* to work the other way... opportunities for the many and tax rates which don't dampen incentive, ultimately leading to a declining need for federal support in the form of entitlements. Our whole system seems contrived to work against this common sense approach. The collective justification given is that "things are more complicated than can be readily understood by the public." Don't you believe it.

I, for instance, can understand one thing perfectly. If banks aren't made to provide funds (opportunity) to those other than at the top of the pyramid, you might not see THE CLOSE OF (ALL) BUSINESS, but Chamber of Commerce's numbers are going to dwindle. And so will jobs, with the reverse happening to entitlements and the deficit... and probably even tax rates, as the government will continue to try and extract more from the wealthy.

The risk of a looser credit market? Without a doubt there will be an inherently higher rate of loan defaults and some institutional failure. However, in the long run, which is more expensive... a certain amount of insolvency at the institutional level or bankruptcy at the federal level. Besides, wouldn't the latter ensure a great deal more of the former taking place anyway? I vote we focus more on the bigger picture. Even a huge number of closures within the banking industry would be a drop in the bucket as compared to what will result

How to Obtain Business Loans

without more efficiently functioning financial intermediaries... such as community banks used to be.

Looking Ahead

Hope for a prosperous future lies with American business, which is dependent upon the national community for sources of capital... and thereby the banking industry. Improper and overregulation have rendered the system far less productive than it was in days gone by. To the point where semi-drastic measures are appropriate.

Such as dropping the deposit insurance program, or at least significantly amending it. Perhaps it is time banks operate independent of the public sector. Or, at least, larger institutions should. Not everyone just *has* to have the "safety" of a government guarantee behind their savings. Look at the flood of money that entered mutual funds during 1993. "Total stock, bond and money market fund assets topped $2 trillion for the first time — double what they were just three years [prior]."[10] Certainly lower interest rates had something to do with the exodus from insured bank accounts. However, this never-the-less shows the willingness of many to leave the *safety and soundness* of the traditional banking system and move into areas devoid of government backstops. Besides, at this point, I think we all recognize that federal guarantees are something of a placebo.

We should also realize wholesale amendment to the banking system isn't likely to take place anytime soon. Neither our government, nor banks, move with great speed. Which is why understanding how to use the current system as effectively as possible is so important. Knowing the rules, and going the extra distance to work within them, will enable you to find success where the majority of others will fail.

As a shining example, I give you Gilbert "Bud" Jackson, a streetwise developer who sustained catastrophic losses in the Texas real estate slide and had to file bankruptcy. Typically, such an occurrence would force a career change, being that a past bankruptcy often prevents many individuals from obtaining sizable commercial credit (at least at palatable terms). Not Bud.

After about a year of sitting things out, he returned better educated as to the manner in which the system worked and applied for financing at my institution. Taking the time to find out who senior management was, meeting with them to explain his past, pulling

Chapter Sixteen

strings as previously described, and supplying (upfront) all the information he knew the bank would eventually get around to requesting... he ultimately found himself with a revolving line of credit in the mid-six figures. And at Prime plus 1.5%! Not bad for someone with a bit more than a blemish on his payment record. How did he do it? By understanding the game to the Nth degree, and by playing according to the new rules. Which proves it can be done... not easily... and not efficiently... but it can be done. Here's to your becoming an example of someone else known for **breaking the bank.**

As the seminar wound down, the speaker mumbled along about the intricacies of the regulatory agencies involved in policing banks and the importance of articulating their value to both customers and prospects. He added that self-promotion of the banking system was vitally important as over the past few years its reputation had been tarnished somewhat. He ended by communicating how critical it was to explain the necessity of close regulation and strict loan policy, otherwise people might simply think the industry was tight with the public's money. (Tough sell.)

Which reminded me of a story. "On a day when a power shortage closed the federal offices of all 'nonessential' personnel, a call came through the switchboard for the head of one of the bank regulatory agencies. The operator's response was particularly poignant. 'I'm sorry only essential personnel are working today.'" [11] (Exactly.)

---

[1]Gills, M. Arthur: "It Ain't All Washington's Fault," *United States Banker*, Vol. CIII, No. 11, November 1993, pg. 88.
[2]Gills, M. Arthur: "It Ain't All Washington's Fault," *United States Banker*, Vol. CIII, No. 11, November 1993, pg. 88.
[3]Gills, M. Arthur: "It Ain't All Washington's Fault," *United States Banker*, Vol. CIII, No. 11, November 1993, pg. 88.
[4]Gills, M. Arthur: "It Ain't All Washington's Fault," *United States Banker*, Vol. CIII, No. 11, November 1993, pg. 88.
[5]Gills, M. Arthur: "It Ain't All Washington's Fault," *United States Banker*, Vol. CIII, No. 11, November 1993, pg. 88.

How to Obtain Business Loans

[6]Gills, M. Arthur: "It Ain't All Washington's Fault," *United States Banker*, Vol. CIII, No. 11, November 1993, pg. 88.

[7]Smith, Ed. "Profitability and Good Cheer," *Bankers News*, Vol. I, Issue 18, December 21, 1993, pg. 7.

[8]Straighter, William W., Editor; "The Future of Banking is Already Here," *ABA Banking Journal*, Vol. LXXXV, Issue No. 11, November 1993.

[9]Paul A. Volcker, Chairman of the Federal Reserve System, Board of Governors, in testimony to Congress on February 20, 1985.

[10]Waggoner, John: "Investors flood mutual funds with cash," *USA TODAY*, January 28, 1994. Section B, Pg. 1.

[11]Dean, Virginia, Communications Director ABA, "Week-ender," *ABA INSIDER*, January 28, 1994, pg. 2.

GLOSSARY

80/20 funding	Of an undertaking's total cost, 80% would be bank financed and 20% would be equity injected.
1031 tax free exchange	At this writing, tax laws permit an owner to sell a particular type of property and not incur a capital gains tax, so long as the proceeds are reinvested in the purchase of a similar type of property within a specified time frame. Also called, "like-for-like" exchange.
AAA bonds	Highest quality ranking for bond issues.
ABA	American Banking Association. The profession's primary industry group.
acceleration	As it relates to development finance, the term refers to the rate at which bank debt is repaid over the salable units involved. (e.g.) $1 million of debt is extended to

How to Obtain Business Loans

	construct 10 condo units (or $100,000 per unit. Assuming a 20% equity position, and no closing costs, the bank receives remittance of $125,000 for each unit closed. The "acceleration" is thus $125,000/$100,000 = 125%.
adverse action	For consumer loan requests and those represented by business concerns with less than $1 million in gross revenues, if the bank doesn't approve the request *as presented*, then by law they must issue the applicant an "adverse action" form indicating how the request must be amended to gain approval... or give reasons why it was denied in its entirety.
amortization	In banking, the term relates to spreading periodic principal payments over the duration of a loan's incremental repayment.
audited reports	Accountant prepared examination of a business's financial statements; tests for accuracy and fair representation.
balloon	The point where a debt owed becomes due in the entirety of its remaining balance. *A maturity.*
Big 8	The vernacular refers to eight of the largest and most prestigious national accounting firms. (e.g.) Arthur Anderson, Peat Marwick, etc.
bk	Slang for bankruptcy. A legal proceeding which prioritizes creditors' claims against a debtor in insolvency. Creditors are generally asked to accept something less than full value of their individual claims.
bonded contract	Banks often require large construction jobs to be "bonded" through a recognized surety. It is a method of *insuring* work under the GC's contract will be completed, and suppliers and subcontractors with lien rights are properly paid for their goods

Glossary

	or services in the process. (e.g.) payment and performance bond.
capital	The investment owners have in any business enterprise or undertaking. Synonymous with *equity* into a deal. Also, in the accounting equation: Assets = Liabilities + Owner's Equity. OE is comprised of the initial investment, plus subsequent retained earnings.
capital adequacy	In banking, the government sets minimum capital levels for banks. This is a safety measure done to help ensure institutions don't overextend themselves and have some cushion to fall back on in the event of operating losses and loan write-offs.
capped	Slang used in reference to capitalizing an income stream to arrive at a value. In terms of income producing real estate, the annual net operating income is derived from the marketplace's current required rate of return for similar properties.
CO	Certificate of Occupancy.
commercial paper	Promissory notes of less than one year, issued in relatively large denominations by high quality business concerns. From the company's standpoint, CP is attractive because the market will often provide "borrowing" rates lower than those available at banks.
commitment	When the bank extends financing for larger credit amounts, particularly in the commercial lending area, formal letters are forwarded to the prospective borrower outlining the terms and conditions of the approved loan. This is done in "commitment letters." A *commitment* is simply an agreement in finance.
Community Reinvestment Act	Legislation designed to ensure banks pump money back into areas from which they garner deposits. Designed to prevent

How to Obtain Business Loans

	redlining (not lending in) underprivileged areas.
consolidated financial statements	Refers to intercompany financials which are combined into one master statement.
consolidating financial statements	Intercompany financials which show operating totals by area before aggregating themselves in consolidated fashion.
contributions and withdrawals	In reference to partnership accounts, K-1s indicate the actual cash transactions ("contributions and withdrawals") and not just taxable income amounts as reported on schedule summaries.
cost center	Large corporations sometimes track costs by the areas in which they originate. Separate points of operation are assigned budgets to which they are expected to adhere in terms of total dollar outlay, and sometimes by individual line item(s).
CPA	Certified Public Accountant. Advanced designation bestowed upon accountants who have met certain criteria and have successfully passed various qualifying examinations.
curtailing	In banking terms, development loans now often carry "curtailment" requirements, whereby borrowers are compelled to make mandatory principal reductions regardless of whether or not the undertaking's salable product is moving.
debt ratio	In banking, this term refers to the relationship between one's total monthly obligations and total monthly income.
doc stamps	"Documentary Stamps." In some states, there is a tax assigned to recorded documents.
DSC	Debt Service Coverage. The relationship between monies available to pay monthly debt installments and other expenses, and the amount of those outlays. Anything over 1:1 means sufficient funds are

Glossary

	available; anything less than 1:1 means there is a shortfall.
Dun's number	Dun and Bradstreet (D&B) is the oldest U.S. agency reporting credit data and ratings on business entities. As a means of tracking, they assign companies identification numbers.
economies of scale	Economic term which refers to operating advantages obtained via size of a concern.
elevations	Structural drawings, completed to scale, depicting something to be constructed.
eminent domain	The government's right, after due process and compensation, to take private property for public use.
environmental audit	A report compiled by specially qualified engineers which comments on the likelihood of possible, or actual, environmental contamination with regard to a property. The site itself is examined, as are surrounding areas, and searches are conducted to determine if past uses on adjacent properties may have caused contamination. Subsequent examinations, as warranted, may also include taking ground water samples.
escrow	Funds, or other assets, held by an unrelated party to a transaction; not to be released until some certain action is undertaken or completed by one of the parties directly involved in the deal. Only if previously described conditions are met to the satisfaction of the assigned escrow agent will funds, or assets, be paid or transferred.
extension	As in "loan." An 80% extension means the credit amount is 80% of the collateral's estimated value.
Federal Deposit Insurance Corp.	Government entity which insures public deposits held in nationally chartered banks and in all state banks that are members of the Federal Reserve system.

How to Obtain Business Loans

Federal Reserve	The United States' central bank. Comprised of all national banks, some member commercial banks, and twelve District FR banks established by the Federal Reserve Act of 1913. Initially designed to oversee monetary policy and overall operation of commercial banks.
FF&E	Stands for Furniture, Fixtures, and Equipment. (e.g.) Restaurants often require FF&E financing. Institutions encumber the assets through Uniform Commercial Code procedures.
FIFO	"First-In, First-Out." Accounting method which assumes merchandise is sold in the sequence in which it is acquired.
FIRREA	Financial Institution Reform, Recovery and Enforcement Act.
FNMA	Federal National Mortgage Association. "Fannie Mae." A government sponsored, but private, corporation which adds liquidity to the residential mortgage market by purchasing loans from institutions. To raise funds to continue making these purchases, "Fannie Mae" packages groups of mortgages to form a *security*, then resells the security to other institutions seeking investments, to private citizens, and also to the U.S. Treasury.
forbearance	An instance when the legal action is not undertaken, and default remedies are not imposed, even though a mortgage is in arrears.
Freddie Mac	Federal Home Loan Mortgage Corporation. A private concern authorized by Congress to buy mortgage loans from institutions and resell ownership certificates in pooled groups of mortgages. Like "Ginnie and Fannie Mae," Freddie Mac provides liquidity to the residential mortgage market.

Glossary

GAAP Stands for Generally Accepted Accounting Principals. The guidelines set by the accounting profession for compiling and presenting company financial statements.

General Accounting Office Agency which completes various audits of financial institutions. The GAO is responsible for examining federal expenditures as well. Reports directly to Congress.

goodwill Intangible asset category used to denote a company's worth in excess of net book value. Often necessary when concerns are purchased in excess of "book." Represented by such things as: reputation, trademark recognition, location, etc. which are believed to have a positive effect on earning power.

Gross Domestic Product A measure of output indicating the total value of all goods and services produced by a nation.

income approach An appraisal method used to calculate rental property's value by means of the stream of cash it produces after expenses. Other methods of evaluation include the Cost Approach and the Market (Comparable Sales) Approach.

indexed Refers to an item which has its value adjusted for inflation based upon a specific time of statistical reference.

infrastructure In terms of residential development, this equates to the roads, water, sewer, electricity, etc. which are completed at the inception of a project... prior to salable lots, condo units, or single family homes being put in place. The infrastructure is the foundation of a project.

joint venture Something taken on by more than a single entity. Generally transpiring out of an agreement between two or more companies. For example, JVs may be

How to Obtain Business Loans

	formed because one entity has an idea and management resources to make an undertaking go, but not the capital to bring it about, which would be provided by the other party(s).
K-1	Tax schedule which discloses the contributions made to, and the withdrawals taken from, a partnership. Also discloses the current balance and ownership percentage of a partner's capital account.
land shortfall	Term used in conjunction with certain types of development financing where the undertaking has phased construction, and sales within the building's first phase do not retire the debt associated with the overall land.
LBO	Leveraged Buy Out. Refers to acquisitions made with little equity infusion. During the '80s, junk bonds (poorly rated subordinate debt) were often issued to raise money for such transactions.
legal lending limits	Along with capital requirements, the government sets maximum amounts banks can lend to a customer. This is done in an effort to ensure risk is spread, rather than concentrated.
letter of credit	A bank-issued document which, basically, guarantees funding to a beneficiary under certain terms and provisions. It is a commitment for financing. An unfunded obligation of the issuing institution.
LIFO	"Last-In, First-Out." Accounting method which assumes the most recently acquired item is the first sold from inventory. During periods of inflation, this causes the dollar value of inventory to be understated in terms of current prices.
MAI	Generally recognized as the highest professional designation for appraisers.

Glossary

                    Stands for Member of the Appraisal Institute.

money market funds   Type of mutual fund which purchases high quality short-term (less than one year) instruments for its investment pool. (e.g.) Government securities and term notes from corporations with the best credit ratings from Moody's and Standard and Poor's.

money supply   Loosely defined as the amount of currency in circulation. More specifically identified by the Federal Reserve in the following categories: M1 — Cash plus demand deposits held in banks. M2 — M1 plus bank time and savings deposits. M3 — M2 plus monies held at mutual savings banks and S&Ls.

monopoly   A market situation devoid of competition. No reasonable substitute for a particular good or service is available for sale in the area of question. Antitrust legislation was contrived to prevent such situations from existing to the detriment of consumers.

multiplier effect   The Federal Reserve controls the reserve positions required of its member banks. When less reserves are required, banks have more money available to recirculate through the economy. This recirculation of money relates to the "multiplier effect."

(net) interest margin   If a bank's cost of funds (what is paid for deposits and borrowed from the Fed) is 4%, and the average yield on its earning assets is 7.25%, then the institution's interest margin is 3.25%.

nonaccrual   In accrual based accounting, revenues (in this case banking, interest payments) are recognized when they are realized (scheduled) rather than when the actual cash transaction takes place. This is allowable when there is a high probability

How to Obtain Business Loans

	of timely receipt of payment. When a loan's regular remittance comes under question, the credit is placed on "nonaccrual," and revenues are no longer recognized according to the repayment schedule.
nonperforming	A loan placed on "nonaccrual" is said to be a "nonperforming" asset. Note: Due to the method in which banks now grade the perceived risks in their loan portfolios, credit which pays on a timely basis can still be placed into "nonaccrual" and "nonperforming" categories.
NSF	Stands for "not sufficient funds." Occurs when a check has been presented for payment and there are not enough funds in the account to cover payment.
OCC	Office of the Comptroller of the Currency. Audits the commercial loan portfolios of nationally chartered banks.
officer calls	Visits made by bankers on prospective customers. Typically, a certain number is required of an officer on a monthly basis.
opportunity cost	As related to ongoing concerns, the effective cost arising from revenues not obtained, and/or costs incurred, as a result of an action not taken. The price of a lost opportunity.
overdraft	A checking account has a $1,500 balance. A check for $1,600 is presented. An "overdraft" has taken place. The account is "overdrawn" by $100.
Paper Reduction Act	Mythical legislation requiring parties (particularly large corporations) to lessen the amount of wasted paper circulated on an annual basis. A conservation effort widely ignored by bureaucratic bodies such as banks.
participation	A credit extension made by a group of institutions acting together. Designed to spread the risk of lending large amounts

Glossary

permanent takeout

of money to single concerns. This type of facility is often made necessary due to legal lending requirements.

Banks sometimes extend financing for the construction of a property (say a shopping center), but do not wish to hold the mortgage over an extended period of time. Rather, they will agree to monitor the disbursement process, providing funds through the completion of construction, so long as a long-term financing commitment ("takeout") has been provided by a third party.

personal debt ratio

The relationship between total monthly cash outflows (principally for the retirement of debt) and aggregate monthly income. The percentage is calculated on both a gross and net of tax basis.

PMI

Private Mortgage Insurance. Banks writing loans to secondary markets (FNMA, GNMA, FHLMC) guidelines extend residential credit up to 80% loan-to-value. Above that amount, PMI is obtained to *ensure* the position extended in excess of 80% LTV. The borrower pays a premium for the bank to have this insurance, and thereby allows the extension of the additional dollars requested.

pro-rata guarantee

A $3,000,000 loan is applied for by a partnership. Four partners have contributed $250,000 each as equity into the deal. A *joint and several guarantee* of the bank's debt would mean each partner is liable for the $3,000,000 loan. A "pro-rata" guarantee would mean each partner, with a 25% share in the undertaking, would guarantee a proportionate percentage of the overall debt — $750,000.

real dollars

Dollar values which are adjusted to a base

How to Obtain Business Loans

	year in order to account for the effects of inflation on purchasing power.
Real Estate Owned	REO. Also called Other Real Estate (ORE). When a bank forecloses on real property, the asset taken back is held in this balance sheet line item until sold.
release provision	Sets the price which must be paid for the bank to satisfy its lien on a particular asset.
rental listing	As in the case where an owner wishes to lease a facility, an agent is sometimes contracted to find a tenant. The agent's advertisement of the available space is a "rental listing."
reserve component	Refers to the portion of bank deposits which must be set aside, as well as a percentage taken against adversely rated loan balances, in order to provide a safety cushion against possible defaults.
revolving credit	With a $100,000 *term loan*, the balance is, typically, disbursed at closing and then repaid over a pre-described period in equal installments... extinguishing the loan. A "revolving debt" is one which allows for the balance to be drawn out in increments, repaid in any fashion, then redrawn again. This can continue for an unlimited amount of times until the obligation itself matures.
S Corp.	More formally, Subchapter S Corporation. Corporate form often chosen by small businesses. Income taxes are not incurred against earnings at the company level. Instead, profits are passed through directly to the owner's personal returns, where they are taxed as regular income.
securitized	Used in two instances. (1) "A loan is securitized by such-and-such collateral." (2) "The mortgages are securitized for sale in the secondary market by Fannie Mae." The process of grouping earning assets into one salable *security*.

Glossary

sole proprietor — A business owned and operated by one individual.

stagflation — The malady existing when inflation occurs during a period of no, or little, economic growth.

submerged land lease — Some states convey the legal rights to build vertically out of coastal waters by means of renting the privilege to parties for extended periods of time (often 99 years). At the end of the lease, the rights are typically rolled over, but may be rescinded if circumstances warrant. The state remains entitled to the submerged property at all times.

subordinate — To place a debt behind, or junior, to another in terms of payment priority in the liquidation of an asset.

title insurance — Obtained by purchasers of real estate to insure bundle of ownership rights being obtained in the conveyance of title.

trading assets — Accounts Receivable, Inventory, and Accounts Payable. The manner in which these areas are managed has a drastic effect on a company's cash flow.

trust — A situation where cash or other assets are held by one party for the benefit of another. They are held in "trust."

INDEX

A
Acceleration rate 230-232
Accountant prepared statements 263
Adjusting Net Worths 266-268
Advertising 54, 56
American Bankers Association 62-63, 73
American Disabilities Act 63-64
Amortization 32, 104, 106
Approval authorities 92-93, 123, 126
APY 102-103

B
Balloon payments 173-175
Bank control 161-171
Bankruptcy risk 6-7, 109-111, 212, 319

How to Obtain Business Loans

Branch manager 47-49, 89-90
Brokered applications 260
Bush, George 311, 313

C
Capital adequacy 11-15, 306-310
Carter, Jimmy 311, 313
Case studies 178-255
Centrust Savings 1-2
Character Loans 77-82
Clinton, Bill 77, 314
Community Reinvestment 111-116, 117, 305, 308
Community service 5-6, 15
Compensating balances 160-161
Compounding 45
Consumer rights groups 61-62
Cost control 18-19, 34-35, 83-84, 304-305
Credit administrator 32, 70, 80-81, 98-99, 123, 125, 128-130, 165, 264, 283-285, 296-300
Credit bureau reports 270-278
Customer service 49-59
Customer service reps 41-44, 49-52

D
Deming, Edwards 54
Deposit rates 46-48, 101-103

E
Employee discontent 285, 290
Ethics 1-2, 10, 44-45

F
Feasibility studies 150-151
Federal deficit 310-321
Fee income 39-44, 61-62
FIRREA 31, 140-156, 165

Index

Five Cs of credit 19-20
Ford, Gerald 313

H
House limits 94-99

I
Interest rate deregulation 6
Interest rate penalties 159, 164
Intermediation 111, 308-309
Internal review 33

J
Johnson, Lyndon Baines 310, 313
Joint & several guarantees 265-266

K
Kennedy, John Fitzgerald 311, 314

L
Legal lending limits 94
Loan applications 260-270
Loan classifications 22-34, 124-125, 130-132, 173
Loan upgrades 13-15, 20-22, 82

M
McCarthyism 110
Milken, Michael 7
Minority holdings 30, 66
Monopolies 6-7

N
Negotiating terms 47-49, 73-77
Nixon, Richard 313

How to Obtain Business Loans

O
Opportunity cost 13, 38-39, 58, 130, 243-244
Over-development 8-10

P
Paul, David 1-2
Payment reserves 30, 129, 160, 168
Political Action Committees 132
Preferred account holders 52-53
Private Mortgage Insurance 149-150

Q
Qualifying 19-20, 65-71, 91-93, 103, 106-107, 120, 142, 147, 181, 192, 273-278, 290-299, 303

R
Reagan, Ronald 313
Re-appraisal 31, 139, 150-156
Regulation DD 101-103, 116-117
Regulatory burden 37-39, 62-73, 79-81, 86-88
Required reductions 32, 160, 169-171
Reserve components 11-15, 306-310
RMA 262-264, 269-270

S
Sales indoctrination 54-56, 301, 304, 321
Secondary repayment sources
S&L bailout 2, 141
Social security 316

T
Taxation 318-319

Index

U
Undesirable loans 115-116, 120
Unemployment 108-110
Unfunded commitments 30, 33, 38-39

V
Volker, Paul 310

W
Whitewater 308